STATION X

THE CODEBREAKERS
OF BLETCHLEY PARK

Michael Smith

First published in 1998 by Channel 4 Books,
an imprint of Macmillan Publishers Ltd,
25 Eccleston Place, London SW1W 9NF and Basingstoke.

Associated companies throughout the world.

ISBN 0 7522 2189 2

Text © Michael Smith, 1998

3 5 7 9 8 6 4

A CIP catalogue record for this book is available from the British Library.

Design by Roger Lightfoot
Typeset by SX Composing DTP, Rayleigh, Essex
Printed by Mackays of Chatham plc, Chatham, Kent

darlow*smithson*

This book accompanies the television series *Station X*
made by Darlow Smithson for Channel 4.
Executive producer: John Smithson
Series producer: David Darlow
Producer/Director: Peter Bate
Picture credits (clockwise from top left): page 1: Barbara Eachus, Mavis Batey, Stuart
Milner-Barry; page 2: Science Museum/Science and Society Picture Library,
Imperial War Museum; page 3: Bletchley Park Trust/Science and Society; page 4:
Barbara Eachus, Joyce Brusa; page 5: Bletchley Park Trust/Science and Society,
King's College, Cambridge; page 6: Barbara Eachus; page 7: Rosamund Tischler,
Harry Hinsley, Valery Emery, Barbara Eachus; page 8: James Thirsk, Barbara
Eachus. The publishers have made every effort to trace the owners of these
photographs and apologise for any omissions.

Bumph Palace

I think that I shall never see
A sight so curious as BP,
This place called up at war's behest,
And peopled by the strangely dressed;
Yet what they do they cannot say,
Nor ever will 'til Judgement Day.

For six long years we have been there,
Subject to local scorn and stare.
We came by transport and by train,
The dull and brilliantly insane,
What shall we do, where shall we be,
When God at last redunds BP?

The Air Force types that never fly
Soldiers who neither do nor die,
Landlubber Navy, beards complete
Civilians slim, long-haired, effete;
Yet what they did they never knew,
And if they told it wasn't true.

If I should die think only this of me . . .
I served my country at BP.
And should my son ask: 'What did you
In the atomic World War Two?'
God only knows and he won't tell
For after all BP was hell.

Anonymous

ACKNOWLEDGEMENTS

The Allied triumph over Hitler's Germany ensured the freedoms we enjoy today. Yet despite the poppies, the war memorials and the annual services of remembrance, the contributions made to that victory by a wide variety of Britons are all too easily forgotten. While once a year we salve our consciences by buying a poppy, the numbers attending the remembrance services dwindle and war memorials are removed and broken up or lost.

With so many battles fought and lives lost, no single group of people can fairly claim to have made the crucial contribution to winning the war. But one particular group could justifiably argue that they made a unique contribution, not just to the Allied victory, but to the way we live today.

The brilliance of the codebreakers who worked at Bletchley Park, the 'most secret' Station X, not only played a major part in the war, arguably cutting the time taken to beat Hitler by up to three years, it also laid the ground for the computer technology that dominates the modern world with the construction of Colossus, the world's first programmable electronic computer.

Throughout this book the term codebreaker is used as shorthand for someone who worked at Station X, regardless of what part they played in the actual codebreaking process. For Bletchley Park was much more than a group of eccentric intellectuals struggling to break Enigma. Thousands of people, the vast majority of them women, worked there during the war. They lived and loved and, despite the demands of their work and the difficulties of wartime life, many still describe it as the time of their lives. It is therefore to all the 'codebreakers' that this book is dedicated. Most people would agree that their remarkable achievements should be commemorated.

Yet the efforts of the Bletchley Park Trust, a small group of volunteers, to preserve Station X as a museum celebrating the codebreakers' ground-breaking successes have met with remarkable apathy. When the wartime attempts to crack the German codes were threatened by indifference on the part of the powers-that-be, Churchill issued a famous order for 'Action This Day'. Similar resolve by those who now benefit from the extraordinary achievements of Britain's wartime codebreakers may be the only way of ensuring that they are not forgotten.

I must thank all of the many former staff of Station X and its outstations who agreed to be interviewed for this book. I am also grateful to Christine Large and the Bletchley Park Trust, and to the staffs of the Public Record Office and Caversham Library who were always extremely courteous and helpful.

Special thanks should go to Charlie Carman and Emma Tait at Channel 4 Books; to Julianna Challenor, Bindu Mathur, Peter Bate, John Smithson and Erika Dodd at Darlow Smithson; to Daphne Walsh whose transcription skills made my task so much easier; to Charles Cunningham, John Herivel, Tony Sale, Jimmy Thirsk and Peter Twinn, who checked parts of the typescript for errors; and to Ralph Erskine, whose advice throughout this project proved invaluable.

CONTENTS

Chapter 1

THE ARRIVAL

Throughout the summer of 1939, as Europe prepared for war, Bletchley Park swarmed with workmen. The roads around the mansion in the centre of the grounds were relaid with concrete. A new water main was put down and electricity cables installed. Post Office telephone engineers were everywhere, laying landlines into the house from the main GPO cable connecting London with the north which ran through Fenny Stratford, a few miles away.

The house itself was a curious mixture of mock-Tudor and Gothic styles, built in red brick and dominated on one side by a large copper dome that had been turned green by exposure to the elements. It looked out over a small lake, rose gardens, even a maze, and reflected the rather odd tastes of Sir Herbert Leon, a London stockbroker who in the late nineteenth century had chosen to build his country home in Bletchley, a small Buckinghamshire town about fifty miles north of London.

Sir Herbert's widow had died a couple of years earlier and the estate had been sold to a syndicate led by Captain Hubert Faulkner, a local builder, who intended to demolish the mansion and build houses on the park. In the spring of 1938, however, it was bought by someone who claimed that it was to be converted into an air defence training school. The *Bletchley District Gazette* told its readers that this story had been dismissed out of hand by its sources in Whitehall. Whatever was going on up at the Park was clearly very hush-hush.

The interest of the locals only increased when 'Captain Ridley's shooting party' arrived. Throughout August 1939, groups of rather odd, mainly middle-aged men, accompanied by a number of young women, began arriving at the Park. They were put up in local hotels, and every morning drove off before returning in the evening, causing something of a scandal among the hotel staff who assumed the men must be up to no good with their 'fancy women'. A chambermaid made her feelings clear. 'It is all right for you,' she told one of the men, 'but some of us have work to do.'

That neither the chambermaid nor anyone else who didn't work at Bletchley Park would discover the true identity of 'Captain Ridley's shooting party' during the war, or indeed right up until the mid-1970s, was a remarkable tribute to the professionalism and dedication of the 'odd people' who began working there that August and the thousands who would later join them to break Germany's supposedly unbreakable Enigma cypher, thereby saving thousands of lives and cutting up to three years off the length of the war.

Bletchley Park had been bought as the War Station for MI6 and its sister organisation the Government Code and Cypher School, the then covername for Britain's codebreakers. The Captain Ridley of the fictitious 'shooting party' was a naval officer in MI6 who had been put in charge of the move.

For several months members of GC&CS had been told to keep a suitcase ready packed until further orders. Malcolm Kennedy, a member of the section dealing with diplomatic codes noted in his diary: 'no one outside the office is to know this except, where necessary, one's wife.' They were ordered to keep a ten-shilling note in their pockets at all times and, on receipt of a telephone message to the effect that 'Auntie Flo is not so well', to proceed across country to Station X.

On 15 August 1939, the main bulk of the codebreakers were sent to Bletchley 'in order to test communications'. They made their way in a mixture of official Ford Utility station wagons and private cars. Diana Russell Clarke was one of a number of members of the staff recruited through family connections. She had no need of the official transport: 'I simply went in my car. I had a Bentley. It belonged to a friend. He said it was better for it to be driven than stuck up on blocks. So I had this beautiful car all through the war.'

Barbara Abernethy, the Naval Section's most recent recruit, was one of those who had to be given a lift to Station X.

> I should think there weren't more than a hundred people in what we called the first wave. Most of us were then billeted in Bedford, I was in the Bridge Hotel, and none of us quite knew what would happen next. War had not been declared and most people thought and hoped that nothing would happen and we would go back to London.

Phoebe Senyard, a middle-aged member of the naval section, had returned to work from her summer holidays to be told she was being sent to Bletchley the next day to work on the German Navy's radio networks. 'Since I knew very little indeed about German naval traffic, with the exception of naval Enigma, I must confess that it was with fear and trembling that I went. Indeed I did try to protest but I was told that it was only for a fortnight so I gave in.'

The house, its carriage sweep and backyards had been fenced off to mark the narrow confines of the area that had been bought for the MI6 War Station. A few prefabricated wooden huts were being erected inside this compound but initially the entire 'shooting party' was crowded into the existing house, its stables and cottages. The top floor of the house was allotted to MI6. The main body of GC&CS, including its Naval, Military and Air Sections were on the ground floor, together with a telephone exchange, a teleprinter room, a kitchen and a dining room for all the staff.

Josh Cooper, a clever but eccentric man in his thirties with wild mannerisms, was head of the Air Section, which had been allocated a large panelled room on the immediate right as one entered the front door. 'Tables and chairs had been provided but there were no cupboards and I remember coming in to a scene of chaos with a great mound of books and papers piled on the floor,' Cooper recalled. 'In the midst of all this I noticed the newly joined Leonard Hooper quietly studying an Italian dictionary while waiting for somebody to give him some work to do.'

There were similar scenes of disorder in the Naval Section, part of which had been put in the loggia to the left of the house with other subsections in the library. 'Chaos is a mild term to describe our condition at the outset,' recalled Edward Green, the office manager. 'We had very few plans, nowhere to lay our heads, no furniture, books for reference, maps, atlases, dictionaries or any tools with which we might be expected to finish the job.'

The German Section, which was to play a crucial role in the naval war, occupied a small corner of the library, said Phoebe Senyard. 'Our equipment was: two small tables, two chairs, a steel box containing the registers for entering intercepted German code messages, a steel filing cabinet, a direct telephone to the Admiralty and a small card index. I was given very little information as to what our function really was. I did not like the work and would have willingly seized any opportunity to press for my return to London.'

There were just four people working on the Enigma cypher. They were led by Dilly Knox, the son of a bishop and so wildly eccentric that he put Cooper in the shade. A fellow of King's College, Cambridge, he walked with a limp, the result of a motorcycle accident, and wore horn-rimmed glasses without which he could see nothing. He and his assistant Peter Twinn were housed in one of the cottages. They at least did not suffer from a shortage of equipment. 'Bearing in mind that in those days we were really doing a pen and ink job, there wasn't much in the way of technical assistance we could ask for,' Twinn said. 'We knew so little of what lay ahead that we could hardly have been expected to tell the powers-that-be before the war had even broken out.'

It was very soon clear that the house and its adjoining buildings were too small to accommodate the number of people for whom office space was needed. Elmers School, a neighbouring boys' school, was acquired and the Commercial and Diplomatic Sections were moved there with such speed that the owner had no time to move his furniture out. The dons had little more time to come to terms with their new home, recalled Nigel de Grey, one of the codebreakers. 'The sight of a professor of some erudition struggling with the unfamiliar task of the blankets on a boy's bedstead in the dormitory is one not easily forgotten.'

For a while, even the fact that the 'odd people' at Bletchley Park were working for the government was to be kept secret. Service personnel wore civilian clothes and staff were instructed not to tell friends and relations where they were. If pushed they were to fall back on the somewhat discredited story about an Air Raid Precautions training school. 'Ostensibly we are now engaged in Civil Air Defence,' noted Kennedy in his diary, 'but this camouflage seems a bit thin and why we can't admit that we are a branch of the Foreign Office, heaven alone knows.'

Their mail was addressed to a post office box number in London and forwarded to Bletchley by MI6 courier. 'The system broke down when large parcels were addressed to the box number,' Josh Cooper recalled. 'In one case a grand piano was consigned in this way.'

Barbara Abernethy was barely eighteen and concerned that she could not even let her mother know where she was.

> There was nothing I could tell her at all really, but there was this man in the Naval Section called A. J. Alan. He was a BBC commentator, his real name was Leslie Lambert. He had a half-hour wireless programme, like nothing today, and he told funny stories in a very sort of blasé accent. Just funny things about life in London. There was nothing I was able to tell my mother. But I said: 'You'll never guess who I work with, A. J. Alan.' From then on my stock went up.

Admiral Hugh Sinclair, the head of both MI6 and GC&CS, had waged a continuous struggle with the Treasury for cash for both organisations. A man of considerable private means and a bon viveur of some repute, he was not above dipping into his own resources to fund intelligence operations. Sinclair brought in a top chef from London to look after the codebreakers and the meals, laid out on long tables in one of the downstairs rooms of the house and with full waitress service, were memorable.

'What I remember very well were the wonderful lunches with which we were served,' said Phoebe Senyard. 'Bowls of fruit, sherry trifles, jellies and cream were on the tables and we had chicken, ham and wonderful beefsteak puddings, etc. We certainly could not grumble about our food.'

For most of the university dons recruited as codebreakers since the First World War this was the life to which they had become accustomed, a mixture of Oxbridge high table and Foreign Office gentility. But to many of the more junior staff it was a world they had never seen before. 'It was beautiful,' said Barbara Abernethy. 'Lovely rose gardens, mazes, a ha-ha, lovely old building, wonderful food.' For a brief moment, Bletchley Park had the relaxed air of a weekend party at an English country mansion.

'There is no moment in time more beautiful than the early days of a fine English autumn such as were the last days of August 1939 and the last days of peace,' wrote Nigel de Grey. 'In such richly romantic atmospheric conditions, even the architectural vagaries of Bletchley Park were wrapt in a false mellowness and almost but never quite achieved the appearance of a stately home.'

Most of the staff still believed that they would soon be back in London and were highly sceptical about the likelihood of Britain becoming involved in war. 'As one cynic put it: "The Poles are going to be sold down the same river the Czechs were sold down last year",' said Henry Dryden, a member of the Military Section. 'There was something of a rude awakening a week later when the Soviet–German Non-aggression Pact was signed and war in Europe suddenly appeared imminent.'

The codebreakers began mounting a 'sleeping watch' with duty officers staying overnight in the few bedrooms that had not been taken over as offices, or simply putting up a camp bed in their own offices. 'The news in the papers was grave enough but there was still nothing in our material to indicate that Germany was on the brink of war,' recalled Cooper. 'Early in the morning of the 1st of September

1939, I met the admiral's deputy, Colonel Menzies, over breakfast in the old dining room in the house. I must have made some fatuous remark about "another quiet night", to which he replied tersely "heavy fighting all along the Polish frontier".'

In the early hours of the morning, the German army had swept into Poland. The Polish infantry divisions were unable to hold back the blitzkrieg launched by the highly mechanised *Wehrmacht*. When the British told Hitler to withdraw, he responded by accusing the Poles of being the aggressors. Neville Chamberlain, the British prime minister, then gave him an ultimatum. If he did not withdraw his troops from Poland, Britain would declare war on Germany. At 11.00 a.m. on 3 September 1939, the deadline set in the ultimatum expired without any response and the two countries were at war. Bletchley Park was now faced with a race against time to break the German Enigma cypher.

Chapter 2

ASTROLOGERS AND ACADEMICS

The British had experience at intercepting the secret messages of their enemies which stretched back more than 600 years to 1324, when King Edward II ordered that 'all letters coming from or going to parts beyond the seas be seized'.

By the sixteenth century the British were infamous for their interception of the correspondence of foreign dignitaries. The Venetian ambassador in London complained that 'the letters received by me had been taken out of the hands of the courier at Canterbury by the royal officials and opened and read'. Perhaps understandably, foreign diplomats, spies and revolutionaries soon resorted to sending their messages in cyphers.

As a result, Sir Francis Walsingham, Queen Elizabeth I's spymaster and the organiser of Britain's first real intelligence service, set up a decyphering department in his London home under the guidance of John Dee, the Queen's astrologer. The main targets of this early equivalent of Bletchley Park were Spanish intrigues and the activities of the banned Roman Catholic Church. Dee was so effective that the Spanish governor of the Netherlands complained that the reports he sent home were read in London before they even reached Madrid.

Walsingham died penniless having put large sums of his own money into funding the intelligence operations. His codebreakers were highly successful, however, perhaps most notably in foiling the so-called 'Babington plot' which aimed to replace Queen Elizabeth with Mary, Queen of Scots, and in providing the evidence which led to Mary's execution.

Under Oliver Cromwell, intelligence gathering was given far greater resources than ever before. The Commonwealth's espionage network was centred on the postal system with John Thurloe, Cromwell's spymaster or 'Number One Argus', taking the role of postmaster-general and installing a 'Secret Man' in the Post Office to open and examine any suspicious letters. The process was enshrined in an Act of Parliament which openly declared that the postal system was the best means 'to discover and prevent many dangerous and wicked designs . . . the intelligence whereof cannot well be communicated but by letter of escript'. The 'Secret Man' was extremely efficient. The French First Minister complained that his government's decisions were known to Thurloe within days.

By the eighteenth century, the 'Secret Man' inside the Post Office had become a Secret Department under the control of the Foreign Office. It monitored the correspondence between foreign embassies and their governments with the aid of its own Secret Decyphering Branch, run by the Reverend Edward Willes, an Oxford don who later became the Bishop of Bath and Wells. For more than 140 years, Willes and his successors ran the decyphering branch as if it were a family concern from their Wiltshire home.

The Secret Department of the Post Office was also manned largely by members of one family. John Ernest Bode, 'Chief Clerk in the Secret Service of Hanover' was brought to England in 1732 in an attempt to improve the operation of the department and promptly recruited two of his brothers and two of his sons. The vast majority of the secret messages they read were Russian, Swedish or French, reflecting Britain's main enemies at the time. How much of this material was of any great value is far from clear, but despite repeated calls for its budgets to be cut in order to save expense, the Secret Department survived well into the nineteenth century.

Its demise came after John Bode's grandson, William, succumbed to pressure from the Home Office to step outside his brief to report on diplomatic correspondence and opened the letters of alleged subversives. Revelations in Parliament that the home secretary had ordered the Post Office to read letters sent to the Italian nationalist Giuseppi Mazzini, a political refugee in Britain, led to a parliamentary inquiry into the Secret Department. William Bode mounted a courageous defence of the work of his staff, in which he provided an early description of the type of person best suited to the work of a codebreaker.

> They must obviously be men of great integrity as well as discretion and diligence. They must be men of good education for besides the delicate, difficult and sometimes hazardous manual operations which are to be performed, a knowledge of many foreign languages is required of them

and that knowledge must be tolerably extensive to enable them to read
and understand the worst writing.

The inquiry was effectively a whitewash, taking no decision on the
future of the Secret Department and concluding that it might be best
'to leave it a mystery whether or not this power is ever exercised'. But
the Foreign Office had found the excuse it needed to save itself the
cost of funding the operations of the Secret Department and its codebreakers.

The department's operations were suspended and the Secret
Decyphering Branch closed down, much to the chagrin of Francis
Willes, the Bishop's grandson, who was pensioned off with Secret
Service money, still protesting loudly at the great financial loss to his
family. The Foreign Office dismissed his complaints, pointing out
that since taking over from his uncle, Willes had cracked 'scarcely
any' codes. According to one official, there were great suspicions that
he was merely 'a fraudulent trickster who leads a life of pleasure and
relaxation at his home in Hanger Hill out of sight of the office'. Not
long afterwards, on 1 January 1847, the Secret Department itself was
abolished and Bode too was pensioned off.

It was not until shortly before the First World War, when the
military began to use wireless communications, that the British again
attempted to break their enemies' codes. The Army began
'censoring' diplomatic communications passed on foreign telegraph
cables, their results enhanced by the actions of the Royal Navy which
cut the German submarine cables, forcing Berlin to use those
controlled by the British.

The War Office set up its own codebreaking section, MI1b, to
decypher the 'censored' telegrams, recruiting a number of eminent
academics. It enjoyed almost immediate success, recalled one of the
codebreakers: 'Nobody could desire more admirable opponents than
the Germans for this class of work. The orderly Teutonic mind was
especially suited for devising schemes which any child could
unravel.'

One of the more notable successes for the MI1b codebreakers came
in December 1916 when a German commander in the Middle East
sent a drunken Christmas greeting to all his outstations. During the
period of Christmas inactivity, the same isolated and clearly
identical message went out in six different cyphers, only one of
which, until then, the British had managed to break.

The Army codebreakers kept track of their targets by means of direction-finding (DF) stations in which a number of radio masts were set up in a circular formation. From the way in which a given signal was picked up by the various aerials it was possible to produce a bearing on the enemy transmitter and by using two or more DF stations against the same target, a number of different bearings could be plotted on a map to determine the precise location of the enemy.

Shortly after the outbreak of the First World War, the Royal Navy followed the Army's lead on the orders of the then First Lord of the Admiralty, Winston Churchill, who henceforth would show a personal interest in the work of Britain's codebreakers. The man he appointed to lead the naval codebreakers was Sir Alfred Ewing, the Navy's Director of Education, who had dabbled in codes and cyphers as a hobby before the war.

'An officer should be selected to study all the decoded intercepts, not only current but past, and to compare them continually with what actually took place in order to penetrate the German mind and movements and make reports,' Churchill said. 'The officer selected is for the present to do no other work. I shall be obliged if Sir Alfred Ewing will associate himself continuously with this work.'

The new codebreaking section was located in Room 40 of the Admiralty Old Buildings. With the assistance of his friend William Russell Clarke, a barrister and radio enthusiast, Ewing set up a series of listening stations around the country, all manned by the Post Office. He also recruited a small number of language experts, first from the naval colleges at Dartmouth and Osborne and then from the country's universities.

One of the first of these naval instructors turned codebreakers was Alastair Denniston, a diminutive Scot known to his colleagues as A. G. D., and by close friends as 'Liza', who was to become the first head of Bletchley Park. By far the most productive source of codebreakers, however, was the universities. Ewing went back to his old college, King's, Cambridge, to bring in two Old Etonians, the eccentric Dilly Knox and Frank Birch, a brilliant comic and famous actor, who later appeared as Widow Twanky in pantomime at the London Palladium.

Other eminent recruits, almost entirely Old Etonians, included William 'Nobby' Clarke, a lawyer whose father had represented Oscar Wilde during his 1885 trial for gross indecency, and Nigel de Grey, a publisher whose diminuitive stature and unassuming nature led the more extrovert Birch to dub him 'the Dormouse'. It was de

Grey who gave Room 40 its greatest First World War triumph, the decyphering of the so-called Zimmermann Telegram.

Written by the German foreign minister Arthur Zimmermann, the telegram suggested that Mexico should join the war on Germany's side in return for 'generous financial support and an undertaking on our part that Mexico is to reconquer the lost territory in Texas, New Mexico and Arizona'. Its publication in US newspapers finally persuaded America to end its isolation and join the war, thereby ensuring the defeat of Germany.

Throughout the war, there had been intense rivalry between Room 40 and MI1b. A small degree of liaison was agreed in 1917 but was confined only to an exchange of results, there was to be no collaboration on the codebreaking itself, Denniston recalled. 'Looking back over the work of those years, the loss of efficiency to both departments caused originally by mere official jealousy is the most regrettable fact in the development of intelligence based on cryptography.' But at the end of the war, the two sections were amalgamated into one organisation called the Government Code and Cypher School (GC&CS) and run by Denniston under the control of Admiral Hugh Sinclair, who at the time was Director of Naval Intelligence. 'It was a very small organisation for the treasury had, throughout the negotiations, been insistent on cutting down the expense,' recalled Nobby Clarke. 'The inevitable had happened. There seemed no longer any need to study the communications of a naval and military nature. The Navy and Army of Germany had disappeared, never were they supposed to rise again.'

All but two of the wartime intercept stations were closed and GC&CS, now based in Queen's Gate, Knightsbridge, was told to forget about military and naval wireless traffic and to concentrate on the diplomatic cables. Its public function was to advise the government on what codes and cyphers it should itself use. But its secret role, and real purpose, was to decypher the secret messages not only of Britain's enemies but also of its friends. 'To show the extent of the change,' Clarke said, 'in the early days of 1920, the strongest section of the GC&CS was the United States Section, to which Knox and a number of lesser lights were attached.'

Perhaps understandably, the Admiralty saw little reason to fund the collection of diplomatic intelligence and Britain's codebreakers were soon placed once more in the hands of the Foreign Office. When Admiral Sinclair was made head of MI6 in 1923, he was told to take charge of GC&CS, Denniston said. 'It became in fact an adopted child of the Foreign Office with no family rights and the poor relation of MI6 where peacetime activities left little cash to spare.' But Sinclair, now known in the tradition of MI6 simply as 'C', did what he could to increase the capabilities of the codebreakers, co-opting a small Metropolitan Police radio interception unit based at Denmark Hill in south London to monitor diplomatic wireless communications.

One of those recruited under Sinclair was Josh Cooper who, like many within British intelligence at the time, was brought in by a family friend, in this case, the novelist Charles Morgan.

> I joined as a junior assistant in October 1925. Like many other recruits, I had heard of the job through a personal introduction – advertisement of posts was at that time unthinkable.
>
> I was one year down from University of London King's College with a first in Russian and had nothing better to do than teach at a preparatory school at Margate. My father was bewailing this at tea with the Morgans one day, and one of Charles's sisters said she had a friend at a place in Queen's Gate where Russian linguists were wanted.
>
> So in due course, I took an entrance exam which had been devised by Oliver Strachey, a former member of MI1b, and included a number of puzzles, such as filling in missing words in a mutilated newspaper article and simple mathematical problems calling for nothing more than arithmetic and a little ingenuity. I wasted a lot of time on these, thinking there must be some catch and so did not finish the paper. Nevertheless I got top marks. I do not think this exam was ever repeated but selection continued on a haphazard basis right up to the war.

Cooper was put to work with Ernst Fetterlein, a shy, bespectacled man with a strong Russian accent, who had been the Tsar's chief codebreaker before the Bolshevik Revolution and still sported a large ruby ring presented to him by his former boss in recognition of a job well done.

> His experience and reputation were both great, and I was fortunate to find myself assigned to work with him on Soviet diplomatic. He took very little notice of me and left it to an Army officer who had been attached to GC&CS to explain the problem. Traffic was scanty and it took me some time to realise that almost every group had two meanings. After about six weeks' work, during which I rubbed holes in the paper with endless corrections, at last I read my first message which was from Moscow to the Soviet representative in Washington and was concerned with repudiation of debts by American states.

Most of the Russian material was being intercepted at an Army out-post in India, by the police operators at Denmark Hill or from the diplomatic cables. But with Sinclair showing a strong interest in the codebreakers' activities, MI6 began obtaining Russian diplomatic telegrams from sources in the Tehran and Peking post offices to aid the codebreakers' work.

Then disaster struck! The extent of the Soviet espionage and subversion operations in Britain, revealed in part by the codebreakers, led the Conservative government to send in the Special Branch. When raids on the Soviet offices in London failed to produce any documentary evidence, the then prime minister Stanley Baldwin and his foreign secretary Neville Chamberlain read out the decyphered telegrams in Parliament. The Russians changed their cyphers and the codebreakers had to begin all over again. It was to be the start of an obsession with secrecy that would dominate their activities.

By now GC&CS had moved into joint offices with MI6 at 54 Broadway, St James's. The codebreakers were on the third floor of the building with MI6 taking the floor above them. 'The structure of the office was pretty hopeless,' Cooper said. 'Recruitment by personal introduction had produced a number of very well-connected officers. At best, they were fine scholar linguists, at worst some of them were, frankly, passengers.'

The codebreakers' regime was extremely civilised. 'There had been a tragic case of suicide shortly before I joined,' recalled Cooper. 'A man called Fryer threw himself under a train at Sloane Square and C had formed the opinion that the work was dangerous and people must not be overstrained.' No doubt reinforced in these opinions by the eccentricity of many of his codebreakers, Sinclair ordered that they should only work between 10 a.m. and 5.30 in the afternoon, with a ninety-minute break for lunch.

Barbara Abernethy joined GC&CS in August 1937 at the age of sixteen. She was fluent in French, German and Flemish and when Denniston asked for a new typist, she found herself dispatched to Broadway.

I was posted over there for a week not knowing what I was doing and told that it was strict secrecy. I was there for a week and they apparently approved of me because I was kept on and I stayed there. Life was very civilised in those days, you know, we stopped for tea and it was brought in by messengers. I was very impressed by this, first job

I'd ever had and it seemed paradise to me. I thought: 'Well this is the life isn't it. Thank God I'm not back in the Foreign Office'.

Diana Russell Clarke, the daughter of Room 40's wireless expert, was typical of the pre-war codebreakers recruited through family links.

My mother simply rang up Commander Denniston, whom we'd known all our lives. She said: 'Liza, have you got a job for Diana?' He replied: 'Yes, send her along,' so that's where I started. We were on the third floor. There were MI6 people upstairs. They were always known as 'the other side'. We didn't have any truck with them.

Henry Dryden, who also joined shortly before the war, was told to report to the War Office.

The junior of two officers who received me donned his bowler hat and walked me across the park to Broadway Buildings, opposite St James's tube station. As we approached it he said: 'All you ever say is "Third" as you get in the lift. Nobody must know where you work. If you have lunch with someone who insists on walking back to your offices with you, proceed to the War Office, say goodbye, count 120 and then walk back here'.

With war fast approaching, the Army, Navy and Air Force had formed their own sections within GC&CS and frantic efforts were being made to try to break the German cyphers, which had been almost totally ignored since the end of the First World War on the basis that they would be unbreakable, Cooper recalled.

Considering what Room 40 had achieved in 1914–18, it seems extraordinary that anyone should believe this. But it was generally assumed that no civilised nation that had once been through the traumatic experience of having its cyphers read would ever allow it to happen again and that, after the wide publicity given to Room 40's results, it would be a waste of time to work on German high-grade systems.

In the wake of the First World War, the Germans had initially gone over to a one-time pad system, regarded by the British as totally unbreakable. Eventually, Cooper recalled, the Americans did decypher it and the machine used to make the one-time pad was reconstructed. 'Only long after this did it emerge that the clue to the system had been in our hands all the time. The inventor had submitted it to GC&CS first and it had been turned down.'

In the late 1920s the Germans began using a new machine-generated cypher. The Enigma machine had been invented by a Dutchman in 1919 in the wake of the success of Room 40. Similar in appearance to a typewriter, the machine's keys sent electrical impulses through three rotatable wheels via a series of electrical contacts and wires to produce the encyphered text.

Despite its appearance, the Enigma machine was incapable of printing anything out. The electrical impulse generated by keying in each letter of the clear text translated it into another letter which lit up on a lampboard above the keyboard. These encyphered letters were then taken down and transmitted in four- or five-letter groups. By typing each letter of the encyphered version into the machine, the operator at the other end was able to see the decyphered message light up letter by letter on his own lampboard.

Naturally, both the sender's and the receiver's machines had to be set in exactly the same way. Alterations in the settings were achieved: (1), by the choice of three wheels from a selection of five; (2), by varying the order of the wheels within the machine; (3), by means of a rotating ring on each wheel which placed different letters over different contacts; (4), by using a plugboard at the front of the machine which introduced further variations to the wiring circuit between the keys and the lampboard, and (5), by setting each wheel in a certain position, indicated by a letter or number in a window in front of the machine.

When the operator entered a letter into the system, the electrical impulse thus created flowed first through the plugboard, then through the wheels before being turned back by a reflector to return through the wheels via a different route. It then went back out through the plugboard again to whichever terminal on the lampboard the circuit now directed it.

To add further to the problems facing the codebreaker, each time a key was pressed the right-hand wheel moved on one of its twenty-six positions, introducing a new circuit for each letter. After twenty-six key strokes, the middle wheel moved round one position of its own, then once it had moved on a further twenty-five positions, the final left-hand wheel moved on one position.

There were sixty possible orders in which the wheels could be placed in the machine, with a total of 17,576 different position settings for each wheel. The plugboard allowed 150 million million changes of circuit. The total number of possible settings for a basic German Enigma cypher machine was, therefore, 159 million million million.

During the 1920s, the machine was taken up and marketed by Arthur Scherbius, a Berlin engineer, and by the early 1930s was in widespread use within the German armed forces. But it was not until the summer of 1936 that any attempt was made by the British to see if the German cyphers were actually as unbreakable as they had always believed.

The codebreaker asked by Denniston to attempt to unravel the Enigma cypher was Dilly Knox, a brilliant man but in the true tradition of GC&CS eccentrics, as Cooper explained.

> Knox had a very powerful intellect but tended to be incomprehensible and intolerant of people who could not understand him. This was partly due to his background which was classical rather than mathematical. He worked at one time on Hungarian, and did not trouble to learn the language, treating the whole thing as an abstract problem.
>
> I remember him coming to me with a piece of paper covered with cypher groups with marks in coloured chalks over them. It was, he said, an account of an interview with an Italian diplomat. Did I have anything in Italian diplomatic cyphers on the same subject? 'This group taken with that one means that either Mussolini or Stalin did, or did not, say that the man named in this group, who may be Sir Samuel Hoare, is going to speak at the League of Nations,' he said. I could only reply that I did not have anything to fit. 'Well, the Hungarian is probably lying anyway,' Dilly said and shuffled out of the room.

In early 1939, Denniston recruited Peter Twinn, a mathematician from Brasenose College, Oxford, to help Knox on the Enigma problem. The classics professors who dominated GC&CS were highly sceptical that recruiting a mathematician would help, Twinn recalled.

> They regarded mathematicians as very strange beasts indeed. They required a little persuasion before they believed they could do anything practical or helpful at all.
>
> The people working on Enigma were the celebrated Dilly Knox and a chap called Tony Kendrick, quite a character, who was once head boy at Eton. There was a slightly bizarre interview with Dilly who was himself a bit of a character to put it mildly. He didn't believe in wasting too much time in training his assistant, he gave me a five-minute talk and left me to get on with it.

A couple of months later, another mathematician joined them, coming in every so often to offer advice. Like Knox, Alan Turing was a fellow of King's College, Cambridge. A painfully shy man who wore unpressed clothes and had a nervous habit of picking at the flesh around his fingernails, Turing was a true genius. A few years earlier, at the age of twenty-four, he had developed the theory of a machine which, by reading a tape of marked or blank squares, could compute anything that could be calculated, the basic principle behind the modern computer.

Despite Turing's assistance, the Enigma team had been unable to overcome a major problem. They had wheel and plug settings for certain days with encyphered messages to go with them but without a machine in front of them, they were unable to work out the order in which the keys were attached to the machine's various electrical circuits, Twinn recalled.

> Dilly, who had a taste for inventing fanciful jargon, called this the QWERTZU, as in the keyboard order familiar to all typists. We had no idea what the order was. We had tried QWERTZU, that didn't work. There are twenty-six letters in the alphabet. Our ordinary alphabet has them in a certain order but the Germans weren't idiots. When they had the perfect opportunity to introduce a safeguard to their machine by jumbling it up that would be the sensible thing to. After all there were millions of different ways of doing it. We hadn't made much impact, indeed no impact at all, until the middle of 1939, when the Poles lent a hand.

The Poles, working in tandem with the French, had been trying to find ways of breaking Enigma for a number of years. Marian Rejewski, a Polish mathematician and codebreaker, had been attempting to decypher Enigma messages since late 1932. During the war, the keys would be changed on a daily basis, sometimes even more frequently. But when Rejewski began working on the problem, the Germans were changing the wheel order every three months.

This was an extraordinary error. Rejewski soon realised that the first six letters of any message were the three-letter wheel setting, the starting position for that message, repeated twice. The specific wheels in use, the order they should be put into the machine, and the positions of each of the rings were laid down in signals instructions that changed daily. Once the lid was closed, the operator had to choose a new three-letter setting, one letter corresponding to each of the wheels.

With his machine set in the *Grundstellung* (basic) position, the operator typed those three letters twice, as in ABC ABC, to obtain an encyphered indicator to allow the other operator to set up his machine. He then set his own machine to encypher the rest of the message. Having received the message, the other operator used the indicator to reset his own machine in order to decypher the rest of the message. Thus both the first and fourth encyphered letters represented the same original letter. Similarly, the second and fifth letter were the same and so were the third and sixth.

By building up a sequence of these letters, Rejewski soon found that they produced closed sequences. If the indicator on one message was DMQVBN, with D and V representing the same letter, he now had only to find a message beginning with V, say VONPUY, to find out that the next encyphered letter in the sequence was P. By continuing this process he could build up a complete closed cycle of encyphered letters all representing just one single original letter, to continue this example perhaps DVPFKXGZYO with the letter following O being D and the whole sequence then repeating itself.

Making the correct assumption that, left to their own devices, operators would choose an obvious combination for the setting such as ABC; a simple three-letter word; or the same letter repeated, as in AAA, Rejewski guessed his way into the text settings for each day. If he found a closed sequence he knew his guess had been correct. Without any knowledge of the internal wiring of the Enigma machine this was still useless. He was in the process of using mathematics to try to work out the wiring when the French took a hand with a somewhat more traditional form of espionage.

They had recruited a spy in the German Army's cypher office, a man called Hans-Thilo Schmidt whom they code-named 'Asché'. His reasons for betraying German secrets were simple. He was a playboy, said Captain Gustav Bertrand, head of the French code-breaking operation. 'He was fond of money, which he needed because he was fonder still of women.'

Over the next seven years Asché was wined, dined and provided with female companions by French intelligence officers in a series of foreign cities. In return, he handed over more than 300 secret documents including instructions for the use of the Enigma machine, the settings used on the Army machine, or keys as the crypto-graphers called them, and a long piece of text in both its encyphered and plain text forms together with the relevant settings.

Bertrand approached both the British and the Poles with this material. Remarkably, the British showed little interest, still believing that the Enigma cyphers could not be broken. But to Rejewski the German instructions and the Army keys were as manna from heaven, helping him to make still further progress in divining the mysteries of the Enigma machine. In what Bertrand later described as 'this incredible adventure, unequalled in any country in the world', Rejewski managed to reconstruct the complete Enigma machine.

The British had no idea of the progress made by the Poles, but they had been exchanging some information with Bertrand. 'The French used to send us files in bright red jackets which we nicknamed Scarlet Pimpernels,' said Cooper. 'Eventually they disclosed that they had a liaison with the Poles and three-sided Anglo-Franco-Polish discussions began on Enigma problems.'

In July 1939, at a meeting in the Pyry Forest just outside Warsaw, Rejewski explained to Bertrand, Knox and Denniston the progress the Poles had made on breaking the Enigma cypher. There had been some early breaks but recent refinements were causing difficulties. Nevertheless, they had the answer to the one problem still holding the British codebreakers back. The first question Knox put to Rejewski was, how were the keys connected to the first wheel? 'What is the QWERTZU?' he asked.

With hindsight, of course, the answer was ridiculously simple, and so obvious that Knox, Turing, Kendrick and Twinn had never considered it as a serious possibility. The connections were in alphabetical order, Twinn recalled.

> It was such an obvious thing to do, really a silly thing to do, that nobody, not Dilly Knox or Tony Kendrick or Alan Turing, ever thought it worthwhile trying it. I know in retrospect it looks daft. I can only say that's how it struck all of us and none of the others were idiots. Assuming our stolen message was genuine, what the Poles had told us was quite sufficient for us to start reading the messages. I'm told that after the meeting, Dilly returned to his hotel in a taxi with his French colleague, chanting, 'Nous avons le QWERTZU, nous marchons ensemble.' I can quite believe it. I wish I had been there.

A few weeks later, the Poles presented Bertrand with two replicas of Enigma machines they had built, one for the French and one for the British. Bertrand later described taking the British copy to London where, having dismounted from the Golden Arrow at Victoria Station, he handed it over on the platform to Colonel Stewart Menzies, the deputy head of MI6, who was swathed in smoke and wearing a dinner jacket with the rosette of the Legion d'Honneur in his buttonhole. *'Accueil triomphal'*, said Bertrand. A triumphant welcome indeed!

Admiral Sinclair had bought the mansion at Bletchley Park in the spring of 1938 as an evacuation site for both MI6 and GC&CS, acting entirely on his own initiative. Having realised that, if it came to war, he would need to protect his staff from the inevitable air raids, he had asked the Foreign Office to pay for a 'War Station'. The FO's response was that it was the War Office which was responsible for war, so the generals should pay. The generals told Sinclair that as a former Director of Naval Intelligence he should go to the admirals, who told him that since he was part of the Foreign Office, the mandarins should pay.

Frustrated by his inability to get a government department to pay the £7,500 asking price for Bletchley Park, Sir Hugh dipped into his own pocket to buy it. 'We know he paid for it,' said one former intelligence officer. 'We're not sure if he was ever repaid. He died soon afterwards so he probably wasn't.' Bletchley Park was given the covername 'Station X', not as a symbol of mystery but simply as the tenth of a large number of sites acquired by MI6 for its various wartime operations and designated using Roman numerals.

Shortly before the Munich crisis of September 1938, some of the codebreakers and a number of MI6 sections moved to Bletchley Park for 'a rehearsal'. Sinclair put a Captain Ridley, RN, one of the MI6 officers, in charge of the operation. 'MI6 provided some cars for transport, but many people used their own cars and gave lifts to others,' Cooper said. 'It fell to my lot to be driven in by Knox who had a remarkable theory that the best way to avoid accidents was to take every cross-road at maximum speed.'

The Broadway tradition of living well was maintained throughout the rehearsal. Sinclair called in his favourite chef from the Savoy Grill and the staff all sat down at a long table to feast on *haute cuisine*. With unfortunate timing, the chef then attempted to commit suicide. Clarke was forced to telephone the Chief Constable of the county in an attempt to keep the story out of the papers and ensure the codebreakers' presence there remained secret. Shortly afterwards, Neville Chamberlain returned from his meeting with Hitler in Munich proclaiming 'peace in our time', Cooper recalled. 'We all trooped back to London with mixed feelings of shame and relief.'

There had always been a general acceptance among the code-breakers that if there were ever another war, 'we should have to mobilise the dons again', Cooper recalled. Denniston now made the rounds of the universities to bring in former colleagues from the First World War and to seek out new talent.

> He dined at several high tables in Oxford and Cambridge and came home with promises from a number of dons to attend a 'territorial training course'. It would be hard to exaggerate the importance of this course for the future development of GC&CS. Not only had Denniston brought in scholars of the humanities, of the type of many of his own permanent staff, but he had also invited mathematicians of a somewhat different type who were specially attracted by the Enigma problem. I have heard some cynics on the permanent staff scoffing at this. They did not realise that Denniston, for all his diminutive stature, was a bigger man than they.

The academics who attended the course were made to sign the Official Secrets Act and told that on receipt of a telegram they should report to Bletchley Park; they would be paid £600 a year and the remainder of their former salaries would be made up by their colleges. On 23 August 1939, Russia signed a non-aggression pact with Germany and it became clear that war was inevitable. Telegrams were sent out calling the dons to Bletchley Park to help to solve 'the Enigma problem'.

Nigel de Grey later recalled how in the first few weeks of the war, the academics recruited by Denniston 'began to drop in with the slightly unexpected effect of carrier pigeons'. They found the staff of GC&CS completely unruffled by the commencement of hostilities. At lunchtime, most of the codebreakers, including Barbara Abernethy, would troop out on to the lawn in front of the house to play rounders.

> We had a tennis ball and somebody managed to commandeer an old broom handle, drilled a hole in it and put a leather strap in it. It was all we had, things were getting a bit tough to get. If it was a fine day, we'd all say rounders at 1 o'clock, we'd all go out and play, just to sort of let off steam. Everybody argued about the rules and the dons just laid them down, in Latin sometimes. We used trees as bases. 'He got past the deciduous,' one would say. 'No he didn't,' another would argue. 'He was still between the conifer and the deciduous'. That was the way they were.

Malcolm Muggeridge, the author and journalist, served in MI6 during the war and visited Bletchley Park. He recalled seeing the codebreakers debate the finer points of the rules.

> They adopted the quasi-serious manner dons affect when engaged in activities likely to be regarded as frivolous or insignificant in comparison with their weightier studies. They would dispute some point about the game with the same fervour as they might the question of free will or determinism, or whether the world began with a big bang or a process of continuing creation. Shaking their heads ponderously, sucking air noisily into their noses between words.

On arrival at Bletchley Park, Denniston's recruits were allocated sections and billets. 'None of the new arrivals had any idea of the general organisation or indeed of what other sections existed beside the one to which they had been appointed and it was no one's business to explain,' de Grey said. 'This was not like reservists rejoining the colours, it was more like the prim first day at a public school.'

Chapter 3

THE FIRST BREAK

If the new boys had no idea of the general organisation of the codebreaking organisation they were not alone. Most of the pre-war codebreakers did not understand the full scale of what was going on, nor indeed did they have any interest in doing so. Their only concern was to find solutions to their own cryptographic puzzles.

Bletchley Park was at the centre of a web of intercept sites around the country where wireless operators carefully logged all German radio messages before sending them to the codebreakers by teleprinter or, in most cases, by motorcycle courier. These Y Service stations were operated by the Army, Navy and Air Force; the Foreign Office; the Post Office; and the Metropolitan Police.

Joan Nicholls talked her way into the female equivalent of the Army, the Auxiliary Territorial Service (ATS), at the age of fifteen by pretending she was two years older. She was posted to one of the intercept sites where she was taught how to operate a radio set and to transcribe German messages sent out in Morse code.

When there was a lot of excitement the wires would be absolutely humming with Morse. They would be transmitting all over the place and we would really have cramp in our fingers sometimes trying to write it down non-stop, because you only had one chance to get it.

We had to get the preamble and the first three blocks absolutely accurate because that was the key to decoding the message. If we missed a letter we had to know exactly what position it was in and if the signal faded and we lost information, we had to know how many blocks we missed. Every one of our sets had access to three aerials. We had what looked like a little switchboard in the set room and, if the reception wasn't good from one aerial, we could switch over to another.

It could be quite exciting but sometimes we had a very quiet shift and not an awful lot happened. Nights were very boring, hour after hour of listening for the station to open. It was a little bit like a cat sitting outside a mousehole waiting patiently for the mouse to appear and that's how we were. We'd be sitting there listening, waiting for them to come to life.

Then suddenly we'd hear the signal of them coming back, transmitting again and then all your adrenalin was running and it didn't matter how tired you were, how sleepy or bored you felt, the minute that station came alive again, you would be alive too, tearing pieces of paper off the pad and scribbling away like mad.

The main Navy intercept sites were at Scarborough and Winchester. The Army site, which was monitoring the bulk of Enigma traffic, was at Fort Bridgelands near Chatham, and there was an Air Force Y unit at Cheadle. In the months leading up to the war, the Post Office had been building a number of other intercept sites for diplomatic traffic to allow the armed forces to concentrate on military and naval traffic and one of these, at Sandridge, near St Albans, was already in place working directly to Bletchley Park. Two more were due to open in Scotland at Cupar and Brora.

'GC&CS had always tended to take too little interest in the radio by which they lived,' Cooper recalled. Similarly the three services had been dismissive of the work of the codebreakers. The Y services believed they produced sufficient intelligence simply by analysing the activities of the radio networks they were monitoring, indeed the RAF site was completely ignoring the Enigma traffic. When Cooper suggested that Cheadle should begin taking Enigma, the head of the RAF Y Service replied: 'My Y Service exists to produce intelligence, not to provide stuff for people at Bletchley to fool about with.'

One of the Cambridge mathematicians brought in to look at Enigma was Gordon Welchman, a Fellow of Sidney Sussex College, Cambridge. A studious, pipe-smoking man in his early thirties with dark hair and a moustache, he was immediately allocated to work on Enigma with Knox. 'During my first week or two at Bletchley, I got the impression that he didn't like me,' said Welchman. 'Very soon after my arrival I was turned out of the cottage and sent to Elmers School.'

Welchman was told to study callsigns, the names used on the radio nets to identify individual stations, and the preambles to the messages, which might include information that would help in solving the Enigma problem.

Previously, I suppose I had absorbed the common view that cryptoanalysis was a matter of dealing with individual messages, of solving intricate puzzles, and of working in a secluded backroom with little contact with the outside world. As I studied that first collection of decodes, however, I began to see, somewhat dimly, that I was involved in something very different. We were dealing with an entire communications system that would serve the needs of the German ground and air forces. These callsigns came alive as representing elements of those forces, whose commanders at various echelons would have to send messages to each other. The use of different keys for different purposes suggested different command structures for the various aspects of military operations.

Welchman was not alone in realising that if Bletchley Park was to be as effective as possible, codebreaking and the process of traffic analysis used by the services to extract intelligence from the wireless messages, had to be coordinated. But he had the drive to make it happen.

No one else seemed to be doing anything about this potential gold mine so I drew up a comprehensive plan which called for the close coordination of radio interception, analysis of intercepted messages, breaking Enigma keys, decoding messages from the broken keys and extracting intelligence from the decodes.

He presented it to Commander Edward Travis, Denniston's deputy. 'Jumbo' Travis was not a codebreaker but the government's main adviser on what type of codes and cyphers to use. Short, stout and bald, with small round spectacles, he was an able and forceful administrator and did not feel himself bound by the traditions of the veteran codebreakers. The innovative nature of Welchman's scheme and the young codebreaker's drive and enthusiasm persuaded Travis it would work. Given that at this stage, just a few weeks after the start of the war, the Enigma messages had yet to be broken, both men were showing remarkable foresight. 'Travis won high-level approval for my plan,' Welchman said. 'And we were able to start recruiting the high-quality staff that would be needed.'

As a result of the problems with the RAF Y Service, Cooper had already decided to attach a number of his staff to Cheadle to allow a liaison officer to be allocated to each shift of wireless operators.

I applied to the Air Ministry for a number of computor clerks. This curious title had nothing to do with electronic computers, which had not yet been invented, but was an echo of an old War Office covername for cryptanalysts – Signal Computor. A successful Computor Clerk watchkeeper was going to need considerable initiative, and would have to fit in with the special world of Cheadle radio operators.

The German-speaking ladies that the Air Ministry sent down to Bletchley pretty obviously failed to meet these requirements. There was, for example, the elderly and very imposing typist-secretary whom the section immediately nicknamed Queen Mary, and a younger rather promising recruit who made her position impossible, scandalising her Bletchley billetors by saying to all and sundry that the only friends she had ever had were Germans.

In the subsection dealing with the German Navy, Phoebe Senyard had also had problems with a number of the temporary clerical staff she had been allocated, some of whom were 'of the most doubtful kind'. The outbreak of war had left her deluged with intercepted messages. But the return of Frank Birch, a veteran of Room 40, who now took charge of the burgeoning German naval subsection, led to a vast improvement.

Birch, a short, bald man who, quite apart from his Room 40 codebreaking exploits, had succeeded in combining fame in the theatre with an academic career, was highly popular. He was not only a great friend of Knox, with whom he had once shared a house, he also managed, like de Grey and Cooper, to transcend the cultural differences between the old codebreakers and the new. Barbara Abernethy recalled his popularity.

> He was a great person. I knitted him a blue balaclava helmet which he wore throughout the war. He was billeted in the Duncombe Arms at Great Brickhill. They had a lot of dons there, Gordon Welchman, Patrick Wilkinson. It was full of dons all the time. All of them having such a jolly time that they called it the Drunken Arms.

Welchman recalled that the darts and billiards room of the Duncombe Arms became a social club for all the Bletchley Park staff who were billeted nearby. 'Our host made us extremely comfortable,' he said. 'The company was extremely enjoyable. Dilly's great friend Frank Birch was the central figure. James Passant, a close friend of mine and the History Fellow at Sidney Sussex College, often joined us. So did Dennis Babbage, another close Cambridge friend from Magdalene. I remember his skill on the billiard table, particularly with strokes played behind his back.'

Birch's arrival brought a dramatic improvement to the German naval subsection's morale, recalled Phoebe Senyard. 'From then onwards, everything began to be properly organised and to take shape,' she said. 'I now became aware, through Mr Birch, of what our functions really were.'

Their main role was to supply the Admiralty's Operational Intelligence Centre (OIC), which was tracking enemy shipping, with any intelligence they could extract from the intercepts of German naval messages via the direct telephone link. Messages in cyphers other than the still-unbreakable Enigma were decoded and passed by teleprinter to the Admiralty.

The Naval Section, under the overall command of Nobby Clarke, continued to work on a number of other codes and cyphers, not least Italian, Japanese, Spanish, and Russian traffic. But Birch's German subsection was becoming something of a cuckoo in the nest and the tiny corner of the library which it had been allocated soon became too small recalled Phoebe Senyard.

> Files were increasing and the numbers of staff were slowly mounting. A colleague and I were working together on a small kitchen table and getting very much in one another's way. Even the floor was used to sort signals into dates and frequencies and it must have been amusing to see us on all fours doing this job. It needs no great effort of the imagination to realise how delighted we were to hear that we were to move into Hut 4.

From that time on the sections took their names from the wooden huts into which they moved, keeping them even when they were transferred into more permanent brick-built offices later in the war. The move to Hut 4, essentially a wooden extension to the left of the main house, came at the expense of a rose garden. 'The Leons who had owned the house had a beautiful rose garden which we had overlooked, and a gorgeous maze,' said Abernethy, 'both of which disappeared when they put up these dreadful huts.'

But that was not the only drawback, as Edward Green, the office manager, soon discovered.

> When we were to emerge from our shell in the library and move into Hut 4, which had almost been built around us to the sound of hammers and electric saws, planes and drill, I rang up the Office of Works and asked for 40 chairs and 10 tables. Our difficulties were increased by the fact that our work was so hush-hush that we were not able to specify the reason for our importunities – for so they were regarded.

I was asked to indent for them on form number etc. and told that 'in due course' I should receive them. When the 'due course' spread into a fortnight, I realised that the ordinary channels led straight down the drain and began to use my own methods. I took the day off, went up to London, connected with a priceless office keeper in our peacetime quarters and returned with two furniture vans of loot. I can well imagine the army of civil servants who are still searching for those tables, chairs, desks, card indexes and so on.

The incident was to earn Green the nickname 'Scrounger' among the occupants of the other huts. It was an alias in which he apparently revelled, largely because of his fondness for the Hut 4 staff, who in turn referred to him affectionately as 'Daddy' Green.

We were a heterogeneous crowd in our section, mostly the product of our older universities, sitting cheek by jowl with lady clerks. Once one had discovered the human end of them, they were worth their weight in gold. If we did strike a dud it was my business to sell him or her. I am told that I once swapped a small and incompetent typist for a large and priceless card index.

As autumn turned to winter, the staff experienced another problem that was to become all too familiar to them. The buildings had not been designed to cope with so many occupants and the heating was woefully inadequate. 'It was dreadful,' said Barbara Abernethy. 'We had an electric stove which didn't work and a very poor heating system. We all froze. We had to wear coats and mittens.'

Given Sinclair's difficulties in getting the funds required to expand the BP operation, the situation was unlikely to improve. 'Soon after we settled in, the Admiral came on a tour of inspection,' said Cooper. 'He complained of the cold in the Air Section and ordered Ridley to put the central heating on. He looked ill, and not long afterwards we heard that he had died.'

It was even colder in the huts, which were bleak after the comfort of the house. Bare concrete floors disguised with a coating of red tile paint, windows with blackout curtains, wooden trestle tables, light bulbs with no shades and inefficient electric heaters, or worse, cast-iron coke stoves with metal chimneys going up through the asbestos roof, said Phoebe Senyard.

They were awful. When the wind was high, long flames would be blown out into the room frightening anyone nearby. Alternatively, the fire would go out and smoke would come billowing forth filling the room with a thick fog. It was a familiar sight to find Mr Green on his hands and knees wearing thick motor gloves endeavouring to light a recalcitrant fire, whilst the shivering occupant would be dressed in a thick overcoat, scarf and gloves endeavouring to cope with his work, with all the windows open to let out the smoke.

Apart from naval signals, and the static Enigma traffic still being monitored by Chatham, the bulk of the messages received from the Y stations in the early months of the war were from the radio networks of the German police who were mopping up behind the advancing German troops in Poland. These were also being intercepted by the French who managed to smuggle Rejewski and his fellow codebreakers out of Poland in mid-September. They were housed in Mission Richard, a large villa on the banks of the Marne at Vignolles, just outside Paris, and exchanged information with Bletchley Park via Biffy Dunderdale, the veteran MI6 head of station in the French capital. Several British codebreakers were sent to France as liaison officers and a number of French officers arrived at Bletchley Park to undertake a similar role.

The Enigma research section, led by Dilly Knox and now including Turing, Twinn and John Jeffreys, a mathematician from Downing College, Cambridge, was getting nowhere. Since the early breaks by Rejewski, the Germans had considerably refined their use of the Enigma machine and began enforcing much stricter operator discipline. Despite the undoubted brilliance of the team, they seemed no closer to breaking the code or, more correctly in the case of Enigma, the cypher.

The first step in breaking any cypher is to try to find features which correspond to the original plain text. Whereas codes substitute groups of letters or figures for words, phrases or even complete concepts, cyphers replace every individual letter of every word. They therefore tend to reflect the characteristics of the language of the original text. This makes them vulnerable to studies of letter frequency; for example, the most common letters in English are E, T, A, O and N. If a reasonable amount, or 'depth', of English text encyphered in the same simple cipher were studied for 'letter frequency', the letter that came up most often would represent E. The second most common letter would be T and so on. By working this out and filling in the letters, some will form obvious words with letters missing, allowing the codebreaker to fill in the gaps and recover those letters as well.

Contact analysis, another basic weapon used by the codebreaker, takes this principle a step further. Some letters will appear frequently alongside each other. The most obvious example in the English language is TH as in 'the' or 'that'. By combining these two weapons the codebreaker could make a reasonable guess that where a single letter appeared repeatedly after the T which he had already recovered from letter frequency, the unknown letter was probably H, particularly if the next letter had already been recovered as E. In that case, he might conclude that the letter after the E was probably the start of a new word and so the process of building up the message would go on.

Machine cyphers were developed to try to protect against these tell-tale frequencies and letter pairings, which is why the wheels of the Enigma machine were designed to move around one step after each twenty-six key strokes. By doing this, the Germans hoped to ensure that no original letter was ever represented by the same encyphered letter often enough to allow the codebreakers to build up sufficient depth to break the keys.

But it still left open a few chinks of light that would permit the British codebreakers to attack it. They made the assumption, correct far more often than not, that in the part of the message being studied the right-hand wheel would not have had the opportunity to move the middle wheel on a notch. This reduced the odds to a more manageable proportion. They were shortened still further by the Enigma machine's great drawback. No letter could ever be represented by itself.

This fact was of great assistance in using cribs, pieces of plain text that were thought likely to appear in an Enigma message. This might be because it was in a common pro forma, or because there was an obvious word or phrase it was expected to contain. Sometimes it was even possible to predict that a message passed at a lower level, on a system that had already been broken, would be repeated on a radio link using the Enigma cypher. If the two identical messages could be matched up, in what was known as a 'kiss', it would provide an easy method of breaking the key settings.

The Germans, with their liking for order, were particularly prone to providing the British with potential cribs. The same words were frequently used at the start of messages to give the address of the recipient, a popular opening being *An die Gruppe* (To the group).

Later in the war, there were a number of lazy operators in underemployed backwaters whose situation reports regularly read simply: *Keine besondere Ereignisse*, literally 'no special occurences', perhaps better translated as 'nothing to report'.

Most cribs could appear at any point in the message. Even *Keine besondere Ereignisse* was likely to be preceded or followed by some piece of routine information. But the fact that none of the letters in the crib could ever be matched up with the same letter in the encyphered message made it much easier to find out where they fitted.

If we take *Keine besondere Ereignisse* as our crib and place it above an encyphered message, divided into the five-letter groups in which they would normally be sent by the German Army or Air Force operators, it is easy to see that the number of places it would fit are limited by the fact that no letter can be encyphered as itself.

KEIN EBESO NDERE EREIG NISSE

GEGOH JYDPO MQNJC OSGAH LEIHY SOPJS MIUKK

Moving the message just one place to the left or right would have one of the first two Es of *Ereignisse* encyphered as itself, an obvious impossibility on the Enigma machine. Moving it even further to the left or right only produces more duplicated letters. In this particular case, and it was only rarely ever that easy, this is in fact the only place in which the crib could fit. Mavis Lever, a member of Knox's team, described the codebreaking process.

> If you think of it as a sort of crossword technique of filling in what it might be. I don't want to give the impression that it was all easy. You did have inspired guesses. But then you would also have to spend a lot of time, sometimes you would have to spend the whole night, assuming every position that there could be on the three different wheels.
>
> You would have to work at it very, very hard and after you had done it for a few hours you wondered, you know, whether you would see anything when it was before your eyes because you were so snarled up in it. But then of course, the magic moment comes when it really works and there it all is, the Italian, or the German, or whatever it is. It just feels marvellous, absolutely marvellous. I don't think that there is anything one could compare to it. There is nothing like seeing a code broken, that is really the absolute tops.

Despite the recognised potential for breaking the cypher, either by using the cribs or by working out the key settings as Rejewski had done, it was almost four months into the war and the British appeared to be no closer to solving the problem. The Phoney War would not go on forever, a solution to the Enigma problem needed to be found quickly.

Travis decided that a more maverick approach might help and that Welchman had the drive and enthusiasm to lead it. The Enigma team was involved in brilliant and vitally important theoretical research. A different, more practical approach, working in parallel, might find an answer to the problem. There was, he said, a chance that 'a chuck-it and chance-it spirit might hook the fish while the more experienced fisherman still considered the colour of his fly'.

As the first Christmas of the war approached, the members of Hut 4 were drawing lots to see who would have to remain at Bletchley Park over the holiday period. Phoebe Senyard was one of those who had to stay.

> I lost and resigned myself to a miserable Christmas, the first for some years that I had spent away from home. When the day arrived, I found that there were more people at BP than I had thought there would be, for the travel ban which had been imposed had prevented quite a number from going home.
>
> Mr Birch invited me to a small celebration and I arrived afterwards in the dining room for lunch feeling quite happy and, being rather late, to find the hall decorated magnificently, with everyone sitting down, wearing the peculiar paper hats one gets from Christmas crackers and blowing whistles which shot out a terrific length of paper. Every seat was occupied with the exception of one round the corner. But there I sat quite happily with a wonderful lunch in front of me.

All the time, new huts were being built. It was bitterly cold that winter with a lot of snow and ice, swiftly turned into mud by the coming and going of the workmen, said Barbara Abernethy. 'Captain Faulkner, who had owned the land and was the local builder, was contracted to put up all the huts. He was very fond of hunting and he would come round in his hunting pink and oversee the construction.'

Once Christmas was over, Welchman drove his blue Austin 7 around Cambridge recruiting former colleagues and students for his codebreaking section, which was to be housed in one of Faulkner's newly constructed wooden huts to the right of the mansion.

Stuart Milner-Barry, chess correspondent of *The Times* and a fellow student of Welchman's at Trinity College, Cambridge, was one of the first to join Hut 6, as it was to be known. He had been in Argentina when the war broke out, playing chess for Britain, along with his friends Hugh Alexander and Harry Golombek. They too soon joined, as did Dennis Babbage, from Magdalene College, Cambridge; John Herivel, a former student of Welchman's; and Howard Smith, like Welchman a Fellow of Sidney Sussex, and later the head of MI5. Continuity with Knox's efforts was provided by John Jeffreys.

The organisation of Hut 6 reflected Welchman's vision of a totally integrated interception organisation. At one end of what would become something of a production line was Bletchley Park Control, which was initially staffed by Travis ringing round the top London banks and begging them to loan him their brightest young men.

Control was manned twenty-four hours a day and was in constant touch with the intercept sites to ensure that their coverage of radio frequencies and networks was coordinated and that as little as possible was missed. Where an important station was difficult to hear, it was to be 'double-banked', taken by two different stations so that the chances of picking up a false letter that might throw a spanner into the works were cut down.

'We were told what we would cover and that came from Station X, the intercept control there would tell us what to cover that day with what priority,' Joan Nicholls recalled. 'They would tell us if they wanted them double-banked, two people to take them, or if one good-quality operator would be sufficient. We didn't know that Station X was Bletchley Park. We never knew where it was: you were only told what you needed to know and we just needed to know that Station X was controlling what we actually monitored.'

While the messages themselves arrived from the outstations by motorcycle courier, Traffic Registers giving the preambles and first six groups of the messages intercepted by the outstations were sent by teleprinter to the Hut 6 Registration Room. Here a number of female graduates recruited by Milner-Barry from Newnham College, where his sister had been vice-principal, tried to establish the specific Enigma cypher in use from the preambles, carefully examining them to see if there was any intelligence that could be garnered before the codebreakers got to work. A description of each message, containing the frequency and callsigns; the number;

whether or not it was urgent; and the first two groups, was carefully logged on so-called B-Lists. These became known colloquially as Blists and the female graduates were dubbed 'Blisters'.

Early Hut 6 attempts to break into the key settings centred on the sheet-stacking room where codebreakers used perforated sheets of paper known as the 'Netz' or 'Jeffreys Sheets' to try to break the key in the same way as the Poles. Once a key was broken, the messages were passed to the Machine Room which contained a number of the British Type-X cypher machines, modified to act like Enigma machines. Here they were decyphered.

'When the codebreakers had broken the code they wouldn't sit down themselves and painstakingly decode 500 messages,' said Peter Twinn. 'I've never myself personally decoded a message from start to finish. By the time you've done the first twenty letters and it was obviously speaking perfectly sensible German, for people like me that was the end of our interest.'

Diana Russell Clarke was one of a group of young women in the Hut 6 Machine Room, decyphering the messages.

> The cryptographers would work out the actual settings for the machines for the day. We had these Type-X machines, like typewriters but much bigger. They had three wheels, I think on the left-hand side, all of which had different positions on them. When they got the setting, we were to set them up on our machines. We would have a piece of paper in front of us with what had come over the wireless. We would type it into the machine and hopefully what we typed would come out in German.

Travis and Welchman realised that once the message had been decyphered it had to be passed on to someone who could make use of it. Since there had been no decyphered Enigma messages to pass on, no system was in place to do this. So a team of what was initially four intelligence officers was set up in Hut 3, an L-shaped building which nestled behind Hut 6. Their task was to use their knowledge of German to work out what should have been in the numerous gaps in the messages, translate them and decide who to send them to.

The original section was headed by Lieutenant-Commander Malcolm Saunders, aided by an Army captain; an RAF squadron-leader, who remarkably spoke not a word of German despite allegedly having acquired his knowledge of the *Luftwaffe* while carrying out 'field work' on behalf of MI6; and F. L. Lucas, a Fellow of King's College, Cambridge.

While Welchman busied himself building up his Hut 6 operation, Turing had gone to France to consult with the Polish contacts. Dilly Knox had promised to give them the results of any research based on their findings and was threatening to resign if he was not allowed to keep his word. Denniston first tried to get the Poles to come to Britain but the French refused to allow this and in the event Turing was sent, partly to keep Knox's promise, but more particularly to try to find out why Bletchley was having so much trouble breaking Enigma. He discovered the main reason immediately. Some of the information the Poles had given Bletchley Park had been garbled.

On his return from France in mid-January, Turing used the correct data to lead an attack on a recent day's worth of the Enigma cypher used by the static German Army command, the *Wehrkreise*, and known at Bletchley Park as 'Green', a result of the coloured crayons used to indicate the various keys used by the different parts of the German armed forces.

The Enigma research team finally succeeded in breaking it. Little imagination is required to appreciate how the codebreakers must have felt. The frustration of the past few months was now over. Their conviction that the mathematical approach would pay off had been fully justified, Enigma *could* be broken. Encouraged by their success, they made their first break into what would become their staple diet for the rest of the war, the main 'Red' Enigma that formed the bulk of Chatham's daily 'take'.

'On a snowy January morning in 1940, in a small bleak wooden room with nothing but a table and three chairs, the first bundle of Enigma decodes appeared,' said Lucas.

> The four of us who then constituted Hut 3 had no idea what they were about to disclose. Something fairly straightforward like German police, or something more like diplomatic – neat and explicit documents straight from the office tables of the Führer and the *Wehrmacht* that would simply need translating and forwarding to ministries?
>
> They were neither. In afteryears, even the Führer's orders were duly to appear. But meanwhile here lay a pile of dull, disjointed, and enigmatic scraps, all about the weather, or the petty affairs of a *Luftwaffe* headquarters no one had heard of, or trifles of *Wehrkreise* business; the whole sprinkled with terms no dictionary knew, and abbreviations of which our only guide, a small War Office list, proved often completely innocent. Very small beer, in fact, and full of foreign bodies.

It was not clear at this stage that Red, rather than Green, would become the most important of the keys. What was obvious was that the Red traffic was not, as had been maintained by the military, an Army cypher. When it first appeared, shortly after the formation of the *Wehrmacht* in March 1935, it was clearly passing traffic between a number of ground stations. The Army had ruled that if it was all ground stations it must be military rather than Air Force and the responsibility of Chatham rather than Cheadle. But once the codebreakers managed to crack it they soon discovered it was being used to encypher communications between various *Luftwaffe* headquarters.

Since the end of 1938, the Red traffic had been the Army's main priority. It came as something of a shock to the generals to discover that for more than a year, they had been funding an expensive operation which should have been carried out by the RAF. The Air Ministry was told in no uncertain terms by both the War Office and Denniston that, like it or not, Cheadle was to put a major effort into 'providing stuff for people at Bletchley to fool about with'.

The first British break in the Enigma cypher led to strict security being imposed around the work going on at Bletchley Park. GC&CS was given the covername 'Government Communications Headquarters' to explain the presence of so many members of different government departments at the Park. Hut 6 and Dilly Knox's Enigma Research Section became 'barred zones' for anyone who was not working there, as did Hut 3.

The potential dividend to be provided by BP's 'Most Secret Source' once the real war began was incalculable, but it hung by a slim thread. The British had managed to penetrate the Enigma cyphers only because the Germans were careless and did not adhere strictly to their signals instructions. If they found out and strengthened or even changed their cypher systems, all the efforts of the codebreakers would have been wasted.

The fact that Enigma had been broken was to remain totally secret to anyone who did not need to know, including the bulk of the people working at Bletchley Park itself. 'We knew nothing about Enigma at all until long after the war,' said Julie Lydekker, one of Cooper's clerks. 'It was a very strange set-up. We were very much in watertight compartments because of the security so one really only knew one's own sections.'

Similarly, those in Hut 6 knew nothing of what went on elsewhere in the Park, said Susan Wenham, one of the codebreakers.

It was a very curious organisation. We were very, very depart-
mentalised. You never discussed your work with anyone except your
little group that you worked with. I hadn't a clue what was going on in
the rest of the Park and nobody else had a clue what we were doing,
except the real high-ups. It was a curious world of its own.

The need-to-know principle was paramount. Gwen Davies had been
sent to Bletchley Park as a member of the Women's Auxiliary Air
Force (WAAF). She was told she was being posted to nearby RAF
Chicksands.

When I arrived at Chicksands I was taken into the administration office
where there was a driver waiting and he said with perfect seriousness:
'Do we blindfold her or do we use the covered van?' and ultimately they
used the covered van, I was shut into the back of a blacked-out van and
taken to Bletchley which struck me as rather absurd because of course
when I was there I had to know where I was, you know, I had to go home
on leave.

Davies was given a security lecture and told never to reveal, even to
her close family, what she did at Bletchley.

I had to sign the Official Secrets Act and I was told that I must never
ever say to anyone where I was working, except to say Box 101,
Bletchley, and that I must never ever tell anyone about any of the work
I was doing. You never talked even to your own watch about your
traffic, about what you were doing. So you talked about personalities,
that was the great thing. Gossip at Bletchley was absolutely wonderful,
apocryphal stories about everybody flew everywhere, personalities
were safe to talk about.

As Hut 6 expanded, Mavis Lever was one of those sent up from the
Broadway headquarters to fill the gap. She had been halfway through
a German degree at University College London when the war broke
out.

I was concentrating on German romantics and then I realised the German
romantics would soon be overhead and I thought well, I really ought to
do something better for the war effort. I said I'd train as a nurse and their
response was: 'Oh no you don't. You use your German.' So I thought,
great. This is going to be an interesting job, Mata Hari, seducing Prussian
officers. But I don't think either my legs or my German were good enough
because they sent me to GC&CS.

She had been working in London Section perusing the personal columns of *The Times* for coded spy messages and using captured codebooks to decode them when Bletchley began to call for more staff.

> I was taken to Dilly Knox's section, in the cottage. It was very much a research unit. Hut 6 was up and running and operational, but Dilly had been one of the great pioneers of it all. He was working on things that hadn't been broken.
>
> It was a strange little outfit in the cottage because, well, organisation is not a word you would associate with Dilly Knox. When I arrived, he said: 'Oh, hello, we're breaking machines, have you got a pencil?' That was it. I was never really told what to do. 'Here you are, here's a whole load of rubbish get on with it.' I think looking back on it that was a great precedent in my life, because he taught me to think that you could do things yourself without always checking up to see what the book said. That was the way the cottage worked. We were looking at new traffic all the time or where the wheels or the wiring had been changed, or at other new techniques. So you had to work it all out yourself from scratch.

Knox had a unique knack of using his imagination to open up codes and cyphers, said Lever.

> He would stuff his pipe with sandwiches sometimes instead of tobacco he was so woolly-minded, but he was brilliant, absolutely brilliant. It just seemed to come naturally to him. He said the most extraordinary things. He was a great admirer of Lewis Carroll: 'Which way does the clock go round?' And if you were stupid enough to say clockwise, he'd just say: 'Oh no it doesn't, not if you're the clock, it's the opposite way.' And that's sometimes how you had to think about the machines. Not just to look at them how you saw them but what was going on inside. That was the only way in which one was really trained. But trained is a bad word because that was the one thing you mustn't be. You have got to look at each thing afresh and wonder how you could approach it.

Chapter 4

THE BATTLE OF BRITAIN

In the early hours of 9 April 1940, the Germans invaded first Denmark and then Norway. The Phoney War was at an end. Almost immediately, a new Enigma key made an appearance. Five days later, the Yellow key (as it had been dubbed in Hut 6) was broken, producing a mass of intelligence on the German operations in Norway.

The intercepted messages told the British virtually every detail of what the advancing Germans were doing. Nothing had prepared the codebreakers for this amount of material and both Hut 6 and Hut 3 began working around the clock to get the intelligence they were producing to London. Until now, all the reports had been bagged up at the end of the day and sent down by van to MI6 headquarters in Broadway, from where they were passed on to the War Office, Air Ministry and the Admiralty.

This was clearly no longer sufficient. Much of the material was urgent and had to be sent to London immediately. Initially, Hut 3 tried to do this by telephone. But it was an open line with no scrambler and was frighteningly insecure. This process was quickly abandoned to be replaced by teleprinters operated by Hut 3's own staff, bypassing the main teleprinter room in the mansion and in direct contact with MI6.

The staff of Hut 3 was expanded rapidly by borrowing people who spoke German from other huts and by recruiting language students from the universities. Each watch consisted of four intelligence officers, a Watch No 1 and three others, together with a number of typists and clerical assistants.

'Hut 3 and Hut 6 were side by side,' said Ralph Bennett, one of the watch intelligence reporters. 'They were linked by a small square wooden tunnel through which a pile of currently available decodes were pushed, as I remember by a broom handle, in a cardboard box, so primitive were things in those days.'

The messages arrived from Hut 6 in batches of between fifteen and twenty and were immediately sorted into different degrees of urgency by the Watch No. 1. They were split into four separate piles, by which the Hut 3 priorities would remain known throughout the war.

Pile 1: The most urgent messages which needed immediate tele-printing to London in the hope that they could be acted on as soon as possible.

Pile 2: Those that needed teleprinting but less urgently in order to arrive in London within four to eight hours.

Pile 3: Those which need to be reported but which could be bagged up and sent to London at the end of each day by van.

Quatsch Pile: Named after the German word for nonsense, this consisted of reports that did not need to be passed on and which were simply held on file in Hut 3.

The rest of the watch dealt with the piles in order of priority. They first attempted to 'emend' them, filling in any gaps left because of radio interference or garbled letters, a process that, like much of the codebreaking, was not unlike solving a crossword puzzle. They then wrote out chits containing intelligence reports, always working from the original German rather than translating it first, in order to guard against the introduction of errors. Once the chits were written out, the Watch No 1 edited them, checked them for accuracy and en-sured that the proper security precautions had been taken before having them teleprinted or sent by bag to London as appropriate. At the end of each shift, the No 1 collected all the chits and again edited them before passing them to typists to be typed up into the German Book, a comprehensive file of all the material that passed through Hut 3 that would later allow more long-term research.

The strict security precautions extended to the way in which the chits were written out. In order to keep the number of people who knew that Enigma had been broken to the minimum, they had to be presented as MI6 intelligence reports, employing the traditional CX serial number that MI6 had used since the First World War. The Hut 3 officers rewrote the messages to remove any evidence of a decyphered radio signal and to give the impression that they had come from Source Boniface, an imaginary British spy with a network of agents inside Germany.

R. V. Jones, an MI6 scientific adviser, was a frequent recipient of reports from Bletchley Park.

They were disguised by some introduction such as 'A reliable source recovered a flimsy of a message in the wastepaper of the Chief Signals Officer of *Fleigerkorps* IV which read . . .', or in the case of an incomplete decrypt, 'Source found a partly charred document in the fireplace of . . .'

I can remember handing a disguised decrypt to Air Commodore Nutting, the Director of Signals, who exclaimed: 'By Jove, you've got some brave chaps working for you.' Inevitably, there was speculation about the identity of the supposed secret agent or agents who were sending back such valuable reports. Gilbert Frankau, the novelist, who had a wartime post in intelligence, told me that he had deduced that the agent who could so effectively get into German headquarters must be Sir Paul Dukes, the legendary agent who had penetrated the Red Army so successfully after the Russian Revolution.

The Norwegian campaign was an exhilarating time for both the Hut 6 codebreakers and the intelligence officers in Hut 3. There was a feeling of triumphant excitement that the system put in place by Welchman and Travis was actually doing its job. The codebreakers were also relieved to discover how much easier it was to crack the Enigma keys when there was a mass of operational signals on which to work.

While Bletchley was now producing valuable operational intelligence, it was not yet appreciated for what it was. There was little confidence among the service intelligence departments in agent reports and among the vast bulk of recipients who knew nothing of the Bletchley secret, Source Boniface was regarded with outright suspicion. Nor had anybody given any thought as to how this intelligence might be passed to the troops on the ground where it could be of some use.

While the Norwegian campaign ended in defeat, it did produce one important side-effect. MI6 managed to set up a secure link to the Norwegian commander-in-chief down which some of the disguised intelligence coming out of Bletchley Park was sent. When the Germans invaded France on 10 May 1940, MI6 set up a mobile Special Signals Unit and sent it out to the front to create a similar link over which the intelligence derived from Enigma could be passed to the commanders in the field.

Despite the vast amounts of traffic being sent by the German troops during their blitzkrieg into France and the Low Countries, the British codebreakers were having difficulty breaking the Enigma cyphers. The main key in use on the traffic intercepted by the British was the

Red key but ever since the first break, Hut 6 had been attacking it with only sporadic success. To make matters worse, the Germans changed their indicator system, making the Jeffreys Sheets useless.

John Herivel had been obsessed with finding a new way into the Red cypher ever since being recruited by Welchman for Hut 6. The young twenty-one-year-old Cambridge mathematician was typical of the new breed of codebreakers coming into GC&CS that Knox disliked. But by combining his mathematical training with the Alice in Wonderland-type thought processes advocated by the Room 40 veteran, Herivel was to have a decisive influence on the Enigma story.

He had arrived at the Park at the end of January 1940 and was taken to the mansion where a naval officer made him sign the Official Secrets Act. 'Then he gave me the address of my digs, which were just down the road from the Park and also he told me where to go, to Hut 6, which of course had been effectively founded by Welchman. I had been recruited by Welchman and I was going to work in his show.'

Unlike Knox, Welchman believed in giving the new recruits like John Herivel some training on the Enigma machine.

> There were two people that instructed me in the mysteries of Enigma and the method which they had been using to solve it from time to time. They were Alan Turing and Tony Kendrick. I don't know how many hours they devoted to us but it didn't all happen in one day.
>
> I do remember that when I came to Hut 6, we were doing very badly in breaking into the Red code. Every evening, when I went back to my digs and when I'd had my supper. I would sit down in front of the fire and put my feet up and think of some method of breaking into the Red code. I had this very strong feeling: 'We've got to find a way into the Red again.' I kept thinking about this every evening and I was very young and very confident and I said I'm going to find some way to break into it. But after about two weeks I hadn't made any progress at all.

Then, just like Knox asking which way round does the clock go, Herivel examined the problem from a totally different perspective.

> Up until the middle of February, I had simply been thinking in terms of the encoded messages which were received daily and which came to Hut 6. Then one evening, I remember vividly suddenly finding myself thinking about the other end of the story, the German operators, what they were doing and inevitably then I thought of them starting off the day.

I thought of this imaginary German fellow with his wheels and his book of keys. He would open the book and find what wheels and settings he was supposed to use that day. He would set the rings on the wheels, put them into the machine and the next thing he would have to do would be to choose a three-letter indicator for his first message of the day.

So I began to think, how would he choose that indicator. He might just take it out of a book, or he might pluck it out of the air like ABC or whatever. Then I had the thought, suppose he was a lazy fellow, or in a tearing hurry, or had the wind up, or something or other and he were to leave the wheels untouched in the machine and bang the top down and look at the windows, see what letters were showing and just use them.

Then another thought struck me. What about the rings? Would he set them for each of the three given wheels before he put them into the machine or would he set them afterwards? Then I had a flash of illumination. If he set them afterwards and, at the same time, simply chose the letters in the windows as the indicator for his first message, then the indicator would tend to be close to the ring setting of the day. He would, as it were, be sending it almost in clear.

If the intercept sites could send us the indicators of all the Red messages they judged to be the first messages of the day for the individual German operators there was a sporting chance that they would cluster around the ring settings for the day and we might be able to narrow down the 17,576 possible ring settings to a manageable number, say twenty or thirty, and simply test these one after the other in the hope of hitting on the right answer.

The next day I went back to Hut 6 in a very excited state and told my colleagues of this idea. 'Oh, brilliant,' they all said. Welchman immediately arranged, very discreetly, for the first message indicators on the Red to be sent early each day to Hut 6. It was a simple matter to look for clusters. The idea, as my colleagues said, was a good one, and it was faithfully tested every day. Unfortunately, it never worked. Not that is until the unleashing of the German blitzkrieg in the West some two months later in May 1940.

I wasn't there, but David Rees, who was on that particular night shift, noticed that among the first messages there were several whose indicators were very close together. So he tried the different possibilities on the different wheels and when I came in at 8 o'clock that morning there was a little group of people around David who had broken the Red. He had got the right wheels and ring settings. Well it was a very exciting moment. Welchman drew me aside and he said: 'Herivel, this will not be forgotten'.

The importance of the break that the Herivel Tip had allowed was not realised at the time. But the Red key would never be lost again. It became Bletchley Park's staple diet. It was used by countless *Luftwaffe* units and, because they needed to liaise closely with both the Army and the Navy in order to provide them with air support, its use gave a good overall insight into all the major German plans and operations.

'From this point on it was broken daily, usually on the day in question and early in the day,' recalled Peter Calvocoressi, one of the members of Hut 3. 'Later in the war, I remember that we in Hut 3 used to get a bit tetchy if Hut 6 had not broken Red by breakfast time.'

The Battle of France produced even more valuable intelligence than had been available during the Norwegian campaign. The creation of the mobile MI6 Special Signals Unit to provide a secure link to the headquarters of the British Expeditionary Force meant that there was a way of getting this intelligence to the commanders in the field but the system was in its infancy and not entirely effective.

At this stage, the reports were still disguised as Source Boniface. Unfortunately the military had such a poor regard for agents' reports that they merely ensured that the commanders did not believe it. The codebreakers were jubilant when they decyphered a message giving eight hours' notice of a meeting between the chiefs of staff and the four *Luftwaffe* formations involved but their joy turned to disappointment when the British commanders ignored it.

Perhaps more importantly than the dismissive attitude of the military at this time to any intelligence report, the battle was already lost by the time Red was broken and, with the Allied troops already in full retreat, even when they did accept that the intelligence was accurate, they were in no position to make proper use of it. Nevertheless, vital lessons were learned allowing the system to be revised to ensure that it would work in any future campaign.

The procedures used within Hut 3 were also altered in the light of lessons learned during the Battle of France. The amount of material coming in had strained its resources to the limit. The number of watches was expanded to provide more cover and both the War Office and the Air Ministry posted their own advisers to Hut 3 to assist in analysing material. Meanwhile, Nigel de Grey was put in charge of a research section. He set about acquiring maps more detailed than the Baedeker tourist guides the Hut had been forced to work with during the campaigns in Norway and France; looked at the various terms used by the Germans, many of which had completely baffled academics more used to translating Goethe than Guderian; and, most importantly of all, began to build up a detailed picture of the structure of the German armed forces.

Hut 3 itself became more organised. It remained centred on the watch room. The members of the watch, or watchkeepers, sat around one side of a horseshoe-shaped table facing the Watch No 1, who was on a rectangular table at the open end of the horseshoe together with the specialist advisers, each one a representative of either military or air intelligence. Once the watchkeeper had compiled his report and it had been checked by the Watch No 1, the relevant service adviser examined it to ensure it made sense and added any notes on background to put it into context or to draw attention to the most pertinent points. They also compiled long-term intelligence reports providing an overall picture of what was going on, said Jim Rose, one of the air advisers.

> Material came in from Hut 3 in more-or-less cablese German and a lot of it corrupt. The head of the watch handed out all these messages to the watch in what seemed to him to be the priority. They had to translate them into English. There was an air adviser and a military adviser sitting alongside and they had access to the index.
>
> One of the great strengths of Hut 3 was the index. Every message was cross-referenced under one or maybe two headings. That gave them their depth of knowledge of whether something of a similar kind had indicated something which was known to have happened earlier. A message was not just a message in itself. It led to all sorts of backwards and forwards intelligence. We were very lucky we had a man called Cullingworth who had worked for Kelly's Directories.
>
> Urgent messages were sent direct to Commanders-in-Chief. All messages went up to the service ministries. If the air adviser or the military adviser had anything to comment he was allowed to do so and then next morning we would send deeper comment to the Commander-in-Chief. Some of the information was tactically immediate, some of it was strategic and some of it was a build-up of order of battle, strength, weaknesses, supplies and so on, which most generals don't know about their enemy. So it was very important in so many ways.

The fall of France cast a dark shadow over everyone at Bletchley Park, but the French liaison officers from Mission Richard were clearly worst affected. 'I remember seeing several of the Frenchmen who were attached to the French Mission here clustered around the wireless set with their ears almost glued to it,' said Phoebe Senyard. 'They were listening to very faint announcements made by the BBC, or getting on to a French station and becoming more and more dejected and downcast with every fresh announcement.'

Mavis Lever was eating her dinner in the mansion dining hall when the news that Paris had fallen was announced.

> We had some Frenchmen working with us at the time and I was sitting next to one of them and he burst into tears. I simply did not know what to do. So, like Charlotte and Siegfried's body, I went on eating my sausages. I mean we weren't going to get any more and it seemed to me there was nothing really I could do if other people were going to burst into tears. I'd got a night shift to work on, so on with the sausages.

Following the German invasion, Bertrand and the Poles set up a new station on a country estate in Provence, in the area under Vichy control. They were supposed to be monitoring British communications with the underground resistance movement but in fact continued working on Enigma and managed to make contact with Bletchley Park, via MI6 contacts. They remained there until the Germans occupied the whole of France in October 1942. Although five of the Polish codebreakers were subsequently captured and held in an SS concentration camp at Schloss Eisenberg, they never gave away the secret that Enigma was being broken.

Neville Chamberlain's association with appeasement and the inadequate response to the German attack on Norway led, at the beginning of May 1940, to his resignation and replacement by Winston Churchill, the man who had ordered Room 40 to be set up during the First World War. The new prime minister soon became obsessed with Bletchley Park, treasuring the intercepts delivered to him each day by Menzies, Sinclair's successor, in a battered old wooden dispatch box covered in fading yellow leather.

With Hitler's next move expected to be an attack on Britain itself, Churchill made a series of speeches aimed at building up 'the bulldog spirit'. They were epitomised by his 'Finest Hour' address to the House of Commons and his warning that the British would defend their island on the beaches. Detachments of Home Guards were rapidly set up around the country and Bletchley was no exception.

Some of the codebreakers were enthusiastic recruits. Malcolm Kennedy recorded in his diary that there had been a wireless appeal 'for volunteers between seventeen and sixty-five to form local defence units against parachutists. I sent in my name to join the detachment which is to be formed at Bletchley, so I may yet have a chance to take a smack at Brother Boche once more!'

One of the more surprising members of the Bletchley Home Guard was Alan Turing. But in typically eccentric fashion, he did it solely on his own terms, joining only in order to learn how to fire a rifle, said Peter Twinn.

> They told him to fill this form in and Turing thought to himself: 'I don't see why I should sign this it won't do me any good and it might be a bit inconvenient.'
>
> So when he'd learned how to fire a rifle and done as much as he thought was of value to him, he thought: 'Well I've got everything I can out of this, I'll just give up going to the Home Guard.' When the officer in charge said he would do what he was told because he had agreed to be subject to military discipline, Turing replied, and I can hear him saying it: 'Well you had better look at my form. You'll see I didn't sign that bit.'

Noel Currer-Briggs, an Intelligence Corps officer, recalled that at one point a mixture of the Home Guard and the regular Army marched into Bletchley as part of an Army recruiting campaign. 'There were lots of oddballs there, people from all over Europe with obscure languages, and there was one chap from Eastern Europe in battle-dress and a bowler hat, much to the dismay of the sergeant who was trying to make us look smart. It made *Dad's Army* look like the Coldstream Guards.'

The second half of 1940 was dominated by growing signs that Hitler would launch Operation Sea Lion, the invasion of Britain. The *Luftwaffe*'s sustained attack on the British defences began on 10 July. Preparations for the Battle of Britain had been picked up by Bletchley Park in messages discussing the extension of airfield runways in Belgium, the Netherlands and France, and the refitting of aircraft in readiness for operations against the United Kingdom.

The interception of *Luftwaffe* low-level communications by Cheadle and a network of small RAF Y units coordinated at West Kingsdown in Kent, provided vital tactical intelligence on the preparations of the German bombers and their fighter escorts. Bletchley gave advance notice of the planned times of raids, the intended targets and the numbers of aircraft involved. But these were often subject to unannounced changes and probably its most important contribution at this time was in providing the true figures of the number of aircraft the *Luftwaffe* lost and had available to replace them, as opposed to the often wildly inaccurate estimates made by air intelligence.

Ann Lavell was a young WAAF in Cooper's Air Section, which at the time was still in the main house but would later move to Hut 10.

> What we dealt with were medium-frequency messages from German aircraft taking off and landing. We had chaps we called the pundits who worked on the codes and tried to reconstruct them. One bit of excitement was when they actually captured a codebook and produced it for us and it had blood on it, presumably from the pilot.
>
> We were all a bit bewildered to be perfectly honest because everything was so compartmented that you never got a proper overview. I was in the operational watch, which collected intelligence from various parts of the Air Section. We reported to Fighter Command at Stanmore. We told them any snippets we could, if there was going to be a raid any night and, if we knew, where. But I never did this, I was much too humble and lowly. I remember being on the evening shift and you had one watchkeeper and one stooge like me and when the watchkeeper went to dinner I was in a state of absolute terror in case Stanmore should ring up and ask something, knowing it could be life or death.

Lavell was appointed as PA to Cooper, a tall, well-built man with a distinctive nervous habit of putting his right hand behind the back of his head and stroking his left shoulder. She found his eccentricity difficult to deal with.

> He was absolutely mad, frightening really. At first I didn't like him at all. I thought he was horrible. But when I got to know him I got quite fond of him. But he was not really one of us. He was on another plane I think. He'd get awfully embarassed and worried when he felt he wasn't acting like an ordinary human being.

Once they were beside the lake and Cooper had been drinking a cup of coffee. When he finished he stood there with the empty cup and was clearly slightly embarrassed by having it in his hand.

> So he just threw it in the lake. There was another time when he kicked over a fire extinguisher and it started foaming. He didn't know what to do. He picked it up and rushed to and fro until a friend of mine went and took it from him and put it out of the window. He wasn't very

practical but once you knew him and got over the slightly forbidding exterior he was very nice and very kind.

Professor R. V. Jones recalled that Cooper was frequently asked to take part in interrogations of pilots. The first time he did this, he and two other interrogators were seated behind a trestle table when the captured *Luftwaffe* pilot, wearing perfectly pressed Nazi uniform and highly polished jackboots, was marched in and halted in front of the them. 'He clicked his heels together and gave a very smart Nazi salute,' said Jones. 'The panel was unprepared for this, none more so than Josh who stood up as smartly, gave the Nazi salute and repeated the prisoner's "Heil Hitler". Then realising that he had done the wrong thing, he looked in embarassment at his colleagues and sat down with such a speed that he missed his chair and disappeared completely under the table.'

Gwen Davies, another member of the Air Section, remembered Cooper as being 'a very, very strange man, who would burst into the watch sometimes and shriek something absolutely unintelligible and burst out again'. Most of the junior members of staff had difficulty understanding what he was saying, but there was no doubting his brilliance, Davies said.

> There was a great degree of tolerance at Bletchley for eccentricities. There had to be because so many of the people were very, very eccentric indeed. At least half of the people there were absolutely mad. They were geniuses, no doubt many of them were extremely, extremely clever, but my goodness they were strange in ordinary life.
>
> So you did have this rather happy atmosphere of tolerance. Very eccentric behaviour was accepted fairly affectionately and I think people worked and lived there who couldn't possibly have worked and lived anywhere else. People who would obviously have been very very ill at ease in a normal Air Force camp with its very strict modes of behaviour and discipline were very happy, very at ease in Bletchley.

Concerns over the possibility of an imminent invasion pervaded the atmosphere at Bletchley Park. 'The sinister covername for an Operation Sea Lion began to appear in the *Luftwaffe* traffic,' said de Grey. 'It did not require much ingenuity to identify this name with the preparations for invasion which continued unabated throughout the late summer and early autumn.' Plans were put in place to set up a mobile codebreaking unit to retreat behind the defending British troops should the Germans manage to cross the Channel. The codebreakers' records were to be evacuated to Canada and there was even talk of moving GC&CS across the Atlantic as well if need be. Phoebe Senyard recalled this as a difficult time.

> The war situation was now becoming very grim. So during the ghastly months of May, June, July and August when the fear of German invasion was greatest, arrangements were made to organise a mobile section of GC&CS. The air was electric with feeling. Those who had been chosen were photographed and supplied with special passports or identification cards and were in a sense excited by the project, although no doubt dismayed by the reason for their evacuation.
>
> I was surprised at the number of people whose feelings were hurt because they had not been included in the list, while certain of the more lighthearted and venturesome of the section came out with suggestions of what we could do should the Germans come and how we could advance our careers under the German *Herrenvolk*. Joking apart, times were very serious and air raid alarms were continuous night and day. We used to use the slit trench at the back of Hut 4 until it was declared unsafe. Special orders were issued about the dispersal of staff should Bletchley Park be attacked and so the gloomy days wore on.

Column BQ, as the mobile unit was to be called, was to comprise around 500 people, 140 of the codebreakers and 360 wireless operators from the various Y stations. The transport was to be a mixture of private cars and four ancient Midland Red buses, hired by the War Office, one of which promptly split along the length of its roof while the other three continually broke down. 'I am told that the petrol consumption is about five miles to the gallon,' complained one of the column's organisers, 'and I think it questionable, if they had to go on a long journey, whether they would arrive at their destination with any degree of certainty.'

Most of the private vehicles were in somewhat better condition, although possibly no less dangerous. One of the cars volunteered as Column BQ transport was the grey Bentley driven by Diana Russell Clarke, who had become renowned for driving it at breakneck speed along the country roads around Bletchley.

> There was one occasion when I was coming back from leave going about sixty-five, which now we would think was very slow, and burst a front tyre. The car went into a frightful wobble. But eventually I got it on to a nice wide verge. There was a car coming from the other direction and the occupant got out to see if I was all right. It turned out

to be Commander Travis. He said: 'My God, I might have realised it would be you Diana.' I'd obviously frightened him to death, he thought I was going to go straight into him.

Fortunately, the invasion never came and neither the Bentley nor the buses were ever needed. The codebreakers were able to remain at Bletchley Park and continue breaking Enigma. Success depended very largely on German operators ignoring the rules. 'We could usually break things when we identified the human error and that was what it was all about,' said Mavis Lever. 'If the Germans had kept to the rule book and done it properly, as they were instructed to do, then of course we wouldn't have been able to get it out.'

The first method of breaking the messages was the work of 'the Cilli Hunters' who relied on the tendency first identified by Rejewski for operators to choose keys that were easy to remember. 'Just occasionally you would get a chap who was rather fond of the same letters,' said Susan Wenham, one of the codebreakers recruited by Stuart Milner-Barry from Newnham College, Cambridge. 'It might be for some personal reason. Perhaps one chap might use his girlfriend's initials for the setting of the wheels or his own initials. Something like that, you know silly little things. They weren't supposed to do it but they did.'

Searching for Cillis, named after one of the operators' girlfriends whose name frequently appeared in the Enigma settings, became something of an art, said Mavis Lever.

> One was thinking all the time about the psychology of what it was like in the middle of the fighting when you were supposed to be encoding a message for your general and you had to put three or four letters in these little windows and in the heat of the battle you would put up your girlfriend's name or dirty German four-letter words. I am the world's expert on German dirty four-letter words!

The other methods were the cribs and 'kisses', messages that had been sent previously – perhaps on a lower-level radio net in a cypher that was already broken – and then turned up in the Enigma traffic, providing a crib for the message. This made it very easy for the codebreakers, though it was an infrequent occurrence. Most cribs were fairly short, although Mavis Lever remembered one occasion when there was a crib for a whole message.

> The one snag with the Enigma of course is the fact that if you press A, you can get every other letter but A. I picked up this message and – one

was so used to looking at things and making instant decisions – I thought: 'Something's gone. What has this chap done. There is not a single L in this message.'

My chap had been told to send out a dummy message and he had just had a fag and pressed the last key of the middle row of his keyboard, the L. So that was the only letter that didn't come out. We had got the biggest crib we ever had, the encypherment was LLLL right through the message and that gave us the new wiring for the wheel. That's the sort of thing we were trained to do. Instinctively look for something that had gone wrong or someone who had done something silly and torn up the rule book.

Within a few months of arriving at Bletchley, Alan Turing had worked out the basic design for a machine that would make it much easier to exploit the cribs. The idea was backed by Welchman, and Travis secured the then spectacular sum of £100,000 to have a number of the machines built by Harold 'Doc' Keen, the head boffin at the British Tabulating Machine Company in Letchworth.

The first of the 'bombes', as they were called, was produced in the space of three months. It was a fast-running electrical machine in a bronze cabinet 6 feet 6 inches high, more than 7 feet wide and 2 feet 6 inches deep, containing a series of 30 rotating drums equating to the wheels of 10 Enigma machines, although later versions simulated the action of 12 machines.

The bombe was a remarkable piece of technology for its time. It was designed to run through all the various possibilities – wheel choice, order, ring position and machine settings – at high speed in order to test that the Cillis or cribs suspected by the codebreakers were actually in use. The codebreakers provided the operators with a 'menu' suggesting possible equations of clear letters to encyphered letters which was fed into the bombe. Each time the machine found a possible match, it was tested by the operator on a replica Enigma machine to see if it produced German text.

If it did, the operator was able to declare: 'The job's up', and pass it back for decryption. If it was garbled letters, as was frequently the case, the process continued until the bombe had either found the right combination or had exhausted all the possibilities, in which case the codebreakers' suspected Cilli didn't work and a new one had to be found.

The first bombe, christened 'Victory', was installed in part of Hut 1 in March 1940, the other end of the hut being the station sick bay.

For five months it was on trial, attempting to break Naval Enigma. Then Turing and Keen incorporated an idea of Welchman's into the design. Called the 'diagonal board' after the chessboard-like device Welchman produced to prove his theory, it exploited the fact that Enigma encryptions were reciprocal. If P produced C, then C would produce P. By wiring up the bombes to test both possibilities simultaneously, the process could be cut in half. On 8 August a second bombe, known as 'Agnus Dei', or 'Agnes' for short, came on stream incorporating the diagonal board and both she and Victory began working operationally for Hut 6.

By the end of September, Bletchley had already reported a number of indications that, with the failure of the *Luftwaffe* to break the RAF, Operation Sea Lion had been postponed. The Germans had switched their air attacks to night bombing of big cities, and in particular London, in what was to become known as 'the Blitz'.

A new Enigma system, nicknamed Brown by Hut 6, began to appear on a communications link between a German experimental research establishment working on navigational beams and a *Luftwaffe* base in France that was using them to direct the German bombing raids on Britain. Professor Frederick 'Bimbo' Norman of Hut 3 called in R. V. Jones, who later credited the material produced from the Brown cypher with playing a major role in helping him to devise countermeasures to the various beams.

Meanwhile, the Red cypher was providing indications of potential German targets and the numbers of aircraft involved in the raids, helped by the Germans considerate use of covernames that began with the same letters as the British towns they were supposed to represent, such as *Bild* for Birmingham and *Liebe* for Liverpool.

While this was a clear error on the part of the Germans, the failure to recognise one of these covernames was to embroil the Bletchley Park codebreakers in the controversy as to whether or not Churchill allowed the devastating bombing raid on Coventry in mid-November 1940 to go ahead rather than risk letting the Germans know that Enigma had been broken.

The earliest signs of an unusually large raid came in a decrypt on the Brown cypher revealing that the beams were to be used for an operation which the Germans codenamed 'Moonlight Sonata', because it was to coincide with a full moon. It gave no further information other than providing a list of four possible targets, all in London and the Home Counties, leading air intelligence to conclude that the target was once again London.

Evidence obtained from a captured *Luftwaffe* pilot gave warning of a major raid due to take place at a full moon; the interrogation report said the raid was codenamed 'Moonshine Serenade' and was aimed against Coventry and Birmingham. The Air Ministry dismissed this information, preferring to believe its own analysis of the German message. It also disregarded navigational beams aimed at the West Midlands, assuming that they were part of German trials of the equipment which had been going on for some time.

It was only later that anyone realised that the use of the previously unknown codeword *Korn*, the German word for corn, in the initial message was in fact the covername for Coventry, which the Germans spelt with a K. While with hindsight the Air Ministry's dismissal of Coventry as a potential target is evidence of the poor coordination of intelligence within Whitehall at the time, it was certainly not ignored to protect the codebreakers' secret.

A week later, Bletchley Park suffered its own bombing raid when a lone aircraft, almost certainly aiming to jettison its remaining bombs on the neighbouring railway junction before heading for home, missed its target. Malcolm Kennedy turned up for work in the Japanese diplomatic section in Elmers School on the morning of 21 November to discover that the building had been hit by one of the bombs. 'Typists' room and telephone exchange in our building were blown to bits by a direct hit and the Vicarage next door damaged by another bomb which landed in the garden,' he recorded in his diary. 'A third exploded in the road outside, while two more landed over at the Park, one of them bursting a bare half dozen paces from Hut 4. By great good fortune there were no casualties.'

The bomb that exploded close to the Naval Section hut broke some of its windows and moved it several inches off of its brick foundations. It also caused some panic in neighbouring houses, recalled Barbara Abernethy.

> I was billeted with this railway guard. The night we heard the bomb, his wife and I said: 'The Germans are coming.' Well he was in the Home Guard and had a big machine gun which was hidden under the sofa. She and I between us managed to drag this machine gun out from under the sofa, and we stood at the door with this stupid gun waiting for a German to arrive. Well the only person to arrive was the railway guard, back from duty. 'What the **** are you doing?,' he asked. 'We thought you were German,' we replied. 'Put that back and don't touch it again,' he said. Very soon after that, the machine gun disappeared.

Chapter 5

THE FIRST BATTLE OF THE ATLANTIC

Harry Hinsley had arrived at Bletchley in late 1939 and was immediately put in Phoebe Senyard's care. Unlike many of the dons, he did not have a privileged background. Hinsley was a grammar school boy from Walsall, in the Black Country. His father was a wagoner who drove a horse and cart between the local ironworks and the railway station. A slight, bespectacled young man with wavy hair, who had won a scholarship to St John's College, Cambridge, he was an immediate hit with Senyard. She recalled his early days at BP:

> I can remember quite well showing Harry some of the sorting and how delighted he seemed when he began to recognise the different types of signals. He joined up with Miss Bostock working on frequencies and callsigns. I then had to pass to Harry any strange, new or unknown signals. If I was in difficulty, I knew I could go to Harry. It was a pleasure because he was always interested in everything and took great pains to find out what it was and why. Those were very enjoyable days indeed. We were all very happy and cheerful, working in close cooperation with each other.

Relations with the Admiralty were less convivial. While Hut 3 worked to the War Office and the Air Ministry, albeit at this stage via MI6, the Naval Section was officially NID12, part of the Naval Intelligence Division, and in direct contact with the Admiralty's Operational Intelligence Centre which coordinated naval intelligence.

But whenever any of the codebreakers attempted to talk to the OIC, they received little attention. 'I used a direct telephone line which I had to activate by turning a handle energetically before speaking,' Hinsley remembered. 'On this I spoke, a disembodied voice, to people who had never met me. They rarely took the initiative in turning the handle to speak to me and they showed little interest in what I said to them.'

At the beginning of April 1940, shortly before the invasion of Norway, the OIC ignored Hinsley's report, derived purely from traffic analysis, of an unusual build-up of German naval activity in the Baltic. As a result, the British were caught completely unawares by the German occupation of Norway.

Two months later, Hinsley reported that a number of German warships were about to break out of the Baltic. Again he was ignored. It was to lead to one of the Royal Navy's worst disasters of the Second World War, the sinking of the aircraft carrier HMS *Glorious*.

'For about a fortnight beforehand, I pretty well rang the OIC once or twice a day and said: "Look you ought surely to pass a signal out on this. Can you possibly pass a signal out?",' Hinsley said. 'They showed some interest. But were not sufficiently convinced to send a warning to the Home Fleet.'

On 7 June 1940, the *Glorious* and her two escort destroyers were spotted by a German flotilla which included the pocket battleships the *Gneisenau* and the *Scharnhorst*.

> On that day more than ever, I was saying to the duty officer: 'For goodness sakes, can't you just persuade them to send an alert or even "It may be the case".' He said: 'I can't because first of all my traffic analysis group doesn't agree with your interpretation. It doesn't see the point, doesn't see there's any evidence, and secondly my boss, the chief of the OIC will not go to the operational chaps and say send this kind of signal out on your kind of information.'

The next day HMS *Glorious* and her two escort destroyers, HMS *Acasta* and HMS *Ardent*, were sunk with the loss of 1500 men. Hinsley remembered the frustration of their warnings being ignored.

> The *Glorious* was capable of making a limited torpedo strike and could have flown defensive patrols if she had received even a qualified warning. But the OIC, for all that it included these indications in its daily bulletin, resisted Bletchley's suggestion that such a warning should be sent to ships at sea. It was not prepared to accept inferences drawn from an untried technique by civilians as yet unknown to its staff.

Bletchley Park's warnings to the Admiralty were the subject of a detailed cover-up. Even today, and despite the fact that Hinsley chronicled the advice given to the Admiralty in the official history of British intelligence in the Second World War, the Ministry of Defence still claims that 'British intelligence sources failed to discover that the German force had sailed'.

After the sinking of the *Glorious*, the OIC began to take more interest in what Bletchley Park said, although some officers clearly resented its very existence. 'There was more than a suspicion of professional jealousy,' noted Charles Morgan, who served in naval intelligence. 'It was almost a point of honour to find the answer from our own records, even if a trifle incomplete, rather than have recourse to a BP telephone extension.'

In an apparent effort to heal the rift, Hinsley was called down to the Admiralty and even sent to visit the Home Fleet at Scapa Flow. This caused some minor problems since the young codebreaker had no smart clothes. Scrounger Green was called in by Birch and told 'to produce a suit of clothes – a hat he would not wear – for a shining light who was summoned to the Admiralty and who had nothing else to wear but a pair of corduroys and a Fair Isle pullover'.

The new liaison had a limited effect, Hinsley recalled.

> They began to realise that in spite of the fact that we were scruffy and young, and civilian, we had something to contribute. They took great pains thereafter always to be in close touch and always to argue and listen to us, taking the trouble to appoint a liaison officer to Bletchley to whom we could always show the facts.

But despite the closer liaison, the difficulties continued. A few months later, Alec Dakin, an Egyptologist from Brasenose College who had been newly recruited into Hut 4, visited the Admiralty and was aghast to discover that the OIC appeared to be deliberately 'obstructive and dismissive' of Bletchley Park.

Asked by Birch and Travis what was behind the problem, Hinsley blamed it on ill-feeling within the OIC towards the codebreakers.

> There is a competitive spirit which instead of being of a healthy type is obviously personal. It couches itself in a show of independence and an air of obstruction. It appears to be based on personal opposition to Bletchley Park. I suspect that another reason for their inadequacy is incapacity pure and simple.

The OIC's tendency to ignore much of what Bletchley Park said reappeared in the late spring of 1941 during an event that was to have a dramatic effect on morale at Bletchley Park – the sinking of the *Bismarck*.

This battleship, the showpiece of the German Navy, had been in the Baltic since her completion the previous September. The Admiralty was watching and waiting for her to break out into the Atlantic to attack the convoys bringing vital supplies to Britain. Early indications that the *Bismarck* was about to leave the Baltic came in decrypts of the Red Enigma which showed that the *Luftwaffe* was mounting a close watch on the activities of the British Home Fleet anchored in Scapa Flow. An MI6 agent was dispatched to monitor the passage of ships through the Kattegat, the narrow strip of water separating Denmark from Sweden and, on 20 May, he reported that two large German warships had left the Baltic bound for the North Sea. The sighting was confirmed by photographic reconnaissance and a few isolated breaks into the main naval Enigma cypher showed that the *Bismarck*, accompanied by the new cruiser the *Prinz Eugen*, was about to attack Britain's transatlantic trade routes.

A British naval squadron was dispatched to hunt the *Bismarck* down. She was sighted on the evening of 23 May and next morning was engaged by the *Hood* and the *Prince of Wales*. The *Hood* was sunk and the *Prince of Wales* hit but not without the *Bismarck* herself sustaining some damage. She parted company with the *Prinz Eugen* and the Royal Navy ships lost contact with her. Throughout the following day, there was confusion as to what direction the *Bismarck* was travelling in.

Bletchley's repeated insistence that the *Bismarck* was heading for the safety of a French port was ignored. Hinsley had telephoned the OIC following the engagement to tell the duty officer that radio control of the *Bismarck* had switched from Wilhelmshaven to Paris, a clear sign that she was sailing south towards France. It was not until the early evening of 25 May, following yet another heated telephone conversation between Hinsley and the OIC, that this reasoning was finally accepted.

The manner and speed of its confirmation was to become a part of the Bletchley folklore. Just minutes after Hinsley's angry exchange with the Admiralty, Hut 6 decyphered a message on the Red *Luftwaffe* Enigma from General Hans Jeschonnek, the *Luftwaffe* Chief of Staff, who was concerned over the fate of a relative, a member of the *Bismarck*'s crew. He was told that the battleship was making for the safety of Brest. Armed with this news, Royal Navy ships of both the Mediterranean and Home Fleets closed in on her. When aircraft from the *Ark Royal* bombed her and succeeded in jamming her rudder on the evening of 26 May, her fate was sealed. In messages decrypted only after she had been sunk, Admiral Lütjens, the officer commanding the *Bismarck*, signalled: 'Ship unmanageable. We shall fight to the last shell. Long live the Führer.'

Malcolm Kennedy was in the dining room in the mansion at Bletchley Park when the news came through on the 1 o'clock news that she had been sunk. 'Spontaneous cheering and clapping broke out from those at lunch when the announcement was made,' he said, 'though some of us had heard the good news slightly before. To give the devil his due, *Bismarck* put up a very good show.'

Years later, Mavis Lever took her son to see the film *Sink the Bismarck*.

> I saw it go down and suddenly I really did feel quite sick. I put my head down and my son said to me after a while: 'It's all right Mummy, it's gone down.' He didn't know. But I was thinking how awful it was that one's breaking of a message could send so many people to the bottom. But that was war and that was the way we had to play it. If we thought about it too much we should never have been able to cope.

Since the sinking of the *Bismarck* involved not just Hut 6 but also the intelligence resources of Huts 4 and 3, news of the codebreakers' role in the affair swiftly got around the Park raising morale and giving them a tangible feeling of making a real contribution to the war effort. It became a standard part of the initial briefing of any new recruit. But it was something of a sideshow compared to the role played by Bletchley Park – and the Enigma codebreakers in particular – in the main naval conflict of the second half of 1940 and early 1941, the first Battle of the Atlantic.

While Army and Air Force Enigma was looked after by Hut 6 and Hut 3, their naval counterpart was receiving little attention. Naval traffic was monitored at Flowerdown, Scarborough and Cupar. Naval Enigma messages were easy to spot. They were sent in four-letter groups with the first two, the indicators, being repeated at the end of each message.

But naval Enigma employed a more complicated procedure for giving the key settings than its Army and Air Force equivalents. The indicators were encrypted before transmission using a pre-determined bigraph table. This meant that there were no Cillis and there was therefore no easy way of working the keys out. What work was done on it was carried out by Dilly Knox's research section and copies of the unbroken messages were stored in two steel cabinets in Birch's office.

The German subsection had no dedicated codebreakers until the spring of 1940, when a 'pinch' of cypher forms from a German patrol boat giving both the plain text and the encyphered version arrived at

Bletchley. Alan Turing and Peter Twinn set up a naval Enigma research group, initially in a couple of borrowed rooms in Hut 4. 'Around about the beginning of April 1940, Mr Birch sent around a circular to the effect that there would be a new cryptographic section formed and that we should probably be very uncomfortable for about a fortnight or more in the endeavours to house them,' Senyard said.

> We put our backs into it in order to welcome the newcomers, by tidying up our files and papers, binding and storing into cupboards all signals and books such as not in current use. Everyone who could be spared temporarily from their jobs was pressed into service and room was made for it, but it was a tight squeeze. We almost felt as if we ought to all breathe in together.

Turing and Twinn were to become quite close. 'He [Turing] was a genius,' Twinn said.

> He was easily the brightest chap in the place. But he would occasionally come round to my digs and play chess and I should think that out of five games, he would win three and I would win two. But I knew very little about chess apart from the rules. I knew absolutely nothing about the tactics or strategy.
>
> It always seemed to me extraordinary that this brilliant chap was absolutely no good at chess at all. It was only because he hadn't given it his attention of course, but it was a rather curious phenomenon. The other thing about Turing is that everyone says he had a stutter. I spent nine months with him in the same room. What I would say is that when he was asked a question which he thought was interesting, he would get very excited. It wasn't stuttering, he was just having difficulty getting everything he wanted to say out.

Turing's eccentricities were legion, Twinn said. He cycled into work wearing a gas mask to stop the pollen sparking off his hayfever, and chained his coffee mug to a radiator.

> He had all kind of crackpot notions based on the fact that he didn't think the currency would stand up to a substantial war. He wanted to keep something of value and he put a lot of money into silver bars. Having extracted them from his bank with the utmost difficulty, he went and buried them somewhere. He had a very elaborate set of instructions for how to find them after the war. But he never did find them. What he'd neglected to think about was that someone might build a new town like Milton Keynes over the site.

At the same time as the naval cryptographic section was formed, Victory, the first bombe, came on line and Turing and Twinn used it to test out various menus as they tried to decypher Dolphin, the 'home waters' Enigma system used by the U-boats.

The naval Enigma system had now become even more complicated than that used by the Army and Air Force. While they could choose any three of five wheels, giving a total number of sixty possible wheel orders, the Navy had added an extra three wheels, producing as many as 336 different wheel orders. In addition, wheels 6, 7 and 8 turned the next wheel twice during each revolution, every thirteen letters rather than every twenty-six. Nevertheless, in early May, Turing broke the keys for several days in April.

The defeat of France in mid-1940 brought an added menace from the German U-boats which now had easy access to the Atlantic from new bases in the Bay of Biscay. Britain was dependent on imports for half its food and all of its oil. These now had to come across the Atlantic from North America and the convoys swiftly became the targets for the U-boats.

The use of convoys, developed during the First World War, gave the British merchant ships a much greater chance of surviving than lone vessels. In order to counter this, the commander of the German submarine fleet, Admiral Karl Dönitz, had devised the wolf pack system under which the U-boats gathered in mid-Atlantic and attacked the convoys en masse, swinging the advantage back in the Germans' favour. The situation for the Atlantic convoys was made worse by the fact that the Germans had broken the Merchant Navy code used by the convoys and were also reading a great deal of the Royal Navy's operational messages. So the wolf packs knew the routes to be taken by the convoys and could lie in wait for them.

The U-boats formed up in long patrol lines stretching north to south across the shipping routes. Once contact was made with a convoy, the closest U-boats shadowed it, sending out homing signals to draw in the other members of the pack. When all the U-boats were assembled, they attacked, frequently using the cover of darkness to slip inside the outer cordon of escort vessels on the surface, where the British sonar could not detect them.

Mussolini's entry into the war in June 1940 had effectively split the German Section. From then on Nobby Clarke, the section head, was fully employed with Italian codes and cyphers, leaving the German material to Birch. A year later, Clarke reached retirement age and Birch took over the whole of the Naval Section. By now Turing and

Twinn were in Hut 8, the naval codebreaking equivalent of Hut 6, where they had been augmented by the experience of Kendrick and the arrival of Joan Clarke, another of Welchman's students at Cambridge and one of the few women ever to get close to Turing. Although he was homosexual, they were for a time totally inseparable and were briefly engaged.

The Hut 8 codebreakers now had pinches of two of the eight wheels from captured U-boats together with a description of how to operate the machine. But it was little help. By September, with attacks on Allied shipping mounting rapidly, the need to find a sustained break of Dolphin had become imperative.

The coordination of the wolf pack attacks required a great deal of radio traffic, which allowed the traffic analysts led by Hinsley to produce detailed intelligence. But it was advance notice of the patrol lines, the points where the U-boats were forming up, that the Admiralty needed. Traffic analysis combined with bearings provided by a network of direction-finding stations could locate the submarines when they left port and once they broke cover. But they spent as much time as they could maintaining radio silence. The only sure way of working out what the wolf packs were planning to do and keeping the convoys away from them was from reading the Enigma traffic between the U-boats and Dönitz's headquarters just outside the French port of Lorient.

With the U-boats enjoying a 'happy time' in the North Atlantic and sinking large numbers of Allied merchant ships, the Admiralty demanded fast results. The codebreakers said that their only hope was to obtain more keys. Admiral Godfrey, the Director of Naval Intelligence, reassured them that he was 'setting up an organisation to arrange "pinches" and I think the solution will be found in a combined committee of talent in your department and mine who can think up cunning schemes.'

One of the people Godfrey had in mind was Ian Fleming, later the creator of James Bond but then a leading naval intelligence officer. He devised an elaborate plan to 'pinch' a set of keys from a German ship with the aid of a captured *Luftwaffe* bomber. In what might have been the first, brief blueprint for the fictional hero who was to make him famous, the then Lieutenant-Commander Fleming sketched out a few of the necessary prerequisites for those taking part in Operation Ruthless. They should each be 'tough, a bachelor, able to swim', he wrote, pencilling in his own name alongside one of the positions.

'Pick a tough crew of five, including a pilot, wireless operator and word-perfect German speaker (Fleming),' he wrote. 'Dress them in German Air Force uniform, add blood and bandages.' These men would then wait until the next German air raid on London and, as the bombers returned home, take off and hide among the other aircraft. On the French side of the Channel, the bomber would send out an SOS. It would then switch off one engine, lose height fast, 'with smoke pouring from a candle in the tail', and ditch in the sea. The team would then put off in a rubber dinghy, having ensured that the bomber sank before the Germans could identify it, and wait to be rescued by the German Navy. Fleming's plan continued: 'Once aboard rescue boat, shoot German crew, dump overboard, bring boat back to English port.'

Frank Birch, always with an eye for the theatrical, gave enthusiastic backing to the 'very ingenious plot'. Fleming duly obtained a captured bomber and took his team to Dover to wait for the next big raid. But reconnaissance flights failed to find any suitable German vessels in the Channel and Operation Ruthless had to be called off, causing immense disappointment at Bletchley Park.

'Turing and Twinn came to me like undertakers cheated of a nice corpse yesterday, all in a stew about the cancellation of Ruthless,' Birch told Fleming. 'The burden of their song was the importance of a pinch. Did the authorities realise that there was very little hope, if any, of their deciphering current, or even approximately current, Enigma at all.'

Faced with the difficulty of finding a decent crib, the codebreakers developed a method known as 'gardening', said Rolf Noskwith, one of the members of Hut 8.

> The RAF dropped mines in specific positions in the North Sea so that they would produce warning messages that would give us a crib. The positions were carefully chosen so as to avoid numbers, especially 0 and 5, for which the Germans used more than one spelling.

The capture of Dolphin key tables for February 1941 on board another German ship off Norway's Lofoten Islands allowed Turing, known as 'Prof' to his Hut 8 colleagues, to break a number of messages over the next few months.

An added problem for the naval crypotographers was that when captured signals documents such as these came in they were frequently saturated with water and in danger of falling apart. Fortunately, Lieutenant-Commander Geoffrey Tandy, who was in charge of captured documents, was a former curator at the Natural

History Museum and had access to special materials used in the preservation of old documents. His presence was doubly fortunate. He had been sent to Bletchley Park because he was an expert in cryptogams, not – as the recruiting officer clearly assumed – coded messages, but mosses, ferns, algae, and fungi.

At about the same time as the Lofoten Islands 'pinch', the code-breakers discovered that messages sent on Enigma were also being sent using a lower-level hand cypher, known by the Germans as the 'Dockyard Key', providing a useful source of cribs. But still there was no continuous break. The search went on for a 'cunning scheme' that would find the crucial 'pinch' to help Turing and his team, now strengthened by the arrival of Hugh Alexander from Hut 6.

The breakthrough came when Hinsley found messages to and from German weather ships among the Enigma traffic. These ships, stationed in two places, north of Iceland and in the mid-Atlantic, would need to have exactly the same equipment and keys as any other ship using Enigma but would be far more vulnerable to raids designed to furnish a 'pinch'. Just as importantly, the same messages were being passed in both the Dolphin Enigma key and the German naval meteorological cypher which was much easier to break and would provide vital cribs throughout the war.

The German weather-ship the *München* was captured in early May, providing the settings for June. A few days later, more material was captured when the U-110 was forced to surface off Iceland. A second weather-ship captured at the end of June gave Hut 8 the settings for July. Turing and his team read through June and July using the captured cyphers. From the beginning of August they were on their own. But as a result of the continuity established over the previous two months, they had built up a library of cribs that, together with those provided by the weather messages, gardening, and a process known as 'Banburismus', allowed them to decypher Dolphin until the end of the war.

Banburismus, so-called because it involved the use of long sheets of paper printed in Banbury, was a brilliant method of decryption devised by Turing as a means of getting over the lack of Cillis on naval Enigma. It was used to identify messages with elements in common that might help to focus the menus and cut down on bombe time.

The Banburismus section of Hut 8 would look for messages sent with the wheel positions close to each other, Noskwith said.

The aim was to identify the right-hand and middle wheels because you could locate the turnover point of the wheel. Most wheels had different turnover points, so if you could show that the middle wheel turned over between E and F that would be, I think, wheel two. Identifying the right-hand and middle wheels meant you had to try fewer combinations on the bombes.

The Banbury sheets were about 10 inches wide and several feet long. They had columns of alphabets printed vertically on them, giving horizontal lines of As, Bs, Cs, etc. Clerks punched holes into the paper to correspond with the encyphered messages; thus, with a message beginning JKFTU, the J of the first column would be punched out, the K in the second column, the F in the third column and so on. They then aligned the sheets of paper over each other on top of a dark-coloured table and moved them to the left or right looking for repeats where the holes coincided and the table showed through.

The aim was to find points in a number of messages where a sequence of the machine coincided. If there were two messages with the indicators equating, for example, to the starting points XYK and XYM, with two letters between them, then the second message would start two spaces on. So if the initial letter of the second message was moved to a position over the third letter of the first message then the letters in each column would be encoded in the same position.

This would show up in an unusual number of repeats. Because more of these letters would have been common German letters like E and N there would be more repeats than in a random position. Alan Turing devised a scoring system which measured the probability of the different positions. The more repeats there were the more likelihood there was of the two sequences having been encyphered in the same position, said Peter Twinn.

If you're lucky and you're lucky pretty frequently, you might come across a four- or five-letter repeat. You would say to yourself 'a five-letter repeat, it's greatly against the odds, there must be a reason for it, what is it?' and the answer is that it represents the encodement of the same German word in both messages and you might be able to make a reasonable guess at what it was, having seen some German messages encyphered in the past.

So that would give you a little start and then you would try and fit a third message on and you might find with a bit of luck that when you staggered it off with both of them, you might find that this third message had two trigrams, one clicked with one of your messages and another trigram clicked with three in a quite different place on the first message.

I'm leaving out a lot of the difficulties, but you gradually build up a selection of twelve or fifteen messages out of the day's traffic which if you make some other guesses and, if you're very, very lucky, you can do one of a number of things. You can for a start cut down the number of wheel orders the bombes need to check. But you can also either find out the wiring of a brand new wheel or you can work out with a reasonable degree of accuracy what these messages might be saying.

There were three rooms in Hut 8, one dealing with cribs, one dealing with Banburismus and 'the big room' where female clerks punched up the messages on the Banbury sheets and decyphered messages on Type-X machines once the wheel order, settings and keys had been recovered.

The codebreakers themselves rarely read the decrypts. Peter Twinn recalled having very little interest in what they were actually saying.

I would have to confess I don't think I really understood the full significance of it. I think I'd have to excuse myself by saying that we lived at that time in a very narrow little world. Remember that I was an inexperienced lad of twenty-four or twenty-five and I'd come into it straight from university, I don't think I had a real grasp of what a major war was all about and we did work very much in a rather monastical way. I don't recall ever having decoded a message from start to finish to see what it said. I was much more interested in the methodology for getting German out of a coded message.

The decyphered messages were passed via Z Watch, the Naval Section's equivalent of Hut 3, over a newly installed teleprinter link to the OIC, giving prior warning of the wolf pack patrol lines and allowing the convoys to be routed away from danger. The result was truly dramatic. Between March and June 1941, the U-boats had sunk 282,000 tons of shipping a month. From July, the figure dropped to 120,000 tons a month and by November, when the wolf packs were temporarily withdrawn from the Atlantic, to 62,000 tons.

The breaking of the naval Enigma was one of the main reasons for this drop in the fortunes of the U-boats, providing the British with a welcome respite during which the vital supplies had a much greater chance of getting through, Harry Hinsley said.

It has been calculated that, allowing for the increased number of U-boats at sea, about one-and-a-half million tons of shipping [350 ships] were saved. This intermission was invaluable for the level of British supplies, the building of new shipping and the development of anti-submarine defences.

Despite the brilliance of men like Turing and Alexander, the naval Enigma could not have been broken without the bombes. Improved versions known as 'Jumbos' had been introduced and, in order to protect them from German air raids, they were dispersed to new outstations at Wavendon and Adstock. At the same time, the Bletchley bombes were moved out of the back room in Hut 1 and into Hut 11, acquiring a number of new operators.

The eight Wrens who arrived on 24 March 1941 were a trial measure. Previously the bombes had been operated by soldiers, airmen and sailors who had worked for BTM before being called up. But male servicemen were at a premium and the number of bombes was being constantly increased to cope with the need to keep the breaks of keys going, so it was decided to try the Wrens out as 'an experiment'.

Morag Maclennan had followed her brother into the Royal Navy at the age of seventeen and was very disappointed to discover that she was being sent to Bletchley rather than Portsmouth or Plymouth.

We got off at the station and somebody met us and we went up a little gravel path, straight into Hut 11. There were all these machines and you were given a thing called a menu with this strange pattern of letters and figures on it. You had to plait up this machine at the back with these great big leads which had to be plugged into different bits.

Then at the front, you had this rack with rows and rows of drums marked up by colour and you were told what combination of colours you were to put on. You would set them all, press a button and the whole row went round once and then moved the next one on. It took about 15 minutes for the whole run, stopping at different times, and you recorded the stop and phoned it through and, with any luck, sometimes it was the right one and the code was broken.

It was very smelly with the machine oil and really quite noisy. The machine kept clanking around and unless you were very lucky your eight-hour watch would not necessarily produce a good stop that broke a code. Sometimes you might have a good day and two of the jobs you were working on would break a code and that was a great feeling, particularly if it was a naval code. Obviously, we hoped to do it for everybody. But there was an extra little surge of pride if it was a Navy one.

Initially, the Wrens were not trusted with any details of what they were doing and it was a boring, frustrating task, she said.

> The job itself was pretty dull. You were just working the machines the entire time. Because if all the bread and butter codes were broken, there were always ones that had got missed from a few days before or trying out more experimental ones. So the bombes were never idle.
>
> But after a bit I think it was thought that it would be useful for our morale to know a little bit more of what the codes were dealing with, what areas they covered and of course the odd successes. Some weren't all that dramatic. They weren't necessarily operational, but they were building up the picture of exactly what Air Force squadrons and tank units were where, or where ships were and what they were doing. But when we were breaking the U-boat ones in particular, we were told about the U-boat sinkings and convoy protection, so we felt good about that.

By the end of the war, there were just under 2000 bombe operators, of whom 1676 were Wrens, at six different locations around the country. They had their own unit, HMS *Pembroke V*, and Wrens had gone on to take up a number of other roles in GC&CS, including codebreaking itself. They were billeted together at a number of beautiful old country homes, including Woburn Abbey, which became known as the 'Wrenneries'. But they never allowed themselves to forget that they were part of the Royal Navy, calling their living quarters, fo'c'sles; their dormitories, cabins; and saluting the areas in front of the country houses in which they were billeted as the quarterdeck.

Their arrival improved the social life and the Wrenneries became renowned for their dances. Barbara Quirk lived in a Tudor mansion called Crawley Grange, an hour's drive away from Bletchley.

> I remember our watch was having a dance in the most glorious ballroom in Crawley Grange, beautiful oak panelling from floor to ceiling, and we were told by our chief officer, who didn't work at Bletchley, that we couldn't have any drink. So we got some of the men who were coming from one of the camps around, they might have been Americans, they might have been British, I can't remember now, to bring some beer. They brought a mobile bar on a Jeep and parked it outside the Wrennery and when the chief officer found out, we were all gated for a month.

Joan Baily was billeted first at Crawley Grange and then at Gayhurst Manor, although she actually worked at Bletchley itself.

I found the atmosphere rather exciting because we had to try to break these codes and if we didn't get the codes up we knew that somebody had had it. If we were on night shift, we had to sleep during the day of course and I remember they had problems with an RAF aircraft flying low over Gayhurst. We found out afterwards it happened to be because my sister was sunbathing on the roof with nothing on.

The codebreakers picked up the first indications of the Nazi occupation of the Balkans in the spring of 1941 from Rocket, the Enigma cypher used by the German railways. Because it was easier to move troops and heavy weapons long distances by train, Rocket was a reliable method of picking up troop movement.

The campaign in the Balkans began well for the British in March 1941, with another success for Bletchley Park. Alerted by the codebreakers, the Royal Navy's Mediterranean Fleet, under Admiral Andrew Cunningham, crushed its Italian counterpart, sinking three heavy cruisers and two destroyers at the Battle of Matapan, off the southern tip of Greece.

Prior to the establishment of Hut 8, attempts to break Italian naval Enigma had, like its German equivalent, been covered by Knox's section in the cottage, Mavis Lever recalled.

We didn't often know the results of our activities, which messages were important. Because you see you might actually break a message which said nothing to report which would give you the settings for the rest of the messages. But the Italian messages were done individually.

The first Matapan message was very dramatic stuff: 'Today's the day minus three', just that and nothing else. So of course we knew the Italian Navy was going to do something in three day's time. Why they had to say that I can't imagine. It seems rather daft but they did. So we worked for three days. It was all the nail-biting stuff of keeping up all night working. One kept thinking: 'Well would one be better at it if one had a little sleep or shall we just go on,' and it did take nearly all of three days.

Then a very, very large message came in which was practically the battle orders for what turned into the Battle of Matapan. How many cruisers there were, and how many submarines were to be there and where they were to be at such and such a time, absolutely incredible that they should spell it all out. It was rushed out to Cunningham and the marvellous thing about him was that he played it extremely cool. He knew that they were going to go out and confront the Italian fleet at Matapan but he did a real Drake on them.

The Italian intention was to intercept British convoys en route from Egypt to Greece. Such was the Royal Navy's superiority over the Italians, that Cunningham did not believe the Italians would dare to carry out these plans. But knowing that the Japanese Consul in Alexandria, who was reporting on the movement of the Mediterranean Fleet, was a keen golfer, the British admiral ostentatiously visited the club house with his clubs and an overnight bag, Mavis Lever said.

> He pretended he was just going to have the weekend off and made sure the Japanese spy would pass it all back. Then under cover of the night, they went out and confronted the Italians.
>
> It was very exciting stuff. There was a great deal of jubilation in the cottage and then Cunningham himself came to visit us. The first thing he wanted to do when he came was to see the actual message that had been broken. I think we had a drink and we were in this little cottage and the walls had just been whitewashed. Now this just shows how silly and young and giggly we were. We thought it would be jolly funny if we could talk to Admiral Cunningham and get him to lean against the wet whitewash and go away with a white stern. So that's what we did. It's rather terrible, isn't it? On the one hand, everything was so very organised and on the other these silly young things are trying to snare the admiral.

Despite the British victory at Matapan, German troops, supported by the *Luftwaffe*, executed yet another blitzkrieg through Yugoslavia and into Greece. British and Greek troops facing insuperable odds were forced to retreat. But the campaign was the first in which the intelligence unearthed by the Bletchley Park codebreakers could be passed on to the commanders in the field direct from Bletchley Park itself rather than through MI6, as had occurred in Norway and France.

A direct Special Signals Link had been set up between Bletchley Párk and Cairo in early 1941 to feed the Most Secret Source intelligence to the British forces in the Middle East and it was extended to the British headquarters in Athens shortly before the German invasion. The Red *Luftwaffe* key provided comprehensive details of the discussions of the German *Fliegerverbindungsoffiziere* or *Flivos*, the air liaison officers who coordinated air and ground operations, and although this had to be passed on in a highly sanitised fashion, it ensured that the British could make an orderly retreat.

It also gave early warning that airborne forces were moving to the

Balkans in preparation for Operation Mercury, the attack on Crete. A series of messages beginning in late March provided the British with every detail of the operation, from the preparations to the complete plan of the airborne assault, and the date, 20 May, on which it was to be launched. The problem was to find a plausible way of camouflaging the source of all this intelligence so as to ensure the Germans did not realise that Enigma had been broken.

On Churchill's orders, Josh Cooper's Air Section produced a detailed report purporting to be a complete dossier of the German plans obtained by an MI6 agent inside the German GHQ in Athens. This was sent to General Bernard Freyburg, the New Zealand Commander in Crete, over the special Middle East link encyphered in the virtually unbreakable 'one-time pad' cypher system. Although he did not have the resources to fight off a sustained attack, the knowledge garnered from the 'German documents' robbed the Germans of any element of surprise – Freyburg allegedly looked at his watch when the German paradrop began and said: 'Right on time'. Alerted by the codebreakers, his men were able to pick off the enemy paratroopers at will, causing carnage and considerably delaying the defeat of the Allied Forces. But the codebreakers were disappointed that the plethona of information they were able to provide couldn't stave off defeat, John Herivel said.

Crete was an example of how knowing a great deal, through the Red, didn't necessarily lead to the correct results. All the German plans, the details for the invasion of Crete were known through Hut 6 decodes on the Red. We all knew about the German plans for the airborne assault on Crete – because there was no attempt to stop the people in Hut 6 from knowing what was in the decodes – and therefore we felt very confident that we would defeat it. But in fact we didn't. What did happen was that they had such enormous difficulty in taking Crete and suffered such enormous losses that Hitler decided he wouldn't try a parachute descent in that strength again.

Chapter 6

'Action This Day'

Throughout the 1941 Balkan campaign, railway Enigma had been indicating a series of movements, named after famous actors and film stars, heading north and east towards Poland. During March, April and May, message after message on links using the Red cypher pointed to a major concentration of German troops and air support converging on an assembly point at Oderberg, near Cracow. While much of the movement could have reflected a German attempt to intimidate Moscow, as many in Whitehall were inclined to believe, the inclusion of a POW interrogation unit and the urgency with which units were being pulled out of the Balkans convinced Hut 3 that the Germans were about to turn on their Russian allies.

> It becomes harder than ever to doubt that the object of these large movements of the German Army and Air Force is Russia. From rail movements towards Moldavia in the south to ship movements towards Varanger fjord in the far north there is everywhere the same steady eastward trend. Either the purpose is blackmail or it is war. No doubt Hitler would prefer a bloodless surrender. But the quiet move, for instance, of a prisoner-of-war cage to Tarnow looks more like business than bluff.

It was not until 10 June, when Malcolm Kennedy's Japanese diplomatic section translated a message to Tokyo from the Japanese ambassador in Berlin confirming that the invasion was imminent, that Whitehall finally accepted the codebreakers had got it right. Twelve days later, Hitler launched Operation Barbarossa, the invasion of the Soviet Union. It was to bring some of the most distressing decrypts the codebreakers had to handle.

Some of the messages of the SS and the *Ordnungspolizei*, the German police who were mopping up behind the German lines during Operation Barbarossa, made chilling reading, providing details of the systematic murder of thousands of Jews.

On 18 July 1941, *Obergruppenführer* Erich von dem Bach-Zelewski, *Ordnungspolizei* commander in the Soviet republic of Belorussia, informed Kurt Dalüge, head of the *Ordnungspolizei*, and Heinrich Himmler, the *Reichsführer*-SS, that 'in yesterday's cleansing action in Slonim, carried out by Police Regiment Centre, 1153 Jewish plunderers were shot.' Three weeks later, he reported that his men had already killed 30,000 'partisans and Jewish bolsheviks'.

On the same day, the SS brigade based in the Minsk area of Belorussia reported having carried out 7819 executions to date. Friederich Jäckeln, *Ordnungspolizei* commander in the Ukraine, told Dalüge and Himmler that on 27 August, with *Ordnungspolizei* Battalion 320 shot 4200 Jews near the town of Kamenets-Podolsk'. In the last week of August alone, 12,361 Ukrainian Jews were murdered, most of them by the police rather than the SS. On 1 September, Jäckeln reported that the same battalion had executed a further 2200 Jews. A month later, he said his men had 'disposed of 1255 Jews, according to the usage of war' near the town of Ovruch.

Alongside this stream of horrific statistics, the Bletchley Park intelligence reporter added the comment: 'The tone of this message suggests that the word has gone out that a decrease in the population of Russia would be welcomed in high quarters and that leaders of the three sectors stand somewhat in competition with each other as to their "score".'

This provoked an angry response from military intelligence in London, where an official noted that the report was tarnished by the fact that 'certain opinions and conclusions are erected on shallow grounds'. But, whatever the War Office opinion of these reports, they left little doubt as to what was going on. The killings that followed the invasion of the Soviet Union are now recognised as the beginning of the Holocaust.

By August 1941, Churchill had become so enraged over the evidence of systematic extermination provided by the police hand cypher and the SS Enigma system, known in Hut 6 as Orange, that he issued an angry warning to the Germans. The British Prime Minister publicly denounced the 'scores of thousands of executions in cold blood' that the German police were committing. 'Since the Mongol invasions of Europe in the sixteenth century, there has never been methodical, merciless butchery on such a scale, or approaching such a scale,' he said. 'We are in the presence of a crime without a name.'

He was taking a gamble that the Germans would assume that their hand cypher was broken rather than the Orange Enigma. It was a high-risk decision which put the Bletchley secret at threat and firmly disproves recent allegations of a British cover-up. Churchill's speech could have completely cut off access to his Most Secret Source, almost certainly lengthening the course of the war. A few weeks after Churchill's speech, Dalüge warned his commanders that the British might be listening and told them to send details of all future 'executions' to Berlin by courier.

Far from covering up information about the massacres, the British appointed two officials, one inside Bletchley Park and one in the Foreign Office, to collect evidence of the German atrocities for the United Nations Commission for the Investigation of War Crimes.

One of those involved in decyphering the plethora of messages coming out of eastern Europe was Charles Cunningham who had been called up into the Army as a private.

> I had read classics, Latin and Greek, at Glasgow. By way of ancillary to that I had taken a short course in German mainly because many of the best texts and commentaries on the Latin and Greek classics are in German. As a result of that very minimal knowledge the Army posted me to Bletchley Park.
>
> On my first day there, I saluted this captain and he turned to me and said: 'Excuse me' – which is not the language normally used by captains to privates – 'Excuse me,' he said, 'What is that noise?' To which I replied: 'That is the air raid siren, sir.' That gives you some kind of an impression of what kind of place Bletchley was. Mad people on all sides.

Cunningham was immediately promoted to lance-corporal and put to work on police communications. 'I was a cryptanalyst working on what was called German police but in fact it included all the security services,' Cunningham said. 'They used a lovely hand cypher system, which was called Double Playfair, named after a British admiral in the mid-nineteenth century who devised it.'

Admiral Playfair's system required the message that was to be encyphered to be split into bigrams so the sentence 'Report to headquarters at once' would be rendered:

RE PO RT TO HE AD QU AR TE RS AT ON CE

The cypher was built in a 5 × 5 square around a keyword. If Phoenix was taken as the keyword, it would be written into the square with the remaining letters of the alphabet filling the rest of the square, omitting J which when encyphering was always taken to be I. A

Playfair cypher using Phoenix as the keyword would therefore appear thus:

P	H	O	E	N
I	X	A	B	C
D	F	G	K	L
M	Q	R	S	T
U	V	W	Y	Z

Each bigram of the divided message is then replaced by a pair of letters from within the square according to pre-set rules. If the letters appear at a diagonal to each other they are replaced by the letters at the other point of a rectangle so formed. In the case of our message, the first bigram RE becomes OS. Bigrams with letters in the same horizontal or vertical line are replaced by the next letter on, making the second bigram of the above message HE. Letters at the end of the line jump to the next one. So the third bigram RT would be rendered SU. The entire encyphered message would then be written in five-letter groups, in this case using four randomly chosen fillers at the end:

OSHES UNRON GIVMG WNSST RCEIN BCVYU

The Germans, having broken this cypher early on in the First World War, decided to adapt it for their own use. They introduced a second square from which the second letter of each bigram was selected and dispensed with the keyword, placing the letters in random order.

This complication obviously made it much more difficult to crack. But since the Germans spelt everything, including numbers, out in full, the codebreakers often got plenty of depth. The German fondness for pro forma traffic in which everything always stayed in its set place also helped to ensure that the Double Playfair system, used as a medium-grade cypher not just by the German police but also by the Army and Air Force, was regularly broken.

Pro forma messages inevitably required each part of the message to be preceded by a sequential number, the first part being 1, the second 2, and so on. Since these had to be spelt out, *EINS*, the German word for one was immediately recoverable and easy cribs were available for the rest of the message. The fact that, when spelt out, the German numbers one to twelve contain all but eight of the letters in the Double Playfair squares made pro forma traffic relatively easy to break.

But while the actual process of breaking the police cypher was an enjoyable and intensely rewarding task for the codebreakers, the results of their labour were often horrific, Charles Cunningham recalled.

> When you're an individual cryptanalyst just working on the intercepts of the day before, you don't have any real overall picture. You only see the bits of paper in front of you and try to break the cypher and having broken it you pass it on to someone else who does the decoding. The business of the cryptanalyst is simply to get the key. When he's done that, he goes on to another batch.

> But there was concern over the concentration camps, which was of course a very inadequate term, and one was aware in the case of stuff coming from these camps that very nasty things indeed were going on. They were run by the SS and they made regular returns of the intake and what the output was and you can guess what the intake was and what the output was. You soon got to have a fairly good idea of what you were dealing with.

> The ironic thing was that these terrible returns, sort of day-to-day status reports, were stereotyped and that is a very good way of getting into that kind of cypher. They provided an excellent crib, which I always thought of as a distinctly unfortunate thing but I suppose it is a kind of way of turning evil into good.

The SS decrypts also revealed the existence of a special SS battalion which, under the guidance of Joachim von Ribbentrop, the German foreign minister, was plundering works of art and sending them back to Berlin. The battalion was attached to Army groups in all the countries invaded by Germany and in Russia made a particular target of the palaces of the former Tsar in Leningrad, suggesting that it may have been behind the disappearance of the wall coverings from the legendary Amber Room, a gold- and amber-encrusted hall in the Winter Palace.

The decrypts showed the battalion becoming involved in a wrangle between von Ribbentrop and Alfred Rosenberg, Minister for Occupied Territories, over what should happen to various works of art looted from Russian palaces, museums and monasteries, most of which made their way into the villas of top-ranking Nazi leaders.

The attack on police and SS cyphers was led by Colonel John Tiltman of the King's Own Scottish Borderers, a tall, rangy pre-war codebreaker and a leading expert on hand cyphers, who was famed for his tartan trews and rather casual approach to military uniform.

William Filby, who worked as a cryptanalyst in Hut 5, the Military Section of which Tiltman was the commanding officer, recalled their first meeting.

My arrival was unforgettable. As I saluted, I stamped the wooden floor in my Army boots and came to attention with another shattering noise. Tiltman turned, looked at my feet, and exclaimed: 'I say old boy. Must you wear those damned boots?' I became the only other rank at BP in battledress and white running shoes, much to the disgust of the adjutant.

Members of the Army and the ATS were quartered at Shenley Road Military Camp, less than five minutes' walk from Bletchley Park, recalled Alan Stripp, an Intelligence Corps NCO working on Japanese cyphers. 'The camp commandant was Colonel Fillingham of the Durham Light Infantry and the DLI provided the camp staff who kept the place more or less clean and tidy,' Stripp said. 'There was a culture gap between them, condemned to this servile role, and us with our hoity-toity ways, our la-di-da talk, our regrettable tendency to wear shoes not boots, and our knowledge of the mysteries of the security area.'

During June 1941, with the number of Enigma decrypts in circulation growing rapidly and the fighting in North Africa opening up their use by commanders in the field to an extent that had not previously been possible, new security precautions were introduced. The codeword 'Ultra' was added to the Most Secret security classification on all reports produced by Bletchley Park. Strict regulations were laid down limiting its circulation and insisting that no action was to be taken on the basis of Ultra unless the information could have been received from another source. The regulations stated that:

Momentary tactical advantage is not sufficient ground for taking any risk or compromising the source. No action may be taken against specific sea or land targets revealed by Ultra unless appropriate air reconnaissance or other suitable camouflage measures have also been taken. If from any document which might fall into his hands, from any message he might intercept, from any word revealed by a prisoner of war, or from any ill-considered action taken upon the basis of such intelligence, the enemy were given cause to believe that his communications are not adequately safe-guarded against interception, he would effect changes which would deprive us of knowledge of his operations on all fronts.

A few months later, Churchill came to visit the codebreakers he was to laud as 'the geese who laid the golden eggs and never cackled'. The prime minister was reputedly startled to be confronted by the eccentricity of the codebreakers, turning to Menzies and saying: 'I know I told you to leave no stone unturned to get staff, but I didn't expect you to take me literally.'

Malcolm Kennedy recorded the visit in his diary entry for 6 September 1941.

> The PM paid us a surprise visit this morning and after inspecting some of the work of BP gave a short talk thanking us for what we have done and stressing the great value of our work. Sir Dudley Pound, the First Sea Lord, paid a similar visit of thanks at the time of the *Bismarck* show. Very decent of these old boys to come down in person to thank us when they themselves must be terribly loaded down with their own work and vast responsibilities. Instructions issued to keep Churchill's visit a secret, but all Bletchley seems to know about it.

One of the first places Churchill visited was Hut 6, where John Herivel was introduced as the man responsible for beginning the continuous break into the vitally important Red key.

> Churchill didn't say anything. He just gave me a deep penetrating look, not a very friendly look, rather a scowl, and then he went on. Later that day, we were told the prime minister wanted to see us. There was a little pile of material which the builders had conveniently left near the end of Hut 6 and Churchill stood up on it and in just a few words, with deep emotion, he said how grateful he was to us for all the good work we were doing in the war effort. So that was our finest hour.

Only a few of the codebreakers were able to hear what Churchill said but there was an immense feeling of pride that the prime minister had visited them and disappointment among those, like Ann Lavell, who were not there to hear him speak. 'I was terribly cross,' she said. 'I was on four to midnight shift that day and when I came up the place was buzzing like an ant-heap. and I'd missed it all, he'd been and gone.'

By now there was far too much work to do and too few people and, just as importantly, too little equipment, particularly bombes and radio sets, to do it. The German and Italian operations in North Africa, the Mediterranean, the Balkans and on the Eastern Front were now generating a massive amount of work for the code-breakers. Welchman expressed his concern that the concentration on the Red Enigma was putting too many eggs in one basket in one of his 'screeds' to the members of Hut 6.

> Since we have neither enough intercept sets to cover all E [Enigma] traffic nor enough bombes to deal with all menus that could be produced we must be very careful to use our resources to the best advantage. Although we must concentrate the greater part of our resources on those colours which are high in the scale, it is most important that we ourselves should not lose interest in any type of E traffic. We should retain a clear idea of what is worth doing, even if we cannot at present do as much as we would wish, and our aim should always be to break every key and to take all steps that may possibly assist future breaking. From the crytographic point of view the breaking of any key may be valuable because key repeats or re-encodements may occur.

As Denniston and Travis struggled to find sufficient recruits to cope with the needs of the various sections, Tiltman set up a training school for cryptanalysts in order to give new entrants a basic grounding in codebreaking. It was called the Inter-Service Special Intelligence School and was initially put into temporary accommodation at an RAF depot in Buckingham before moving into the gas company show-rooms in Ardour House where it swiftly became known to locals as 'the Spy School'.

A comprehensive building programme was put in place in anticipation of a staff of around 3000 – at the time, with the number of staff still some way short of 1000, a highly optimistic figure. The first priority was a canteen to replace the old dining hall in the mansion which was now far too small, leading to long queues at mealtimes. There were also to be a number of custom-built brick blocks to house the necessary expansion. But there was still no sign of the manpower needed to fill them. The armed forces refused to let fit, young recruits join intelligence. They were needed to fight the war.

Without further resources, not just people but also equipment like bombes and radio sets, the codebreakers knew they would be totally unable to cope. Denniston and Travis were doing what they could in Whitehall, but since so few people were allowed to know the Ultra secret they were unable to make clear the importance of the work being done at Bletchley Park. Nor did Denniston, the head of an obscure Foreign Office department, wield the necessary power or weight of personality to force the issue. The requests for more resources were getting nowhere.

Welchman, Milner-Barry, Turing and Alexander, 'the wicked uncles' as they were known among their junior staff, decided to go straight to the top. On 21 October 1941, they wrote a letter to Churchill reminding him of his visit and his praise for their work. 'We think, however, that you should know that this work is being held up, and in some cases not being done at all, principally because we cannot get sufficient staff to deal with it,' they said. 'Our reason for writing to you direct is that for months we have done everything that we possibly can through the normal channels and that we despair of any early improvement without your intervention.'

They emphasised that they had written the letter entirely on their own initiative and were careful to stress that the problem lay with the Foreign Office and the service ministries.

> They seem not to understand the importance of what is done here or the urgent necessity of dealing promptly with our requests. No doubt in the long run these particular requirements will be met, but meanwhile still more precious months will have been wasted. If we are to do our job as well as it could and should be done, it is absolutely vital that our wants, small as they are, should be promptly attended to.

Fearing that if the letter were sent through Denniston or Menzies, it would never reach Churchill, they decided that Milner-Barry should go to Downing Street himself to deliver it. There he received a small taste of the problems faced by Denniston in getting Whitehall to provide what the codebreakers required. Brigadier Harvie-Walker, Churchill's principal private secretary, insisted that no one saw the prime minister without an appointment and demanded more details of this matter of supposed great national importance. Milner-Barry, who had not thought to bring any official identification with him, was equally insistent that he could not discuss it with anyone who was not authorised to know about it.

Eventually, Harvie-Walker agreed to pass the letter on to Churchill, whose immediate response was a minute to General Hastings Ismay, his Chief of Staff. 'Make sure they have all they want extreme priority and report to me that this has been done,' Churchill wrote, scrawling across the minute the ominous warning: 'Action this day.'

From that point on, resources began to flow into Bletchley Park. The Ministry of Labour was ordered to hold a meeting with Denniston and Menzies at which the needs of the codebreakers were to be considered favourably. The service chiefs were instructed to provide more clever young men and to enlarge the Y service immediately to provide the coverage that Welchman, Milner-Barry, Turing and Alexander demanded. Expensive new orders for many more bombes were placed with the British Tabulating Machine Company and the Royal Navy agreed to supply additional Wrens to operate them.

The military resorted to unusual methods to bring in the right type of recruit to Bletchley Park. Stanley Sedgewick's job as a managing clerk with a firm of city accountants was classified as a reserved occupation which meant that call-up was deferred for six months at a time. Every day, he travelled into London by train.

I became quite good at solving the crossword puzzles appearing in the *Daily Telegraph*. Towards the end of 1941, the appearance of a crossword marking a milestone in the history of the *Telegraph* inspired several letters from readers claiming they had never missed them, or never failed to solve them, or never took more than so many minutes to solve them.

A Mr Gavin, Chairman of the Eccentrics Club, wrote saying he would donate £100 to the Minesweepers' Fund if it could be demonstrated under controlled conditions that anyone could solve the *Daily Telegraph* puzzle in less than twelve minutes. This prompted the editor to invite readers wishing to take up this challenge to present themselves at the newspaper's offices in Fleet Street on a Saturday afternoon. I went along, to find about thirty other would-be fast solvers. We sat at individual tables in front of a platform of invigilators including the editor, Mr Gavin, and a timekeeper. The editor then selected a sealed envelope out of a stack of seven, each containing the puzzles due to appear the following week.

Four of those present completed the puzzle correctly in 7 minutes 57.5 seconds; 9 minutes 3.5 seconds; 9 minutes 52.5 seconds; and 10 minutes 38.5 seconds. I was one word short when the 12-minute bell rang, which was disappointing as I had completed that day's puzzle in the train to Waterloo in under 12 minutes. We were then given tea in the chairman's dining-room and dispersed with the memory of a pleasant way of spending a Saturday afternoon.

Imagine my surprise when several weeks later, I received a letter marked 'Confidential' inviting me, as a consequence of taking part in 'the *Daily Telegraph* Crossword Time Test', to make an appointment to see Colonel Nichols of the General Staff who 'would very much like to

see you on a matter of national importance'. Nichols was the head of
MI8, the military intelligence department concerned with Bletchley
Park and the Army's Y Service.

I arranged to attend at Devonshire House in Piccadilly, the
headquarters of MI8, and found myself among a few others who had
been contacted in the same circumstances. I think I was told, though not
so primitively, that chaps with twisted brains like mine might be
suitable for a particular type of work as a contribution to the war effort.
Thus it was that I reported to 'the Spy School' at 1, Albany Road,
Bedford.

On completion of the course, I received a letter offering me an
appointment as a 'Temporary Junior Assistant' at the Government
Communications Centre and started at BP.

Sedgewick worked in Hut 10, Josh Cooper's Air Section, on German
weather codes. 'The results were used – usually currently – to permit
weather forecasts to be made for operational use by Bomber
Command,' Sedgewick said. He was unaware until long after the
end of the war that they were also used as crucial cribs for the naval
Enigma.

The Y Service was gradually expanded by around 1000 wireless sets
and, since these were to be manned 24 hours a day, seven days a week,
by more than 4000 operators. As a result of Chatham's vulnerability to
German air raids, new Army stations had been built at Harpenden, in
Hertfordshire, and at Beaumanor, near Loughborough in Leicester-
shire, while the need for the RAF to monitor as much of the Red
Luftwaffe traffic as possible had led to the contruction of another Air
Force interception site at Chicksands Priory, not far from Bletchley.
This was now expanded rapidly and a new GPO site to augment the
work of Sandridge was opened in a rambling old rectory at
Whitchurch in Shropshire.

There were also a number of Y Service interception stations abroad
in Palestine, Egypt, Malta, Gibraltar, India and South Africa as well
as the Far East Combined Bureau, based in Singapore until the
Japanese invasion when it moved to Ceylon. Joan Nicholls was based
at Beaumanor.

The Y Service was an amazing organisation. It began with a few people
before the war and ended up with thousands of us. Wherever the
Germans were we were listening. Berlin, Essen, anywhere in Germany,
anywhere in Russia, all over the Continent, Holland and so on. At
Beaumanor, there were 900 female ATS intercept operators and 300

The *Daily Telegraph* Crossword Competition

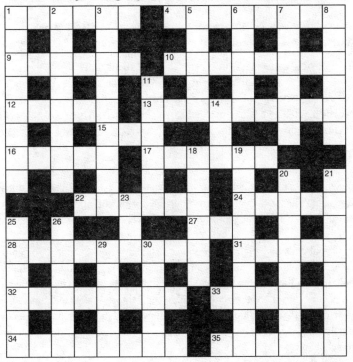

ACROSS

1. A stage company (6)
4. The direct route preferred by the Roundheads (two words – 6, 3)
9. One of the evergreens (6)
10. Scented (8)
12. Course with an apt finish (5)
13. Much that could be got from a timber merchant (two words – 5, 4)
15. We have nothing and are in debt (3)
16. Pretend (5)
17. Is this town ready for a flood? (6)
22. The little fellow has some beer: it makes me lose colour, I say (6)
24. Fashion of a famous French family (5)
27. Tree (3)
28. One might of course use this tool to core an apple (9)
31. Once used for unofficial currency (5)
32. Those well brought up help these over stiles (two words – 4, 4)
33. A sport in a hurry (6)
34. Is the workshop that produces this part of a motor a hush-hush affair? (8)
35. An illumination functioning (6)

DOWN

1. Official instruction not to forget the servants (8)
2. Said to be a remedy for a burn (two words – 5, 3)
3. Kind of alias (9)
5. A disagreeable company (5)
6. Debtors may have to this money for their debts unless of course their creditors do it to the debts (5)
7. Boat that should be able to suit everyone (6)
8. Gear (6)
11. Business with the end in sight (6)
14. The right sort of woman to start a dame school (3)
18. 'The War' (anag) (6)
19. When hammering take care to hit this (two words) – 5, 4)
20. Making a sound as a bell (8)
21. Half a fortnight of old (8)
23. Bird, dish of coin (3)
25. This sign of the zodiac has no connection with the Fishes (6)
26. A preservative of the teeth (6)
29. Famous sculptor (5)
30. This part of the locomotive engine could sound familiar to the golfer (5)

Solution on page 90

civilian intercept operators, the men, so there were 1200 of us manning four setrooms twenty-four hours a day and that was only one station.

The operators sat chasing the stations up and down the frequencies, mainly at Bletchley Park's behest, identifying them by a mixture of direction-finding; radio finger-printing, a technique that identified wireless transmitters from their individual idiosyncracies; and simple operator skill at recognising the style and technique of the German signallers, Nicholls recalled.

> The transmitter itself has a sound. Some of them were deep, some of them were light and tinny, and the man who is actually transmitting the Morse, he has his own particular way of sending letters, the rhythm of the dots and dashes would be made in a certain peculiar way by each person.
>
> It is like a voice. When a member of your family comes through the door and says something to you, you don't have to look to see who it is because you know the voice. You recognize the voice of your friends and family on the telephone because the minute they speak you know it's them and it's the same with the operators. They each had their own particular sound, that lilt or staccato way of sending morse dots and dashes.
>
> So if they changed frequency and we lost them, we would go looking for them and we would listen first of all for the sound of the transmitter and then we would tune in to that transmitter and listen for the operator and the minute we found him, that was him, there was no question of 'We think we have him'. As soon as we heard the sound of our man, the way he sent the letters, he was our man.

The Y operators developed a curious relationship with the German signallers, Nicholls said.

> In my off-duty time, I was hostile to the Germans and the things that were happening that were in the papers and on the news, very hostile because at that age everything is good or bad, there is nothing in between. But I wasn't hostile to the operator I was listening to. You had a rapport with him. Not a feeling of friendship or anything, but certainly not a feeling of hatred.
>
> You would hear them when our side were there outside their door. We had one man who wanted to get a message to his family to say what had happened and the control station was saying: 'In code, in code' and he was saying: 'The Tommies are outside the window.' You aren't actually there but you feel part of it, knowing that outside are the Allies

about to shoot him, capture him or whatever and he's thinking of his mother and trying to get a message to her. You're sat there safe and sound in England and you feel sorry for him.

Hundreds of Wrens were drafted into Bletchley, not just to look after the new bombes, but also to work in a number of other codebreaking and intelligence roles. They were allocated their own trade, 'Special Duties X', and a new bombe outstation was opened up at Gayhurst Manor, north of Bletchley.

The increase in numbers of people arriving put a strain on the administration, which had to find billets for them all. 'Many more service people came in, many more Wrens,' said Mavis Lever, one of the civilian codebreakers.

> The more people came, the further you had to go out to villages, right over beyond Woburn and into Bedfordshire and around Buckinghamshire and a vast system of taking people in and out and so on, whereas before we were all very locally billeted.

When the shifts changed over at 9.00 a.m., 4.00 p.m. and midnight, swarms of people descended from a variety of vehicles, many of them driven by young female Motor Transport Corps volunteers, young society women who had no need to be paid for their war work. 'The MTC drivers were really very attractive girls,' said Barbara Abernethy. 'They were usually quite wealthy and they had to buy their own uniforms, which were beautifully cut, and they were all pretty. But they worked very, very hard.' The staff coming on shift had been brought in from various billets all over the surrounding countryside and those going off shift were taken home in the same fashion. Morag Maclennan was one of the Wrens working in the Hut 11 bombe section.

> We would do eight-hour shifts. You would come out of your transport, buses or shooting brakes. They were the great things, shooting brakes dashing all over the villages of Buckinghamshire bringing people in. Huts were being built all the time and extra pieces of equipment being installed. Things were going on in the far reaches of the Park that I didn't know very much about.

Some of the vehicles were extremely old and unreliable, said Julie Lydekker, a junior assistant in the Air Section.

> They laid on extraordinary old seaside charabancs, with doors all down

the side. One of the people who used to come on this charabanc was A. J. Alan. He used to be in the Hunt Hotel, Lindslade, and when the buses broke down, he would take us in and give us ginger wine. He was always very amusing.

In an attempt to relieve the pressure for new billets, the servicemen and women were moved into military camps, recalled Ann Lavell.

We were hauled out of our billets, many of us wailing and screaming mightily, and by this time we were all dressed up as flight sergeants. A flight sergeant is really quite somebody in an ordinary RAF station but we were nobodies. We were put into these frightful huts that took about twenty-four people and had these dangerous cast-iron stoves in them that got red hot and sent out smoke everywhere.

There was a terrible feeling between the camp authorities and the Bletchley Park people. They couldn't bear it because they didn't know what we did and because we could get in past the sentries. The guards actually said: 'Halt, who goes there?' If you arrived at night, they did the bit about 'friend of foe' and you said 'friend' and they said 'advance friend and be recognised'. The camp people absolutely hated not knowing what was going on and some of the officers tried to bully out of the junior people what they were doing.

By now most people, apart from the dons, wore uniform. There was a period when the hierarchy, such as it was, was completely chaotic, said John Prestwich, one of the Hut 3 intelligence reporters.

Some people were group-captains, some people were lieutenants and so on. So for a longish period we all wore civilian clothes and we were perfectly happy about it, uniforms were uncomfortable. Then some wretched admiral came down and said: 'Where are my Wrens?' and there were these girls in skirts and jumpers and he said: 'It's disgraceful. My Wrens should be jumping up, hands down seams of skirts.' So we were all made to wear uniform.

A branch of the Corps of Military Police known as the Vital Points Wardens mounted guard on the camp. The VPWs wore a distinctive blue cap cover rather than the standard MP red-cap until somebody pointed out that this gave away the fact that Bletchley Park was a 'vital point' and the blue cap covers were removed.

Among the new staff recruited as a direct result of Churchill's 'Action this day' minute, were the members of the central index in Hut 7 which housed an enormous automated Hollerith punch-card sorter. Under the direction of Frederick Freeborn, the former head of Hollerith's Letchworth factory, women clerks cross-referenced every piece of information passing through Bletchley on to punch cards. A request for details of a radio station, unit, codeword, covername or indeed any type of activity would swiftly produce every card containing any previous mention or occurrence.

Marjorie Halcrow, a twenty-two-year-old graduate from Aberdeen University, was one of those recruited by Freeborn to work in Hut 7.

> The cards were actually punched up on a machine about the size of a typewriter. There was a room containing about twenty or thirty of them called the punch room where girls copied the coded messages on to these punch cards. The main room contained much larger machines, about the size of a small piano, called the sorting machines, which could read the cards and sort the hundreds of thousands of messages into different categories. There were loads of sorters and there were collating machines that were even larger. The whole department was filled with machinery. It was a very noisy place, all banging on all night and day long.

This frequently forgotten part of Britain's wartime codebreaking operations was also used in the decyphering process, although not always as efficiently as it might have been. 'The cryptanalytical sections would have had a better service if they had simply discussed their needs with Freeborn instead of dictating to him,' recalled Welchman. 'This would have given him the chance to programme the overall use of his equipment and staff in a way that would have been advantageous not only for each individual problem solution, but for the overall service he was providing.'

By the end of 1941, the increase in the numbers of people had brought a dramatic improvement in the social life. Phoebe Senyard spent her first Christmas of the war at home. 'I returned on Boxing Day to find everyone gradually returning to normal after having spent a riotous time, everyone going out of their way to make everyone else enjoy themselves.'

The Christmas of 1941 was the last to be held in the old dining hall in the mansion with a traditional dinner, followed by a fancy dress dance in the school hall. The highlight of the festive period was the revue, run by Bill Marchant, a former German master at Harrow who became deputy head of Hut 3. 'The revues took place once a year about Christmas or New Year,' said Barbara Abernethy. 'They were produced by Bill and his wife and they really were excellent because they had good people who wrote the stuff like Patrick Wilkinson and a man called Patrick Barraclough, who was Hinsley's tutor at St John's.'

The revues were not only popular with the staff, recalled Travis's daughter Valerie. Her father would invite senior service officers to Bletchley as a means of improving relations between the code-breakers and Whitehall.

> My father always used to have a tremendous party, inviting all the top brass down from London for the revue and they loved it. The little man who was the caterer for Bletchley Park had a wonderful line in the black market and he used to produce the most sumptuous feasts.

Christine Brooke-Rose was a young WAAF officer working in one of the Hut 3 research sections.

> There was a sort of hall just outside Bletchley Park itself, a brick hall with a stage with shows once a year at Christmas. We would go up to London to see a play or a concert. There were people like Peter Calvocoressi who would give musical evenings in their billets. I remember Brin Newton-John, an RAF officer in Hut 3 whose daughter Olivia became a well-known pop star, would sing German lieder. People went cycling around the countryside and there were a lot of love affairs going on.

There were a number of debutantes working in the various indexes or as volunteer bus drivers who determined to liven Bletchley Park up including Pamela Gibson, head of the naval index where many of the girls worked.

> We gave what we thought were splendid parties. A girl called Maxine Birley, the Comtesse de la Falaise as she now is, was a great beauty and mad about France and I remember her giving a party at which we all had to be very French. People would change partners quite a lot. We were rather contained in a way out place and you could only travel if you managed to get transport so there was a good deal of changing of partners.

Stanley Sedgewick organised twice-weekly dances, many of them fancy dress, and also provided modern dance lessons. 'This was in the Big Band era of Glenn Miller and I engaged the dance bands of

Above: Members of Captain Ridley's Shooting Party arriving at Bletchley Park in August 1939.

Below left: Hugh Alexander, the British chess champion who became one of the leading codebreakers.

Below right: Dilly Knox, the eccentric veteran cryptographer who broke the more complicated Enigma machine used by German intelligence.

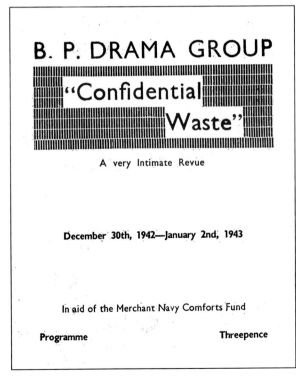

B. P. DRAMA GROUP

"Confidential Waste"

A very Intimate Revue

December 30th, 1942—January 2nd, 1943

In aid of the Merchant Navy Comforts Fund

Programme   **Threepence**

Above: The cast of the final Bletchley Park revue held in January 1945.

Left: The cover of one of the revue programmes.

Above: The control panel of the MkII version of Colossus, the world's first programmable electronic computer which was used to break the Fish encyphered teleprinter traffic.

Right: Alan Turing, the revered Cambridge mathematician who not only played a leading role in breaking Enigma but also laid down the principles behind the modern computer.

Top: Playing rounders on the lawn in front of the mansion *(l to r)* George McVittie; Dick Bowen; Daphne Bradshaw.

Above: Codebreakers watching a game of rounders during the last days of the Phoney War in Spring 1940: *Standing (l to r):* Phillip Howse; Stephen Wills; Captain Ridley; John Barns; George McVittie; Marjorie de Haan; Alastair Denniston. *Seated (l to r):* E. M. Smith; Edmund Green, Barbara Abernethy; Patrick Wilkinson; Alan Bradshaw.

Right: Codebreakers skating on the lake at Bletchley Park during the Phoney War winter of 1939–1940.

Top left: Harry Hinsley, the leading naval intelligence analyst in Hut 4.

Top centre: Gordon Welchman, whose reorganisation of GC&CS created Huts 3 and 6 and formed the basis for the modern GCHQ.

Top right: Commander Edward 'Jumbo' Travis, who took over from Alastair Denniston as head of Bletchley Park.

Below: Alastair Denniston, the original head of Bletchley Park (left), with Professor E. R. P. Vincent, one of the Hut 4 Italian experts (centre), and Colonel John Tiltman, the brilliant codebreaker whose many achievements included the first break into the Fish encyphered teleprinter traffic.

Above: Members of Huts 6 and 3 celebrating VE Day. *Standing (l to r):* Joan Watkins; Elizabeth Granger; Jean F. Davies; Jane Morris; Pat Dewning; Bob Roseveare; unidentified; Harold Fletcher; George Davis; Asa Briggs; Molly Bruce; Pam Bevington; Jessie Proctor; Sheila Dunlop; Jean Proctor; Joyce Robinson; Major J. C. Manisty; Honour Poss; Daisy Genge; Gwen Thomas; Margaret Bradshaw; Hope Wallace. *Sitting or kneeling (l to r):* Ioana Jay; Winifred Mary Smith; Maureen F. Kewley; Major Neil 'Willy' Webster; Peggy Rawlings-Smith; Major J. G. Monroe; unidentified; Mary Groves; Major Edward Rushworth; Audrey Cocking.

Right: Dennis Babbage, one of the Hut 6 codebreakers, getting married to Diana Russell Clarke who worked in the machine room deciphering Enigma messages.

the RAF at nearby Halton and a USAF bomber base and demonstrations of jitterbugging.'

On one occasion, a bus-load of the debs and Wrens, including Adrienne Farrell, were invited to a dance in a hangar at a nearby US Air Force base where Glenn Miller's band was playing.

> The hangar was crowded and in semi-darkness, lit only by swirling coloured spotlights and resounding with the superb but deafening noise of the band. As each of us entered we were grabbed by one of the waiting line of airmen. After the first dance, I looked eagerly round for my next partner. Alas, we were expected to stay with the same person all evening. I think my partner was as disappointed as I was. On the way home, I noticed with some puzzlement that the bus was half empty.

More erudite tastes were catered for by the Bletchley Park Recreational Club which included a library, a drama group, musical and choral societies as well as bridge, chess, fencing and Scottish dancing sections.

Hugh Foss, one of the old Broadway codebreakers and head of the Japanese Section, was in charge of the Scottish dancing in which Denniston himself took part. 'I used to do choral singing and Scottish country dancing in the evenings which was wonderful exercise,' said Valerie Travis. 'With Hugh Foss, who was a member of the Chelsea Reel School, in command we did it properly. I danced an eightsome reel with the 51st Highland Division at one of the Wrenneries. The Wrens gave marvellous dances out at Woburn.'

Ann Lavell recalled that the choral society was also run by an expert, James Robertson, the conductor.

> There was a little church just behind the Park and they did a little Sunday service for the workers and Julie Lydekker and I sang in that and then, right at the end of things James Robertson ran a choir. He was quite a well-known conductor. He conducted at Sadlers Wells when he escaped from GCHQ. He went to Australia and died there. So it was quite an excitement being in his choir.
>
> Then there was Angus Wilson who was really quite a considerable novelist and was one of the famous homosexuals at Bletchley. He wore a bow tie, which was a bit unusual in those days, and I can picture him in the Beer Hut, where there was a bar and people went for a booze in the evenings or lunchtime, quite a haunt. He had a very funny high voice and I remember hearing this above the hubbub in there. Even

then he was known as a novelist but he became really quite considerable, very well thought of.'

The eclectic mix of people based at Station X was an eye-opener for many of the young men and women who found themselves there. Diana Russell Clarke had the time of her life at Bletchley Park.

> We all had a marvellous time, all these young men, not attached. We had a very gay time going out to pubs for supper together when we were free. A lot of romance went on, very definitely a lot of romance. The whole thing was absolutely tremendous fun. It's rather awful in the middle of the war. We had to be there, it was an emergency and I think we all put our hearts into it. But I think we all enjoyed being there.

Solutions to Crossword on page 83

ACROSS	DOWN
1. Troupe	1. Tipstaff
4. Short cut	2. Olive oil
9. Privet	3. Pseudonym
10. Aromatic	5. Horde
12. Trend	6. Remit
13. Great deal	7. Cutter
15. Owe	8. Tackle
16. Feign	11. Agenda
17. Newark	14. Ada
22. Impale	18. Wreath
24. Guise	19. Right nail
27. Ash	20. Tinkling
28. Centre bit	21. Sennight
31. Token	23. Pie
32. Lame dogs	25. Scales
33. Racing	26. Enamel
34. Silencer	29. Rodin
35. Alight	30. Bogie

Chapter 7

THE NORTH AFRICAN CAMPAIGN

Bletchley Park's problems with lack of staff had not been helped by a tug-of-war over Hut 3. The breaking of the Red key had provided the RAF with a good deal of interesting material on the *Luftwaffe* and air intelligence regarded the codebreakers as a prime source of information. But partly because of an inherent distrust of intelligence and partly because there was so little Army Enigma being broken, the War Office had shown no real interest in the rather strange civilians at Bletchley Park. The ability of intelligence to influence the fighting in the Balkans and North Africa had been a revelation, said Ralph Bennett, one of the Hut 3 intelligence reporters.

When Enigma was broken in 1940 nobody really knew what it was going to do. It is important to understand that up until then intelligence was not rated very highly by the ordinary Army chap. It is difficult now to remember but before May 1940 when Enigma was first broken, military intelligence of all kinds was in the same state it had been at the Battle of Hastings.

If you wanted to know what the enemy was going to do, the only way you could find out was by getting an agent to disguise himself with a beard and spectacles and tell him to go and have a look, come back across the lines, which he might not do, he might be caught, and anyway he would be a bit late because it would take him a long time to do this.

The intelligence world changed completely in May 1940. There were, of course, not enough people who understood this. But the theory of the thing had changed completely. You could now get absolutely reliable information immediately across the lines, because radio waves are no respecter of armies. But the old bull-headed generals paid no attention to Enigma. They couldn't understand it. When they realised what they'd missed they began to gripe about it and tried to get it.

Under pressure from the War Office and the Air Ministry, the heads of the Hut 3 military and the air advisers attempted to expand their role to the control of all reporting, usurping the role of the Watch No. 1s who, not unnaturally, were unhappy at having their authority questioned. A mixture of overwork and lack of recognition fuelled a turf war between the two factions during the latter part of 1941 and early 1942.

From handling around fifty decrypts a day when the Hut 3 system was first put in place and about 250 a day during the German advance through the Balkans, the watch was now having to process some 1300 pieces of decyphered traffic with very few extra staff. A measure of the anger and frustration building up can be gauged from one extra-ordinary moment when two erudite middle-aged academics squared up to each other in the middle of the hut.

The whole affair was not helped by a clash of personalities between Commander Malcolm Saunders, the head of the hut, and Group-Captain Robert Humphreys, the chief air adviser, and by the additional interference of the main military adviser, described by R. V. Jones as 'a charmingly naive plagiarist' and in somewhat less polite terms by other members of Hut 3.

It was the role of air intelligence and Humphreys in particular that was the most critical, F. L. Lucas recalled.

> Humphreys had the highest technical qualifications through his real mastery both of intelligence and of German, but unfortunately he aimed at securing control over the organisation for himself. Moreover, he tried to set up within Hut 3 a semi-independent and almost rival organisation, responsible to himself and through him to Air Ministry. It cannot be doubted that he made a great contribution to our work and also to getting it taken seriously at the highest levels. Nevertheless, he caused great dissension and disturbance.

An attempt to resolve the situation by giving the military and air advisers a veto over both the circulation of the reports and their content, only increased the problems and resulted in an 'imbroglio of conflicting jealousies, intrigue and differing opinions,' said Nigel de Grey. The atmosphere in the hut became 'tense and unpleasant' and, with the standard of output being affected, Menzies himself was forced to intervene on a number of occasions.

No doubt influenced in part by this and in part by the discontent that had led to the joint letter to Churchill, Menzies decided that Denniston had neither the political nous nor the force of personality to control the rapidly growing organisation. In order to resolve the problem, he moved him to one side, putting him in charge of diplomatic and commercial codebreaking as Deputy Director (Civilian) with the more dynamic Travis as Deputy Director (Services) in charge of the military sections, Ralph Bennett recalled.

> Denniston had spent his life in the time of the Battle of Hastings dealing with hand codes and not much information that you could use militarily. Then he found himself in charge of a huge growing organisation, a lot of us younger and in some ways thinking along different lines, and he got a bit outdated in some ways and was shunted out. It was a bit of bad luck for him because he was a very good chap but he was overtaken by events.

Travis acted almost immediately, insisting that Humphreys be replaced. The Air Ministry in turn insisted that Saunders must go. Both seem to have agreed at least on the wisdom of posting the senior military adviser away from Bletchley and creating more watches to ease the problems of overwork.

The whole affair rumbled on into the summer of 1942 with Hut 3 being run by a committee led by Lucas. But despite the don's undoubted ability, Travis felt strongly that the lingering discontent among the remnants of the opposing camps needed a firm hand on the tiller. He found it in Squadron Leader Eric Jones, an air intelligence officer who had been sent up from London to investigate the problems and had succeeded in impressing all sides, Jim Rose recalled.

> There was an inter-service rivalry there and jockeying for position. Jones was just ideal. He had left school at fourteen and had been in the cotton business in Manchester. He was very intelligent, didn't know German but understood organisation very well. He gave people a free hand. It all became crystal clear. Quite a lot of brainy people had the habit of resigning when they were miffed. We used to keep a graph of when we expected one or two of them to resign but Jones dealt with them.

Jones augmented the Hut 3 system with a team of duty officers who would lead each shift, effectively replacing the Watch No. 1s, said Ralph Bennett, one of the newly appointed duty officers.

> Under his firm but understanding rule, we could concentrate on our work undisturbed by internal conflict. The watch received the raw decoded messages straight from Hut 6 with all the corruptions and they translated it into English. Then the translations went to either the air or

the Army desk to be put into military sense. These chaps passed it to the duty officer for final vetting and for checking for security. No signal could go out of Hut 3 without the initials of the duty officer.

The manning problems were eased in May 1942 by the transfer of a War Office traffic analysis unit, known for cover purposes as No. 6 Intelligence School, from Beaumanor to Bletchley to 'fuse' information gained from the ordinary radio communications with the material produced from decryption. Operator chat could be invaluable in helping the codebreakers. They would frequently joke between themselves over Cillis or clarify parts of encyphered messages that would provide cribs for Hut 6. But because the operators and traffic analysts were not in on the Ultra secret much of this was being wasted.

The traffic analysts had built up complete pictures of radio networks, much in the manner advocated by Welchman shortly after his recruitment. They were able to keep track of the individual stations by their callsigns and radio fingerprinting. They also knew from direction-finding where stations were located and had normally worked out what units they represented, information that was frequently not available to the Hut 3 watch but would enhance their reporting considerably. It made sense to bring them to Bletchley.

Some of the officers were used to reinforce the badly understaffed Hut 3 watch system. The remainder formed a section called Sixta, short for Hut 6 Traffic Analysis. Jimmy Thirsk, a twenty-seven-year-old librarian who had been in the Royal Artillery before transferring to the Intelligence Corps, was one of the log-readers working in Sixta.

> Our job was to analyse the operator chat. If you had a section of the *Luftwaffe*, say they were in France with their headquarters in Dijon, and perhaps they had ten outstations in that area. Every morning they would start up. Each station had a three-letter callsign and they would change that at midnight according to a pre-set pattern which could be predicted by using the 'Bird Book' which Sixta had compiled in the early days after prodigious efforts. Then they would call up the outstations just to make contact, just to make sure they were all awake and working, and they would occasionally chat to each other in clear German. This operator chat was going on all day long and the intercept operators logged it all down.
>
> Most of the messages were teleprinted from the intercept stations but the logs used to be brought mainly by motorcycle dispatch rider. You would be allocated a number of nets. If they were small ones you might

have two or three but you might have just one. Each day you would plot the radio net. We had coloured pencils, and you made a circle with a dot in the middle as the HQ. The outlying stations were round the circumference of the circle with a line drawn from each of the outstations to the centre and you would note the number of messages passing on each link. Then at the end of the week you had to compile a report summarising the week's activities. It was pretty dreary stuff at times.

The Sixta log-readers did not know that the Enigma cypher had been broken, and we had often speculated about this. At last, about nine months after we arrived at Bletchley, Gordon Welchman gathered us all together and told us the history of the breaking of Enigma. It was certainly a morale booster now that we knew that the messages we recorded on our network charts were providing valuable information.

The other things I remember most about Bletchley are the friendly atmosphere and lack of discipline; stumbling to the canteen in the middle of a pitch-black night; the long rides back to the billet in the buses which ran twenty-four hours a day; and the mad dash to the station to catch the 4.54 to London.

Longer-term traffic analysis was carried out in the Hut 3 Fusion Room which used all the information produced by various parts of Bletchley Park to build up as complete as possible a picture of the enemy radio networks. Joyce Robinson had a degree in French and German and after a brief spell in the Civil Service, joined the ATS and was posted to Bletchley where she was allocated to 'fusion'.

It was really a sort of consolidation of information from a lot of quarters after material had been dealt with operationally. It was department-mentalised according to networks, or keys, where a group of one, two or more people considered the behaviour of certain things so that you knew your network. You were sometimes able to help Hut 6 when they had difficulties with decoding, with a change in the wheels.

One of her ATS colleagues was Jean Faraday Davies, who after reading French and German at Manchester University was sent to Bletchley. The Fusion Room coordinated information produced by the log-readers with the intelligence from the decyphered messages, she said. 'Our function was to take these two sources and feed it out in two directions to enable interception to go on or to help decoding.'

The new canteen was completed in the spring of 1942 and the builders began work on the larger blocks which would replace the wooden huts. Throughout 1942, wave after wave of new recruits

arrived at Bletchley. Despite the departure of Denniston's Diplomatic and Commercial Sections to London, the numbers had more
than doubled since the end of 1941. Malcolm Kennedy was moved
from diplomatic cyphers in London to the Japanese Naval Section in
Elmers School on 14 December 1942, recording his return to the War
Station in his diary. 'Great changes since I left for town in March,' he
reported. 'From a mere 200 or so at the start of the war, there are now
over 3500 there. No wonder the war costs so much.'

By now the new purpose-built blocks had been constructed and
the latter half of 1942 and early part of 1943 saw a mass exodus into
the new accommodation where a pneumatic tube system, commonly
known as 'the spit and suck', carried messages between the various
huts, ensuring that even fewer people knew what was going on
outside their own office. Sarah Norton was one of the debutantes
working in the naval index.

> We moved from Hut 4 which we loved into a horrible concrete
> building. To be totally perverse, we insisted on still calling the new
> block Hut 4. It had a long wide corridor which ended in a T-junction.
> One afternoon, we decided to give Jean Campbell-Harris, who later
> became Baroness Trumpington, a ride in a large laundry basket on
> wheels that was normally used to move secret files. We launched it
> down the long corridor where it gathered momentum by the second. To
> our horror, at the T-junction Jean suddenly disappeared, basket and all,
> through some double swing doors crashing to a halt in the men's
> toilets. A serious reprimand was administered and our watches were
> changed so we were distributed among a more sober group. But this
> fortunately did not last long.

The fighting in North Africa had begun with a sweeping victory over
the Italians by General Archibald Wavell, Commander-in-Chief
Middle East, in early 1941. Signals intelligence had played no great
role in the campaign although Wavell had received some assistance
from a mobile Army Y unit attached to his troops and from the
Combined Bureau Middle East, an offshoot of GC&CS based in the
former Flora and Fauna Museum at Heliopolis, near Cairo.

Almost immediately after the Italians' defeat, an Italian Air Force
message referring to *Luftwaffe* escorts for convoys between Naples and
Tripoli was decyphered at Bletchley Park. Hut 4 inferred from this that
the convoys were German and that Hitler must be sending troops to
support his beaten ally. The codebreakers' views were dismissed in
both the Admiralty and the Air Ministry, and the report did not make

its way to Cairo. A few days later British troops had their first contact with the Afrika Korps under General Erwin Rommel, the 'Desert Fox'.

Rommel's arrival in North Africa coincided with the installation of the direct Special Signals Link to Cairo. Hut 3 could now send their reports direct to Wavell. The link had not had time to establish itself before the Germans began a rapid offensive. The available Enigma decrypts appeared contradictory. Some suggested that Rommel had been told to build up his strength before launching an attack. But the *Luftwaffe* key used by *Fliegerführer Afrika*, broken by Hut 6 at the end of February and designated Light Blue, pointed to an immediate advance.

Ignoring his orders and despite only having a limited force, Rommel attacked immediately and was soon pressing home his advantage against the poorly prepared British troops, taking the Libyan ports of El Agheila and Benghazi before surrounding the Australian garrison at Tobruk. But here he came to a standstill.

Given Rommel's maverick disregard for his original orders, General Franz Halder, the Army Chief of Staff, sent his deputy, General Friedrich Paulus, to Tripoli to agree on a strategy, which was then passed back to Berlin, and to Bletchley Park, via the Red *Luftwaffe* Enigma. The decrypts also disclosed that the failure to secure the port of Tobruk had stretched Rommel's supply lines too far and left him desperately short of fuel.

Churchill pushed Wavell to take advantage of this position. But two attempted counter-offensives failed in the face of the German 88mm anti-aircraft guns, converted by Rommel for use as anti-tank artillery, which had an unrestricted view of their targets across the flat desert terrain. The link from Bletchley Park was of little use, partly because the Hut 3 reporters were still learning their trade and partly because of the time it took to carry out the whole process of interception, decryption and the production of an intelligence report.

During a land battle, the Bletchley Park reports rarely arrived in Cairo in what the military called 'real time'. All too frequently the fighting had moved on before the intelligence could be given to commanders, said Ralph Bennett. 'Very occasionally, the process could be completed in about three hours, but six hours may have been nearer the average.'

The failure of the second counter-offensive, codenamed 'Battleaxe', led Churchill to transfer Wavell to India, replacing him with Sir Claude Auchinleck, known as 'the Auk'. The Light Blue cypher had been providing some details of Rommel's resupply convoys from Italy

since his first arrival in North Africa. But the information derived from
these intercepts was rarely good enough to allow the Royal Navy or
the RAF to take action against the convoys, a problem that was not
helped by the continuing delay in information reaching Egypt.

Then in July 1941, Hut 8 managed to break an Italian Navy
machine cypher, designated C38m, which provided a flood of
detailed information about the convoys. The Light Blue cypher gave
indications of when a convoy was going to cross the Mediterranean
and what it would be carrying while the C38m provided details of
vessels involved and the route. Since collating and analysing this
information was a job in itself and the information it produced was
required by both the Royal Navy and the RAF, it was carried out
initially through collaboration between the Hut 4 'Z Watch' and the
Hut 3 research section led by Lucas.

'From now until May 1942, longer-term research had to yield place
to the more exciting duties of handling operational signals on Axis
convoys to Africa,' Lucas said. 'The essential part of the work lay in
the identification of covernames, or covernumbers, for turning
points on the routes.' The routes taken by the convoys would have
on average half-a-dozen legs on the journey to North Africa. The
length of each leg could be worked out from the speed and sailing
times specified in the message. The difficulty was in locating the
turning points, Lucas recalled.

> Pins were stuck into a string at distances equal to the lengths of the legs
> on the map. The string had its ends pinned to the ports of arrival and
> departure. Any intermediate points already known were also pinned.
> The rest of the slack was shifted about by trial and error to give the
> various alternative possibilities until a general shape of route was
> obtained that made sense and corresponded with our experience of
> Italian naval habits, for example a respectful detour to the east or west
> of Malta. Life in the research section was never dull but nothing again
> ever quite equalled the excitement of angling for Axis convoys with
> pins and string.

The convoy reports went to Cairo via the Special Signals Link and also
to the Navy in Alexandria and the RAF in Malta. The protection of the
Ultra secret was paramount. No offensive action could be taken unless
there was a clear secondary source, overwhelmingly created by aerial
reconnaissance. Even this could not be directed solely against the
convoy lest the Germans noticed the change in routine reconnaissance
patterns. But the material supplied by Bletchley Park allowed the

Royal Navy and the RAF to wreak havoc among Rommel's supply convoys as Jim Rose, one of the Hut 3 air advisers, recalled.

> Ultra was very important in cutting Rommel's supplies. He was fighting with one hand behind his back because we were getting information about all the convoys from Italy. The RAF were not allowed to attack them unless they sent out reconnaissance and if there was fog of course they couldn't attack them because it would have jeopardised the security of Ultra, but in fact most of them were attacked.

By the time Auchinleck launched 'Crusader', a successful counter-offensive which relieved Tobruk in November 1941, the RAF and the Royal Navy were regularly sinking Rommel's supply ships, causing him major problems. The arrival in Malta in late October of Force K, comprising the cruisers HMS *Aurora* and *Penelope*, together with two destroyers, heralded a two-month period when supplies to the Afrika Korps were brought to a virtual standstill.

The *Luftwaffe* keys had revealed Rommel's own plans for an attack on Tobruk, but the first break into Army Enigma in North Africa confirmed that the failure of supply ships to get through made it unlikely that any attack would take place in the near future. The proliferation of Enigma keys as the Germans sought to improve signals security had led to a change in the nicknames given to them by Bletchley Park. The main keys that had already been broken retained their colour designation. *Luftwaffe* keys were named after flowers or insects, Army keys after birds and naval keys after fish.

Chaffinch, as the new Army key was called, provided details of the Afrika Korps' shortages of food, fuel and water as well as ammunition for the 88mm 'anti-tank' guns. It also gave Auchinleck full details of how many tanks Rommel had at his disposal and useful information on the German dispositions.

This information could be passed direct to commanders in the field by a Special Signals Unit sent out to North Africa in mid-1941. Based on the units first introduced during the Battle of France, it received Ultra reports direct from Hut 3, encyphered using the highly secure one-time pad system and sent via the RAF com-munications centre at Leighton Buzzard. The title was soon changed for security reasons to Special Liaison Unit since the abbreviation SSU and the presence of Intelligence Corps officers in the unit had led to it being jokingly described as 'the Secret Service Unit'.

The intelligence officers serving in the SLUs had to control the use of Ultra strictly to ensure that only those who had been indoctrinated knew of its existence. They also had to enforce the regulations on its use, making sure that it was never acted upon without a secondary source being available, and to liaise with Hut 3 on any queries from commanders.

Despite the presence of the SLU at the headquarters of the British Eighth Army, the Crusader offensive proved beyond doubt that the best use of Ultra was in providing details of enemy strength and dispositions, and often future plans, rather than in tactical information during the heat of the battle. The sheer length of time it took for reports to get from Bletchley to Libya meant that Hut 3 could not compete with the mobile Y Special Wireless Sections of Royal Signals and Intelligence Corps personnel in armoured cars who were at the Front. Bill Williams served as an intelligence officer in North Africa.

> Despite the amazing speed with which we received Ultra, it was of course usually out of date. This did not mean that we were not glad of its arrival for at best it showed that we were wrong, usually it enabled us to tidy up loose ends, and at worst we tumbled into bed with a smug confirmation. In a planning period between battles its value was more obvious and one had the opportunity to study it in relation to context so much better than during a fast-moving battle such as desert warfare produced.

Auchinleck's defeat of Rommel forced the Afrika Korps back to El Agheila. But within a few months, the Germans had regained much of the ground they had lost and were back in Benghazi. This was at least in part the result of a serious misreading of a decrypt from the Italian C38m cypher which was wrongly seen as suggesting that the Afrika Korps did not expect to reach Benghazi. But it was also a result of the failings of the British tactics.

'The troops on the ground on our side were still not used to receiving high-level information,' Bennett said. 'They were also using the wrong tactics. The gunfire was never sufficiently massed to do enough damage to the enemy until Auchinleck managed to change it under pressure in the late summer of 1942.'

Although the Red *Luftwaffe* Enigma gave good warning of a German offensive scheduled for the end of May and aimed ultimately at regaining Tobruk, Hut 3 was unable to provide any information about Rommel's precise plans, either before or during the Battle of Gazala. By mid-June Auchinleck had decided to withdraw across the Egyptian border to a stronger position at Alam Halfa, leaving the 2nd South African Division to hold Tobruk as a fortress inside the enemy camp.

Within a week, it had surrendered. Churchill, who was in Washington conferring with Roosevelt, was bitterly disappointed. 'I did not attempt to hide from the President the shock I received,' he would later recall. 'It was a bitter moment. Defeat is one thing; disgrace is another.'

But the tide was about to turn, and as a direct result of a dramatic improvement in the work of the codebreakers at Bletchley Park. Up until now the delay in breaking Chaffinch, the main Afrika Korps Enigma, had been up to a week. From the end of May, they were able to break it daily, albeit with some delay. Another *Panzerarmee* Enigma, designated Phoenix and broken briefly at the end of 1941 following the capture of three machines and a number of keys, was read continuously from 1 June. A third Army Enigma, Thrush, giving details of air supplies, was also broken.

Hut 6 was able to read all the *Luftwaffe* keys, including the Red which had been continuously broken since May 1940; two relatively minor keys called Locust and Gadfly; and two much more important keys which, in an extraordinary security blunder by the Germans, were closely linked. Primrose, the cypher of the *Luftgau Afrika*, the air formation responsible for administration and supply of the *Luftwaffe* forces in North Africa, was not only an important source in its own right, its keys were also used later by Scorpion, the cypher used for communications between the *Flivos* and the ground forces.

During the campaign, Primrose became as high a priority as the Red cypher, as Susan Wenham one of the Hut 6 codebreakers recalled.

> It was very important. Every day the key was changed and about 3 o'clock in the morning Primrose used to send a tuning message through, a very short little message. It was always on the same wavelength and it was always recognisable. So people on the night shift would watch out for this message and, when they got it, they would tinker about with it and we could quite often break on that message. Red had an enormous quantity but it didn't have a nice convenient tuning message that you could find.

Since Scorpion's keys were now predictable, Hut 6 decided that it could be decyphered in Heliopolis, making it available to the commanders far quicker than any other material. Because the *Flivos* needed to keep in close contact with the battle in order to coordinate air attacks with the movement on the ground, Scorpion provided more details of the fighting, the troop positions and air activity than any of the other cyphers had before.

Meanwhile, during July and August the number of mobile Y units in North Africa was doubled and they became much better integrated into the command structure. Traffic analysis and direction-finding was improved and the Intelligence Corps and RAF codebreakers attached to the Special Wireless Sections expanded their exploitation of enemy tactical codes and cyphers.

Ultra was now totally in the ascendant. In the first nine months of the Special Signals Link to the Middle East, between March and November 1941, Hut 3 had sent just over 2000 signals to Cairo. Between November 1941 and July 1942, it had sent five times that figure.

Desperate for a victory and fully aware of the information from Ultra that was now available, Churchill decided it was time for change. Auchinleck was a fine general but did not have the necessary killer instinct. He brought in General Harold Alexander as Commander-in-Chief Middle East and appointed General Bernard Montgomery to take command of the Eighth Army.

Within days of his arrival, Montgomery was the beneficiary of a major piece of Ultra intelligence that was to change the military's view of the codebreakers. On 15 August, Rommel explained to Hitler what he planned to do next. The details of the plans had to go first through his direct commander, Field Marshal Albrecht Kesselring, the German Commander-in-Chief South, and because Kesselring was a *Luftwaffe* officer, they were transmitted using the Red cypher, which Hut 6 had no problems reading.

Two days earlier, Montgomery had outlined what he believed the Desert Fox would do. It matched the signal sent to Kesselring almost to the letter. Rommel intended to attack around the time of the full moon due towards the end of August, swinging south around the end of the British lines before striking north to come up behind the Eighth Army, cutting it off from Cairo. But to do so he would have to cross a major obstacle, the Alam Halfa ridge, Ralph Bennett explained.

Monty arrives in the middle of August and is told not to go and take charge until the next morning. He goes up to Alam Halfa to have a look round, one day before he is going to take over. He sums up the situation and realises that if Rommel is going to attack he will almost certainly do so on a route that will take him through the Alam Halfa ridge.

A few days later, Rommel tells Hitler what he is going to do, which is exactly that. We get this signal and we tell Monty. So there is Monty, the new boy, who has just made a pep talk to his troops, now knowing that his hunch as to what Rommel will do is exactly right. He can't tell anybody about it but when Rommel attacks Monty is ready.

Two other new developments at Bletchley Park also helped Montgomery. Hut 3 had just started receiving reports decyphered from the Chaffinch cypher, giving a complete breakdown of the fighting strengths of the Afrika Korps and comprehensive returns on the availability of tanks. Meanwhile, its joint operation with Hut 4 to detect the Axis supply lines had been improved, partly by the decision to place Royal Navy advisers inside Hut 3 to track the convoys and, more importantly, by Hut 8's breaking of Porpoise, the German Navy's Mediterranean cypher.

Throughout the second half of August, the RAF and the Royal Navy redoubled their attacks on the Axis convoys. Meanwhile, the codebreakers were able to monitor a series of high-level exchanges between the German commanders. Those between Kesselring and Rommel showed that the two were barely on speaking terms. They also revealed that the Desert Fox was unwell. Then came the approval, first by Hitler and later by Mussolini, of Rommel's plans.

More importantly perhaps, given the Desert Fox's predilection for ignoring orders, Bletchley and Heliopolis were able to chart the regrouping of the German forces in readiness for the attempt to out-flank the Eighth Army as well as the problems and delays to the operation caused by the non-arrival of two of the supply ships. Montgomery had briefed his troops on what Rommel was about to do. Then the supply problems led to a four-day postponement. Bill Williams was the Eighth Army commander's chief intelligence officer.

> Believing that the confidence of his men was the prerequisite of victory, he told them with remarkable assurance how the enemy was going to be defeated. The enemy attack was delayed and the usual jokes were made about the 'crystal-gazers'. A day or two later everything happened according to plan. The morale emerging from the promise so positively fulfilled formed the psychological background conditioning the victory which was to follow.

After finding his way through the Alam Halfa ridge blocked, Rommel was forced to retreat for lack of fuel. From then on, Ultra played a privileged part in Montgomery's plans. He allowed Williams access to his command post day or night with any new information the codebreakers produced.

Ralph Bennett was sent out to the Middle East to report from Cairo on the Scorpion traffic.

> Imagine the situation in the desert in the late summer of 1942. There is Montgomery. He's got a little truck park with his own command truck and the Army and the Air commanders forming three sides of a little square. Then the fourth one is the wireless truck to receive the Ultra signals so that Williams can make immediate contact with Montgomery and the other commanders to give them the urgent Ultra information.

Ultra played no significant part in the Battle of El Alamein itself. But Montgomery knew from Chaffinch and Scorpion the precise numbers of troops and tanks he faced, while the sinking of the supply ships, 50,000 tons in October alone, nearly half of the cargo which left Italy for North Africa, had a crucial influence on the Afrika Korps' ability to resist. So tight were its margins of supply that the sinking of an Axis convoy during the battle itself had a direct influence on the fighting.

On the afternoon of 2 November, with Montgomery having punched two holes in the Panzer Army's defences and about to force his way through, Bletchley decyphered a message from Rommel to Hitler asking permission to withdraw. '*Panzerarmee ist erschopft*', he said. The Panzer Army was 'exhausted' and had precious little fuel left. The response from Berlin was that Rommel should stand his ground at all costs. He was to 'show no other road to his troops than the road leading to death or victory.'

But in the face of far superior troops, the Fox was forced to retreat along the coast road towards El Agheila. Why he wasn't pursued at speed and destroyed either by intensive RAF bombing raids or Montgomery himself remains a puzzle. Chaffinch revealed on 10 and 11 November that one of his Panzer divisions had just eleven tanks while the other had none at all.

Five days later, with all attempts to resupply the German troops being frustrated with the aid of Ultra, the Red Enigma carried a special situation report from Rommel to Hitler in which he described his fuel supplies as 'catastrophic'. Montgomery's inaction at this point provoked fury among the pundits in Hut 3 who were telexing this information to Cairo.

'After the war, I found my initials at the bottom of the signals giving details of three supremely important tanker movements at the time of El Alamein,' said Edward Thomas, one of the naval officers in Hut 3. 'Their sinking was largely responsible for Rommel's long and halting retreat westwards. I well remember the frustration that exploded from our Hut 3 colleagues at Montgomery's failure to overtake and destroy him.'

Their anger was clearly shared by Churchill. Following the victory at El Alamein, he had said: 'This is not the end. It is not even the beginning of the end. But it is, perhaps, the end of the beginning.' Now he bombarded Alexander with pieces of Ultra suggesting that the Eighth Army kill the Afrika Korps off for good.

'Presume you have read the Boniface numbers QT/7789 and QT/7903 which certainly reveal a condition of weakness and counter-order among the enemy of a very remarkable character,' one signal from the prime minister stated with obvious impatience, while another pointed out: 'Boniface shows the enemy in great anxiety and disarray.'

But Montgomery feared that Rommel's greater mobility might allow him to turn the tables on the British yet again and decided to be cautious, ignoring the repeated suggestions of Churchill, Alexander and Air Marshal Tedder, the commander of the Middle East Air Force, that the Desert Fox should be pursued and annihilated.

'Unfortunately after Alam Halfa, Monty was inclined to be a bit boastful about having got it right,' said Ralph Bennett. 'He was inclined to think he was right all the time. At El Agheila, he insisted on being cautious, which of course was Monty's great thing most of the time, although he knew perfectly well, because we had told him over and over and over again, that Rommel had inferior defences and very few tanks.'

A few days later, Operation Torch began. British and American troops under General Dwight Eisenhower occupied French North Africa and pushed east with the aim of linking up with Montgomery. Meanwhile the Axis forces began pouring troops into Tunis, a reinforcement chronicled in some detail by Hut 3 from the *Luftwaffe* Enigma, the Italian C38m and Porpoise, the German Navy's Mediterranean cypher.

Plans were put in place well in advance to keep the Torch commanders supplied with Ultra. They were agreed at a conference in Broadway attended by Nigel de Grey, representing Travis; Harry Hinsley, on behalf of the Naval Section in Hut 4; and Eric Jones, the head of Hut 3. Four separate Special Liaison Units were set up to pass the material on, one to serve Eisenhower's headquarters, one with the forward elements of the troops pushing eastwards and two others with the occupation forces in Oran and Casablanca.

A number of codebreakers from Bletchley Park, including Noel Currer-Briggs, a member of Tiltman's military section, were sent out to reinforce a mobile Y unit, 1 Special Wireless Section. Their role was to help in breaking the Double Playfair hand cypher that was used by the German Army for its medium-grade messages, while Bletchley concentrated on the *Luftwaffe* cyphers and a new Army Enigma introduced for the campaign which Hut 6 designated Bullfinch.

The mobile Y unit set up its base in an old Foreign Legion fort at Constantine in eastern Algeria, Currer-Briggs recalled.

> Fort Sid M'Cid was built in true Beau Geste tradition on top of a hill above the astonishing gorge which bisects the city of Constantine. It may have looked romantic, but it was the filthiest dump imaginable. One of my most vivid memories of it is cleaning the primitive latrines, a row of stone holes set in the thickness of the wall over a fifty-foot drop which had to be emptied through an iron door set in the base of the ramparts. It would be a good punishment if somebody had done something wrong but nobody had. So the adjutant and I said: 'Let's get on and do it,' and we started shovelling shit. I can still smell it. I also recall, with more pleasure, reading Virgil on the battlements. Hardly typical of military life but in the true tradition of BP.

The Tunisian campaign was to be dominated by Rommel's last two throws of the dice. In the first, during which Ultra was unable to play any useful part, he trounced the Americans in the Kasserine Pass, a vital communications link through the Atlas mountains, before turning round and heading east with the intention of taking on Montgomery, who had advanced to Medenine in eastern Tunisia.

Ultra gave Montgomery full details of Rommel's plans to throw the whole of the Afrika Korps against the Eighth Army positions. Throughout the last week of February and the first week of March, information from Bletchley and from 1 Special Wireless Section, now moved closer to the British commanders, built up a complete picture of Rommel's plans.

'This was a most exciting time for us,' said Currer-Briggs. 'Traffic was coming in thick and fast. We were theoretically working in shifts but there was so much to do that we hardly ever took time off, and frequently worked when we should have been resting. It was far too exciting to twiddle one's thumbs in idleness.'

By the time Rommel's 160 tanks and 200 guns attacked the Eighth Army positions on the morning of 6 March, they were faced by a solid wall of 470 anti-tank guns, 350 field guns and 400 tanks. Fed by the codebreakers with every detail of his planned assault, the British simply sat and waited for him. By evening, his tanks largely reduced to burning wrecks, Rommel called the battle off. Three days later, he left Africa, never to return.

The fighting in Tunisia continued for two more months but the North African campaign had effectively ended and the British were already making plans for one of the unhappier aftermaths of victory. The Ultra-led attacks on the Axis supply convoys had been carried out with the future need to be able to feed a large number of prisoners in mind, said Edward Thomas. 'While those with cargoes of tanks, fuel and ammunition had been selected for attack, ships known from the decrypts to be carrying rations had been spared.'

Although Montgomery claimed them as his own, it was the Bletchley Park contribution to the victories in North Africa that finally persuaded the British Army and the RAF that Ultra was an extremely powerful weapon and one that could win the war.

Ultra was one of the main reasons behind the British defeat of the Afrika Korps, said Jim Rose.

If you look at the position at the Fall of Tobruk in July 1942, that's only a few months before El Alamein, Rommel was really in the ascendant. Things looked desperate when Churchill was with Roosevelt and he heard about the fall of Tobruk, but then six months later they had completely changed. That would not have been possible without Ultra.

For the codebreakers themselves, two and a half years of hard slog had enabled them to create an efficient organisation capable of ensuring that, while individual keys might occasionally be lost, the bulk of the German's top secret communications would be read, and that the information they contained could be passed to the men who were able to make best use of it, the commanders in the field.

'Until Alam Halfa, we had always been hoping for proper recognition of our product,' said Ralph Bennett of his return to Bletchley Park in March 1943. 'Now the recognition was a fact of life and we had to go on deserving it. I had left as one of a group of enthusiastic amateurs. I returned to a professional organisation with standards and an acknowledged reputation to maintain.'

Chapter 8

THE SHARK BLACKOUT

Bletchley Park's early successes against the U-boats in the Battle of the Atlantic and the ease with which the Allied shipping convoys were evading the wolf packs had led Admiral Dönitz to suspect that something was very wrong. Either the British had a very good intelligence network in western France and had managed to infiltrate the U-boat control system or Enigma had been broken.

He recalled ordering the German codebreakers to look at the Enigma system themselves. Was it really impregnable, he asked.

> We found ourselves bound to admit that we had not succeeded in finding with our reconnaissance sweeps the convoys for which we had been searching. As a result of these failures, we naturally went once more very closely into the question of what knowledge the enemy could possibly have of our U-boat dispositions. Our cyphers were checked and rechecked to make sure they were unbreakable and on each occasion the head of the naval intelligence service adhered to his opinion that it would be impossible to decypher them.

Nevertheless, when Dönitz was given a chance to make the submarine cypher even more secure, he jumped at it. The plan involved a slight internal re-design of the Enigma machine. A new, thinner reflector with different wiring was introduced, leaving space for an extra wheel that would add a further factor of twenty-six to the number of possible solutions, thus surely making it impossible for anyone to break.

The first sign of the fourth wheel came in early 1941, in a captured document. In August of that year the U-570 surfaced south of Iceland only to find that a British Hudson patrol aircraft was directly above her. The pilot, Squadron Leader J. H. Thompson dropped four depth charges, two on either side of the U-boat, causing so much damage that the commander was forced to surrender. Inside the U-boat was the casing of an Enigma machine with a fourth indicator window.

References to the fourth wheel soon started to appear in decyphered messages and, on occasions, operators used it in error. By the end of the year, the wiring of the wheel had been recovered from a number of messages sent first using the fourth wheel and then, after the other operator pointed out the mistake, with just three wheels.

On 1 February 1942, the U-boats introduced the fourth wheel, creating a new cypher dubbed Shark by the Bletchley Park codebreakers. The extra wheel had rendered Banburismus useless, recalled Shaun Wylie, head of the crib section in Hut 8. While they could continue to get Dolphin out, they were now unable to do anything with Shark. The vital intelligence the OIC had been using to re-route the Atlantic convoys had disappeared.

> We were dismayed when the fourth wheel appeared. We knew it was coming. But it was a grim time. We were very much frustrated, the things that we'd hoped to use went bad on us. We realised that our work meant lives and it ceased to be fun. We did what we could, of course, and we got on with what there was but we kept an eye out for any possibility on Shark that might present itself. There was a lot of pressure and we were trying all we could but we didn't have many opportunities. We had to get Dolphin out, but Shark was the prime target, the focus of our interest.

The problems caused by the Shark 'blackout' were exacerbated by the fact that the number of U-boats now in the Atlantic had risen to forty and by the breaking by the *B-Dienst* – the German equivalent of BP – of the Royal Navy's Naval Cypher No. 3, which was used for most of the Allied communications about the Atlantic convoys.

A week after Shark came into force, the OIC's Submarine Tracking Room admitted that it was at a loss to say where the U-boats were. 'Since the end of January, no Special Information has been available about any U-boats other than those controlled by Admiral Norway,' it reported. 'Inevitably the picture of the Atlantic dispositions is by now out of focus and little can be said with confidence in estimating the present and future movement of the U-boats.' A break into Shark was desperately needed if the U-boats were not to be given a completely free hand in the North Atlantic.

With a great deal of work, Hut 8 did manage to solve the keys for two days in late February and one day in March. But it took six of the bombes seventeen days to solve each of those settings. Banburismus was useless on a four-wheel cypher. Noskwith recalled that there was a feeling of deep disappointment but while the codebreakers were doing everything they could to solve Shark, 'there was an acceptance of the fact that until we had better bombes, faster bombes that could work through the twenty-six times as many permutations we wouldn't really be able to cope with it.'

The bombe section had been further expanded with the addition of a new outstation at Stanmore, in Middlesex; increased recruitment of Wrens; and two different development programmes put in place to produce an upgraded bombe that could cope with the four-wheel Enigma machine. Doc Keen began work on a high-speed machine with an additional row of wheels that could complete a standard three-wheel run in less than two minutes. But the first experimental 'Keen Machine' could not be produced before March 1943.

The other development programme was led by Dr C. E. Wynn-Williams of the Telecommunications Research Establishment at Malvern, where a team of GPO engineers had started working on a high-speed bombe. This had a long snake-like attachment to replicate the fourth wheel which led to it being nicknamed the 'Cobra'. But it could not be brought into operation until early 1944.

The codebreakers' acceptance that their best chance of breaking Shark was through bigger and better bombes led to further conflict with the OIC which, as one naval intelligence officer recalled, was unable to look at the problem with such scientific detachment.

> There was a danger of BP's researches being too academic. Their researches though brilliantly conducted were more like a game of chess or the arrangement of the jigsaw puzzle. They set the known against the unknown and proceeded to a dispassionate consideration of deductions.
>
> We saw the problem in a different light, for us the merchantmen and MTBs, the patrol vessels and the *Sperrbrecher* [specially reinforced escort vessels] lived and moved and had their being in a world vibrant with the noise of battle. It was almost as though with a finger on the enemy pulse we brought a warmth and a sense of reality to our research work which was noticeably lacking from many similar efforts by BP.

Two factors prevented the U-boats from running riot in the North Atlantic in the spring of 1942. First, the Germans did not realise that Enigma had been broken and were therefore unaware that the introduction of the fourth wheel had left the OIC unable to route the convoys around the wolf packs. Second, they had found a new and much easier target. The U-boats were enjoying their second 'happy time' off the eastern sea-board of the United States.

America's entry into the war in December 1941 had given the Germans the opportunity to attack Allied supply ships at the point where they ought to have been safest, as they travelled along the coast of the United States. The Atlantic was divided into zones in which either the British, Americans or Canadians had complete control over all naval and merchant shipping. The eastern seaboard was obviously a US-controlled zone. The Americans declined to accept British advice that escorted convoys were safer than individual ships. The US Navy disliked the defensive acceptance that some ships would be sunk but most would get through, preferring to send merchant ships along the coast one by one, protected by an offensive programme of routine patrols designed to frighten off the U-boats.

The result was predictable to all but the Americans. In an operation codenamed 'Drumbeat', the U-boats simply avoided the patrols, waiting for them to pass before picking off the supply ships one by one. In the first three months of 1942, U-boats sank 1.25 million tons of shipping off the US east coast, four times the rate they had been achieving in the North Atlantic in 1941. But by mid-1942, a convoy system had finally been put in place, the US Navy had established its own submarine-tracking room, and the Liberty Ships, bigger and faster than the pre-war freighters, were being built at a phenomenal rate. Dönitz decided to pull the U-boats back into the North Atlantic.

It was probably fortunate for Bletchley Park that they had not been there when Shark was first introduced, said Harry Hinsley.

> Had the U-boats continued to give priority to attacks on Atlantic convoys after the Enigma had changed, there would have been such an improvement in their performance against convoys that the U-boat command might have concluded that earlier difficulties had been due to the fact that the three-wheel Enigma was insecure.

The OIC was not totally blind as to the presence of U-boats in the North Atlantic. Details of new submarines being built and tested in the Baltic could be had from Dolphin and from the medium-grade Dockyard cypher. Bletchley Park usually knew when a U-boat was leaving the Baltic or the Bay of Biscay on an operational cruise and when it was coming back. But once the U-boats were in the Atlantic, the only indications of what was going on came from direction-finding and radio-fingerprinting techniques, and knowledge of the U-boats' typical behaviour, capabilities and endurance, none of which were reliable.

The wolf packs resumed their attacks on the convoys in August 1942 with eighty-six U-boats, four times as many as when Shark was introduced. One of the first attacks came over five days between 5 and 10 August when the *Gruppe Steinbrinck* pack of eighteen U-boats attacked a convoy of thirty-three ships, sinking eleven, a total of 53,000 tons of shipping.

During August and September, the U-boats located twenty-one of the sixty-three convoys that sailed, sinking forty-three ships. They destroyed 485,413 tons of shipping in September, and in October, when there were more than a hundred U-boats at sea, sank 619,417 tons, the first time they had destroyed more than 500,000 tons of merchant shipping in a month. At the same time, the number of U-boats sunk dropped to just five in August and three in September. It rose to eight in October but by the third week of November, only two U-boats had been sunk while the number of Allied ships lost that month was rising steadily towards the one hundred mark.

The Admiralty began to step up the pressure on Bletchley Park to break Shark. The OIC urged Hut 8 to pay 'a little more attention' to the U-boat cypher. In a tersely written memorandum, it complained that the U-boat campaign was 'the only one campaign which Bletchley Park are not at present influencing to any marked extent and it is the only one in which the war can be lost unless BP do help.'

There was no need to push the codebreakers any harder than they were pushing themselves. Turing and Alexander were obsessed with the Shark problem to the detriment of security as John Herivel recalled.

> I was standing on the platform at Bletchley station one day. Alexander and Turing were standing, not all that close, and I could hear them talking at what seemed to me to be the tops of their voices about some matter in connection with Bletchley Park. But it was a cryptographical matter. So they were probably quite safe because no one would have known what they were talking about. On the other hand, if there had been an intelligent German spy on the platform, he might have twigged that it was something to do with cryptography.

Although Turing was in theory head of Hut 8, he spent a great deal of 1942 working on other matters. The hut was effectively run by

Alexander but without the full authority that he would have had as head of the hut. Following the OIC's complaint, Alexander was put in charge of Hut 8. One of his first acts was to institute daily 'U-boat meetings' with the Naval Section. He also increased pressure for the introduction of the new bombes designed to cope with the four-wheel Enigma machine.

But the solution to Shark was already in place. Two days after the Admiralty memorandum, a pinch of two German 'short signal' codebooks arrived at Bletchley providing new cribs for the U-boat messages. The books had been recovered from the U-559, which had been scuttled by its crew after being attacked by the British destroyer HMS *Petard* off the Egyptian coast. Lieutenant Anthony Fasson and Able-Seaman Colin Grazier swam to the submarine before it sank and managed to recover its signal documents. They were joined by a sixteen-year-old Naafi boy, Tommy Brown. He stayed by the conning tower and succeeded in getting out with the codebooks. But Fasson and Grazier went down with the submarine. They were both awarded the George Cross posthumously. Brown, a civilian, received the George Medal. The medals were well-deserved; their heroism was vital in helping to end the U-boat blackout.

Hut 8 codebreakers decided to put all their efforts into breaking Shark, Shaun Wylie recalled. 'We knew that we had a good chance and we certainly put a tremendous amount of effort into it, bombe time and all that sort of thing. Looking back on it I think we might have chanced our arm and hoped to be lucky, but we did decide to give it everything.'

Wylie took over the codebreaking shift in Hut 8 at midnight on Saturday 12 December. All night they continued the tedious process of looking for cribs from Hut 10's weather reports that might fit the short U-boat weather messages. Wylie was in the canteen the next morning when one of his colleague's came running in.

'I was having breakfast and somebody rushed in and said: "We're back into the U-boats",' Wylie recalled. 'I asked which it was and it was the one that meant we were going to be able to go on getting into the U-boat traffic. That was terrific, it wasn't just a one off, we were going to be able to do it steadily. It was a great moment. The excitement was terrific, relief too.'

When the Germans designed the fourth wheel, they had taken into account the fact that anyone using it might have to talk to other stations equipped with only the three-wheel machine. So in one of its twenty-six positions it replicated the action of the old reflector, turning the four-wheel machine into the equivalent of a three-wheel machine. When the U-boats communicated with the shore weather stations they had to use the three-wheel set-up, making the keys for the first three wheels relatively easy to break. Once they were broken, there were only twenty-six options to try out on all the other messages to find out the setting of the fourth wheel.

'We found that certain types of signals still used three wheels,' Noskwith noted. 'These were certain short signals and weather signals from U-boats. The time when we found these short signals was a very exciting time.'

Once Wylie had checked it was out, he was under instructions to inform Travis immediately. There were celebrations in the Hut and at the Admiralty. 'We were elated,' Wylie said. 'We knew that from then on we had good prospects of keeping in with it. We knew we were in with a chance. I was told to ring up the boss as soon as it came in and Travis was going to ring up Menzies who would ring Churchill.'

Within a few hours, Hut 8 had broken the day's keys and decyphered messages began to arrive in the Submarine Tracking Room where Lieutenant Patrick Beesly was on duty. 'They continued to do so in an unending stream until the early hours of the following morning,' he said. 'It was an exciting and exhausting night.'

Pat Wright was one of the young women working in the Big Room at Hut 8, decyphering the messages. She had been recruited earlier that year.

I was just approaching my eighteenth birthday. I had a letter at home asking me if I would go for an interview at the Foreign Office. There were several other girls there. They told us that they wanted us to do something but they couldn't tell us what it was and that we would be hearing from them. So I went home and my mother said: 'What did they want you for?' and I replied: 'Well I haven't the faintest idea.'

Eventually we received a letter and train passes to go to Bletchley. We were taken to the Big House and were lectured by a very ferocious-looking security officer and we signed the Official Secrets Act. They said: 'The job we want you to do is decoding.' Well everybody knows the Foreign Office has codes. It didn't seem very secret. We trailed over to Hut 8 where they said: 'Well, the thing is it's German naval codes, we've broken the codes and we want you to do the decoding' – collapse of several young ladies in a heap. None of us were fluent German speakers.

It was then read out to us in no uncertain terms that on no account

were we to tell anybody what we were doing. Nor were we to say we
were on secret work. It wasn't secret. We were the evacuated office of
the Foreign Office and we were copy typists. It was explained to us that
the German codes had been broken by this super machine that had
been invented. At the same time every day, the Germans transmitted
this weather message beginning exactly the same way. This was of
course not anything that we lesser mortals had to worry about. This
was the brainy boys' department.

The 'copy typists' in the big room operated Type-X machines
decyphering the messages that came in. They had to wait for the
codebreakers to break the keys first.

Sometimes we had to wait a long time. Sometimes it was done quickly.
But there was always a backlog of work so we were never not having to
do anything. There were four wheels out of a box of eight which were
put into the machine and then turned to the right letter of the alphabet
and then there was a plugboard with plug leads that went everywhere.

You started off typing and then with a bit of luck you suddenly saw
something you could recognise as German. There were of course very
clever interpreters there who, if you got into a real fix, where the
German went off into garble, would help you. Because not many of the
messages were wholly intercepted. Bits were missing or not picked up.
So it wasn't a case of just typing straight through.

Anybody who works a computer now that has this light touch would
be horrified. The keys had to be pressed right down and came up with
a clankety bang. It was very, very noisy. It printed out on to a long strip
of sticky tape a bit like you used to get on old-fashioned telegrams.
When we finished we took the message and stuck it on the back like an
old telegram. Then we would send it through and say shall we go on
with this and they would say: 'Yes keep going', or 'No, don't bother'.

She and the other women working in the Big Room were well aware
of the importance of what they were doing. 'Clothing was rationed,
soap was rationed, sweets were rationed and the Atlantic convoys
coming across were being sunk quicker than they could take up with
thousands of men and we were just told that if they could just keep
these messages decoded then they would keep the submarines away
from the convoys.'

The decyphered messages were sent via the 'spit and suck' to Z
Watch in Hut 4. One of those working there was Sarah Norton, who
had been promoted from the index to translating German decrypts.

She remembered the time of the blackout as a very depressing period. 'It was a terrible, terrible time because all our shipping was going. We could have starved, actually, and eventually when they broke it the volume of work was just unbelievable because every signal had to be translated. It might just be a floating mine. It might have been something terribly important like a U-boat attack some-where. So it all had to be done and we had to work extremely hard.'

Their efforts were rewarded with a dramatic drop in the number of successful U-boat attacks. But when Shark was lost in early March, following the introduction of a new short weather code, it looked as if a new blackout had begun. But by concentrating all available bombes on the problem and with the assistance of the first 'Keen Machine', Hut 8 broke the keys out within ten days.

From that point on, the new-found confidence in Hut 8 and the arrival of the faster bombes ensured that naval Enigma was never as difficult to break again. The Allies had been lucky that Dönitz had chosen to concentrate on the eastern seaboard of America. If he had not, the U-boats might well have pushed Britain to the brink of starvation, Frank Birch said.

> The only comforting thought about those ten months is that at the time British resources were so meagre that even with all the information in the world only moderate immunity could have been obtained. By March 1943, when Special Intelligence was coming along strong, though not yet at full strength, the Germans had become incapable of reading our stuff and in the great showdown of that month the U-boats were, as a result of Special Intelligence, driven off the convoy routes for six months.

The break into Shark was not the only deciding factor in the Second Battle of the Atlantic, the introduction of the Very Long Range Liberator aircraft, centimetric radar, the Huff-Duff shipborne DF system, and new naval support groups, including aircraft carriers, made life altogether too dangerous for the U-boats. But it was the ability to read the U-boat messages that allowed the Allies to use these new-found resources to conduct a war of attrition against them, trading the loss of merchant ships for the destruction of a U-boat, Beesly recalled.

> Decisions had to be taken, never lightly, never without due thought, but taken none the less and one had to accept the consequences. We were far removed from the sea but it did not require a great deal of

imagination to picture tankers going up in flames, seamen being drowned or maimed, or invaluable cargoes being lost.

The only possible way to treat the matter was as though it were a game of chess. Ships or U-boats were pawns. When one of them was sunk it was removed from the board. One side or the other had gained a point, but the game was not over and one had to turn immediately to consider the next move, to try to save the remainder of one's pieces and to take out some of one's opponents.

Hut 8's ability to read Shark also confirmed that the *B-Dienst* had been reading the Naval Cypher No. 3, ensuring that communications security was improved and the Germans were unable to predict the convoys' routes.

Nearly a hundred U-boats were sunk in the first five months of 1943. As the battle swung towards the Allies, Harry Hinsley and the Hut 4 intelligence reporters detected increasing signs of nervousness among the U-boat commanders. They began to report torpedo failures, made exaggerated claims and expressed widespread fear of Allied aircraft. By April, their morale appeared to have gone into terminal decline, with the Shark decrypts containing 'increasingly frequent references to their fear of air attack and to the efficiency of the Allied surface escorts in following up aircraft sightings.'

By May, the Allied successes against the U-boats had soared to a level that threatened to wipe them out completely. On 23 May, after hearing of the loss of the forty-seventh U-boat that month, Dönitz ordered the wolf packs to be withdrawn from the Atlantic, giving the Allies the respite they needed to get supplies across to Britain in preparation for the invasion of mainland Europe.

The successes against Shark were marred by the death, in February 1943, after a long struggle against cancer, of Dilly Knox. But before his death he had made a momentous breakthrough that allowed British intelligence to achieve one of the great espionage triumphs of the war – the Double Cross System.

Although Knox's research section carried out a great deal of vital work that helped the codebreakers of Hut 6 and Hut 8, he felt sidelined and remained angry that the pre-war GC&CS was being turned into a production line by the young mathematicians that Denniston had insisted on bringing in. While the mathematicians were only interested in obtaining the keys to a cypher before moving on to the next problem, Knox was frustrated by his inability to see the decyphering process through to the end. This, combined with the effects of his cancer, made him increasingly irascible.

Mavis Lever recalled tensions between Knox and Welchman over the way in which the latter had wrested control of the codebreaking operation away from him.

> Dilly was usually at loggerheads with somebody or other. He rather resented, I think, that other people were having all these operational units and felt he could have done it. But then of course he wouldn't have been able to cope. So I think it was best as it was.
>
> Dilly was a Greek scholar and an Egyptologist, looking at papyri and hieroglyphics and things. He didn't go in for technology at all. In fact, he absolutely turned his nose up at all these young men who were coming in from Cambridge, one of them being my husband-to-be, because he said they really didn't know what they were doing. As far as he was concerned, it was all a question of having an imaginative approach. Of course, imagination would not have got him the whole way and he knew that.

Nevertheless, he continued to rail against the mathematicians and their 'monstrous' new methods. At the end of 1941, Knox wrote to Denniston complaining yet again about the fact that he was unable to follow the codebreaking process through to the end.

> As a scholar, for of all Bletchley Park I am by breeding, education, profession and general recognition almost the foremost scholar, to concede your monstrous theory of collecting material for others is impossible. By profession and in all his contracts a scholar is bound to see his research through from the raw material to the final text.
>
> From 1920 to 1936, I was always able to proceed as a scholar. I simply cannot understand, nor I imagine can the many other scholars at BP understand, your grocer's theories of 'window dressing'. Had these been applied to art scholarship, science, and philosophy, had the inventor no right to the development and publication of his discourses, we should still be in the Dark Ages.

Denniston's response belies his reputation as a poor man-manager.

> If you do design a super Rolls-Royce, that is no reason why you should yourself drive the thing up the house of a possible buyer, more especially if you are not a very good driver. Do you want to be the inventor *and* be the car driver? You are Knox, a scholar with a European reputation, who knows more about the inside of a machine than

anyone else. The exigencies of war need that latter gift of yours, though few people are aware of it.

Within days of this exchange, Knox had made a major breakthrough, working out the internal mechanisms of the radically different Enigma machine used by the *Abwehr*, German military intelligence, and reading a message that had been sent on it. 'Knox has again justified his reputation as our most original investigator of Enigma problems,' Denniston told Menzies in early December 1941. 'He has started on the reconstruction of the machine used by German agents and possibly other German authorities.'

Knox seems to have thrived on the confrontation with Denniston and Welchman. But he was just as likely to have gained the inspiration for the break of the *Abwehr* Enigma in the bath. Professor E. R. P. Vincent, one of the Hut 4 Italian experts, recalled that Knox claimed a steamy atmosphere was highly conducive to cracking codes. 'At his billet, Dilly once stayed so long in his bathroom that his fellow-lodgers at last forced the door,' Vincent said. 'They found him standing by the bath, a faint smile on his face, his gaze fixed on abstraction, both taps full on and the plug out. What was passing through his mind could possibly have solved a problem that was to win a battle.'

This particular battle was to control the *Abwehr*'s activities against the British. The Double Cross system had originated from a plan devised by MI5, the British domestic Security Service, under which any German agents uncovered during the war were to be left in place and 'turned' to work as double agents for British intelligence. MI5 would be able to keep complete control over all German espionage activities in Britain and, as a welcome side-effect, the information the agents asked for would tell the British what the *Abwehr* did and did not know.

The first opportunity to turn a German agent came shortly before the outbreak of war when Arthur Owens – a businessman and part-time MI6 agent or 'stringer' – was found to be working for the Germans. He was arrested and agreed to work as a double agent under the covername of 'Snow'. His controller was Lieutenant-Colonel Tommy 'Tar' Robertson of MI5. Through Snow, Robertson acquired a number of other agents and a new section called B1a was set up to run them.

The messages from the agents to their controllers were monitored by the Radio Security Service based at Hanslope Park, just north of

Bletchley. The medium-grade hand cypher the agents used was broken in March 1940 by Oliver Strachey's section at Bletchley Park. The decyphered messages, known as ISOS after the name of Strachey's section – Intelligence Services Oliver Strachey – enabled MI5 to keep track of the messages of the double agents and spot any other German spies arriving in the country. Soon a whole team of *Abwehr* agents had been intercepted and turned by the British to operate under MI5 control.

A special committee was set up to decide what information should be fed back to the Germans. Its small select membership included representatives of MI5, MI6, naval, military and air intelligence, HQ Home Forces and the Home Defence Executive, which was in charge of civil defence. The committee was called the XX Committee, although it swiftly became known as the Twenty Committee, or more colloquially the Twenty Club, from the Roman numeral suggested by the Double Cross sign. It met every Wednesday in the MI5 headquarters at 58 St James's Street, in the heart of London's clubland.

The Twenty Club's job was to decide what information could be fed back to the *Abwehr* without damaging the British cause. Initially, with the threat of a German invasion dominating the atmosphere in London, it was decided that the 'intelligence' provided by the double agents should be used to give an impression of how strong Britain's defences were. But by the beginning of 1941, it was clear that more could be done with the double agents. They could be used to deceive the Germans, to provide them with misleading information that would give Allied forces an advantage in the field.

Most of the material passed to the Germans was 'chicken-feed', unimportant information that would give the *Abwehr* a feel that its agents were doing something and had access to real intelligence without telling them anything really harmful. But mixed among this were key pieces of specious or misleading information designed to build up a false picture of what the British were doing.

While the response of the agent handlers helped the Twenty Club to work out where the gaps in the Germans' knowledge lay, it did not tell them whether or not the misleading intelligence picture they were attempting to build up was believed in Berlin. The only way of finding this out was by decyphering the messages passed between the *Abwehr* outstations and their headquarters. But these links used an Enigma machine cypher and it was clearly a different machine from that used by the other German services.

Knox's unravelling of the *Abwehr* Enigma allowed Bletchley Park to read the high-level *Abwehr* messages revealing that the Germans believed the false intelligence the Twenty Club was feeding them. The messages, known as ISK (Intelligence Services Knox), also showed whether or not individual double agents were trusted or under suspicion, in which case steps could be taken to remedy the situation. One of the double agents, the talkative 'Treasure', was run long after her operational usefulness had come to an end because her verbose reports were passed on verbatim by her *Abwehr* controllers, thus providing the codebreakers with a regular, and very long, crib for the *Abwehr* traffic.

The information collected from the Bletchley Park decrypts built up such a good picture of *Abwehr* operations in Britain that Robertson was soon able to state categorically that MI5 now controlled all the German agents operating in Britain. The Twenty Club could watch the Germans making arrangements to send agents to Britain and discussing the value of their reports, Robertson wrote. 'In two or three cases we have been able to observe the action (which has been rapid and extensive) taken by the Germans upon the basis of these agents' reports.'

By the spring of 1943, the Double Cross system had developed deception into a fine art. But one of the Twenty Club's most famous achievements did not involve a double agent at all. The Allied forces were now mopping up in North Africa and preparing to invade southern Europe. The most obvious stepping stone was Sicily, just a short hop across the Mediterranean from Tunisia. The problem was to find a way of giving the Germans the impression that General Eisenhower and his British colleague General Alexander had other plans, forcing the Germans to reinforce other areas and weakening the defences in Sicily.

The Twenty Club devised Operation Mincemeat, a plan based on the known level of collaboration between the Spanish authorities and the Germans. They would release the body of a dead 'British officer' off the coast of Spain as if he had come from a crashed aircraft. He would be carrying documents indicating that the main thrust of the Allied attack would be somewhere other than Sicily. The Spanish would pass these on to the Germans who would reinforce their garrisons in the suggested targets at the expense of the real one.

Ewen Montagu, the Royal Navy representative on the committee, took charge of the operation. He acquired a suitable body from a London hospital and gave it the identity of Major William Martin,

Royal Marines, an official courier. Attached to Martin's wrist by a chain was a briefcase containing a number of documents, including a letter from a senior British general to Alexander discussing planned assaults on Greece and an unspecified location in the western Mediterranean, for which Sicily was to be a cover. A further letter from Lord Mountbatten, the Chief of Combined Operations, referred jocularly to sardines, which was rightly thought enough of a hint to make the Germans believe the western thrust of the attack was going to be on Sardinia.

The body was floated ashore from a submarine near the southern Spanish town of Huelva. The Allies now had to find out if the Germans had swallowed the bait and the only sure way of knowing was from Ultra. Noel Currer-Briggs was still in Tunisia with 1 Special Intelligence Section.

> We were stationed at Bizerta on top of a hill just outside Tunis and I remember we were inspected one day by Alexander and Eisenhower. There we were working away at the German wireless traffic coming from the other side of the Mediterranean and we were saying: 'Oh yes. They've moved that division from Sicily to Sardinia and they've moved the other one to the Balkans' and these two generals were jumping up and down like a couple of schoolboys at a football match. We hadn't a clue why. We thought: 'Silly old buffers'. It wasn't until 1953 when Montagu's book *The Man Who Never Was* came out that we realised we were telling them that the Germans had swallowed the deception hook, line and sinker.

The ability the Allies now had, through Ultra, to tell whether or not the enemy had been fooled by deception operations was another crucial contribution made by the codebreakers to Allied intelligence operations, said Ralph Bennett. 'No other source could have proved the efficacy of the deception planners rumour-mongering so conclusively, relieving the operational commanders' minds as they prepared an amphibious undertaking on an unprecedented scale.' Even two months later, when the invasion of Sicily had been launched, German intelligence continued to insist that the original plan had been to attack Sardinia and Greece and that it had only been changed at the last moment.

The Italian surrender and the Allied landing in Italy in September 1943 provided Ultra with its first strategic test. Hitler's reaction was uncertain. Would he take the logical course and retreat to the Alps saving men and material or would he fight every inch of the way?

Bletchley Park was able to follow his decision-making as he initially hesitated and then decided to make a stand on successive defence lines all the way up the peninsula. 'This was the strategic prize of the greatest moment,' said Ralph Bennett. 'It enabled the Allies to design the Italian campaign to draw maximum advantage from the willingness Hitler thus displayed to allow Italy to drain away his resources.'

With the tide finally turned in the Allies' favour, Christmas 1943 was a time of real celebration, particularly in Huts 4 and 8 which had come successfully through the Shark blackout. Phoebe Senyard recalled the occasion.

> Mr Birch gave a wonderful luncheon party. We toasted the Naval Section and anything else that came into our heads. It was great fun and by the time we went into the room where the luncheon was served, we were prepared for almost anything but not for the wonderful sight which met our eyes. The tables were positively groaning with Christmas fare. They were arranged in a T-shape. The top of the T was loaded with turkey, geese and chicken while the table down the centre at which we all sat was decorated with a game pie, and fruit salad, cheese and various other dishes. We set to and thoroughly enjoyed ourselves and I know that I was still beaming by the end of the day.

Pat Wright was working in Hut 8 and was not one of those invited to Birch's lunch. At the end of her shift she returned to her billet.

> I remember it was the first house I had come across that had a toilet in the garden and I had spent five minutes of my first evening there with my toilet bag touring around looking for the bathroom. But Mrs Tomlin was very good to me. She had an engine driver husband and a fireman son and she never took the tablecloth off. She always had food on the table.
>
> She was a very capable woman with a range of language I had never encountered before. I had been brought up fairly strictly and she used words I hardly knew the meaning of. I was working Christmas day and so I finished work at four o'clock and went back to my billet. Christmas dinner was over by now but she said: 'Hello duck, saved you a bit of Christmas pudding. Here you are, this'll make your shit black.' I didn't know whether to laugh or what to do. So I said thank you very much and ate it.

Chapter 9

THE AMERICANS

The Christmas festivities were topped off by the annual revue. By now, the amateur talents had been augmented by some professionals, including some very good actors, singers, musicians and writers. Pamela Gibson had been an actress before joining the Naval Section index.

> I spoke German quite well and I had a letter from a rather interfering godmother who said she was sure I was doing splendid work entertaining the troops but she knew a girl who had just gone to a very secret place and was doing fascinating work and they needed people with languages.
>
> That made me feel I was fiddling while Rome burnt. So I wrote off to the address they sent me and thought no more about it. I had just been offered a part in a play when I got a telegram from Frank Birch asking me to meet him at the Admiralty. He gave me several tests and said: 'Well I suppose we could offer you a job' and I said: 'Well you know about the stage, what would you do if you were me?' He said: 'The stage can wait, the war can't.' So I went to Bletchley.

It was while taking part in one of the revues that she met Jim Rose, her future husband, who had written a sketch in which she was acting. 'No one who wasn't in it was allowed to go to rehearsals,' said Jim Rose. 'But at that time, just before Christmas at the end of 1943, I was going to Washington so they let me in and this glorious vision of loveliness all in green stepped down from the stage and said: "Your sketch isn't bad".'

The fact that so many clever people were gathered in the one place meant that even if the performances were sometimes not up to professional standards, the scripts were always good, Pamela Rose said.

> There were a lot of people with talent there who wrote bits and there

were a few actors doing their bit for the war and a lot of amateurs. It was like a university revue, like Footlights. We thought they were splendid. I've no idea if they really were. The performances may not have been so great but I think the scripts were fairly good because there were a lot of very bright people there.

The end of 1943 was memorable for another reason – the 'invasion' of the Americans and the commencement of sustained cooperation between British and US codebreakers. The first tentative moves had begun in the summer of 1940, at the height of the Battle of Britain and amid widespread fears that a German invasion was imminent. The Americans were offered access to British cryptographic 'equipment and devices' in return for 'secret information of a technical nature which our experts are anxious to have urgently'.

An exchange of information on codebreaking was agreed by senior US and British representatives in Washington in December 1940. The following month, nearly a year before the Japanese attack on Pearl Harbor brought the Americans into the war, a four-man American delegation – comprising two US Army officers, Captain Abraham Sinkov and Lieutenant Leo Rosen, and two US Navy officers, Lieutenant Robert Weeks and Ensign Prescott Currier – set sail for Britain carrying 'certain packages'. At least one of these packages contained a so-called 'Purple machine', designed to unravel the main Japanese diplomatic machine cypher. Barbara Abernethy was then working as Denniston's personal assistant.

It must have been early 1941. Commander Denniston said: 'Please come in for a minute, I've got something important to tell you. At twelve o'clock, there are going to be four Americans who are coming to see me, and I require you to come in with the sherry. You are not to tell anybody who they are or what they will be doing.'

Now the sherry consisted of a great big cask which I could barely lift. It came from the Army & Navy Stores. So at twelve o'clock the bell rang and I went in and I somehow managed to pour glasses of sherry for these poor Americans, who I kept looking at. I'd never seen Americans before, except in the films. 'What were they doing here?', we said to ourselves. So anyway I plied them with sherry, that was the end of my role.

I didn't know what they would be doing, I wasn't told. But it was very exciting and hushed voices, and I couldn't hear anything. I was just told not to tell anybody. I guess it wasn't general knowledge that the Americans had got any liaison with Bletchley. It was before Pearl

Harbor, you see, and presumably Roosevelt was not telling everybody there was going to be any liaison at that stage.

Currier recalled that the Americans were given an extensive briefing on the work taking place at Bletchley.

There was complete cooperation. We went everywhere, including Hut 6. We watched the entire operation and had all the techniques explained in great detail. We were thoroughly briefed on the latest techniques in the solution of Enigma and the operations of the bombes. We had ample opportunity to take as many notes as we wanted and to watch first hand all operations involved. Many of our evenings were spent at the home of one or another of our British colleagues. Food and liquor were both rationed, especially liquor, and it was not easy for them to entertain. Whisky and gin were generally unavailable in the pubs and most people had to be satisfied with sherry.

The Americans were also taken to a number of intercept sites and to London where they were put up in the Savoy and introduced to Menzies, he said.

I remember standing in a doorway while a few bombs went off, none close, and walking up a narrow stairway to a little reception room with comfortable chairs and a fireplace in which a coal fire was burning. We were served tea and talked briefly about our mission. I was not clear at the time just what role the head of the British Secret Intelligence Service played in the Sigint business nor precisely why we were talking to him. I recall having the impression that he thought we knew a lot more than we did since he spent some time telling us of the difficulty of running agents and collecting intelligence from enemy territory.

We were taken by one of the Royal Navy officers to the Café de Paris, an underground London night club on Leicester Square. It was a favourite with Londoners for the very reason that it was underground and relatively safe during a bombing raid. On the evening we were there it was very crowded and noisy, filled with men in uniform dancing to the music of 'Snake Hips' Johnson, a West Indian band leader. The only thing I remember particularly about that evening is a tricycle race across the dance floor between the actor David Niven and some of his fellow officers. The following night a delayed action bomb crashed through the four or five floors of the building over the club and exploded on the dance floor killing most of the dancers together with 'Snake Hips' and his band.

Despite subsequent claims that the mission was not as successful as the Americans had hoped, the only real threat to transatlantic cooperation appears to have come during a visit to the Marconi factory at Chelmsford in Essex. 'We were stopped at a road block in a small village,' Currier recalled.

> When the local constable saw two men in civilian clothes, obviously not British, riding in a War Department staff car, he reacted quickly and asked if we would 'mind getting out and accompanying him to the police station'. This infuriated our diminuitive Scottish driver who jumped out and confronted the policeman: 'Ye can nae do this, they're Americans on a secret mission.' This had no discernible effect on the constable and it took us the better part of an hour to convince our captor it was all right to let us proceed.

Amid continuing concerns over American security the British did hold some things back. Denniston told Menzies that Currier and his colleagues had been 'informed of the progress made on the Enigma machine' during their visit to Station X. But as Menzies stressed to Churchill, the information they were given was 'confined to the mechanised devices we utilise [the bombes] and not to showing the results'. They were not given any of the actual decrypts.

The Americans were interested mainly in Japanese cyphers and it was agreed that all liaison on this should be carried out in the Far East between the British Far East Combined Bureau in Singapore, which did most of the work on Japanese codes and cyphers, and its US equivalent at Corregidor in the Phillipines. Menzies also took the opportunity to post one of his officers, Tim O'Connor, a former merchant banker, to Washington to liaise on cryptographic matters.

Exchange of Enigma represented real security problems but by mid-1941, the wolf pack attacks on the Atlantic convoys had led the Admiralty to start passing U-boat decrypts to the US Navy. Denniston flew to America in August of that year, striking up a particularly friendly relationship with William F. Friedman, the leading US cryptographer, that was to ease the initially stilted cooperation between the two sides.

Friedman had been born in Kishinev, the capital of Moldavia, in 1891. When he was still a baby, his parents had emigrated to the United States. At university he studied genetics and he was offered a job in the laboratories of the wealthy textile manufacturer George Fabyan. It was here that he first began to take an interest in cyphers, as a result of Fabyan's obsession with proving that Shakespeare's plays were actually written by Francis Bacon. After doing some codebreaking work for the US Government during the First World War, Friedman became head of the US Army's small cryptography unit.

Denniston's friendship with Friedman was very useful in the early days of the wartime alliance. Some US codebreakers were extremely sceptical of cooperation with what they saw as the conservative, class-ridden and technologically deficient British. But a series of exchange visits between the two sides followed Denniston's trip to America.

Joe Eachus, a young US naval lieutenant, was sent to Bletchley by the US Navy's codebreaking section Op-20-G. He arrived in March 1942 after the Japanese attack on Pearl Harbor had brought the Americans into the war. 'My nominal task was to tell Washington what was happening at Bletchley Park,' he said. 'And in that role I got around to see more of Bletchley Park than a lot of the people who were part of it.'

Nevertheless, the mutual mistrust continued on both sides. 'As a liaison officer I was occasionally asked to get specific stuff and on one occasion I was asked by Washington for an organisational chart of Bletchley Park. I went to the man in charge and said could I have a chart of the organisation. He paused and said "I don't believe we have one." I didn't pursue this with him, but I was never quite certain whether he meant we don't have a chart, or we don't have an organisation.'

Throughout 1942 a series of exchange visits took place. The British were suspicious and the Americans, perhaps understandably, were resentful that they were not being trusted. Tiltman, who had been appointed liaison officer, spent some time in Washington attempting to smooth over the differences. But when an officer from the US Army Signal Intelligence Service toured Bletchley Park and its outstations in August 1942 and was openly excluded from certain parts of the operation, his report reflected his anger and caused 'some offence', de Grey recalled. 'The matter is negligible except that it tended to place the Americans in a bad light and made their advent the less welcome.'

If relations with the US Army were difficult, those with the Navy were on a somewhat firmer footing. Travis flew to America in October 1942 to meet Captain C. F. Holden, the US Navy's Director of Communications. They signed the so-called Holden Understanding, which committed both sides to cooperation on the breaking of the German naval cyphers, and in particular Shark. The daily keys and any messages that were broken were sent across the Atlantic on US bombers in what became known as 'the bomber bag'.

A few weeks later, Hinsley went to Washington as Assistant to the Director GC&CS, a title designed to give him greater credibility with the Americans than a youthful civilian might otherwise have enjoyed, and put forward plans for an agreement that would share out responsibility for various targets between Arlington Hall and Bletchley Park, rather than have each just duplicate what the other was doing.

In his role as Birch's chief intelligence officer, he was already heavily involved in the informal relationship that had been set up between the naval section and Op-20-G. He soon found his attempts to broker a similar deal with Arlington Hall foundering, at least in part, on the jealousy between the US Navy and the US Army. 'The Navy didn't like me talking to the Army,' Hinsley said. 'But I wasn't allowed to tell the Navy any details because the Army would have been furious.'

Meanwhile, Joe Eachus had begun working in Hut 8 as a naval codebreaker.

My official duty was to report back to Washington what was happening at BP. But that was not a full-time job, so I undertook to be a cryptanalyst while I was there. It had been a hobby of mine before the war. Some of the British had been in the FO as professional codebreakers for some years, but there were no US Navy guys who fitted that description. Everybody had been amateurs before.

We were working on German Enigma and often-times we were reading stuff currently. Other times, something would happen and we were not and there was just a feeling of gloom around when we would go for a week without reading things, very downhearted. Then it got going again and you would see the smiles in the corridors. That was very noticeable that people there took a personal interest in the work.

As an officer I was permitted to circulate a good deal more than most of the people who worked there, I had a good excuse, and there were a lot of academics there, particularly from Cambridge. I met professorial types on an equal footing in a way I would never have otherwise done. They were always a level or two above me. I found their attitude towards life very interesting. They were academics primarily and their personal life was secondary. My view had always been the other way round, my personal life was the primary thing and my professional life was a way of making a living.

By the end of 1942, Eachus was one of seven American officers at Bletchley Park. Two of them were from the US Navy's Op-20-G, the rest from the Army's Special Branch and Signal Intelligence Service, which was exchanging information on breaks into the Japanese cyphers with Bletchley Park and the FECB.

But the British reluctance to allow the decrypts to cross the Atlantic for security reasons continued to mar the relationship. General George Strong, who as G-2 was the US Army officer in charge of signals intelligence, remained highly suspicious of British motives. 'The picture that emerges is of G-2 and the British authorities walking around each other and eyeing each other like two mongrels who have just met,' wrote Ted Hilles, one of the senior US Army officers at Bletchley Park. 'Presumably and quite naturally, the ministries in London were reluctant to risk sources' necks sharing this precious information with an unproved and shadowy group in Washington.'

Throughout the early months of 1943, intense negotiation took place with Bletchley Park seeking American technology to improve the effectiveness of the bombes but refusing to allow its US Army equivalent at Arlington Hall, Virginia, access to the finished Ultra material and doing all it could to stop the Americans from working on Enigma themselves.

'We make available to any properly accredited representative of the [US] War Department all the processes and results of cryptographic investigation at the Government Code and Cypher School,' Tiltman told Field Marshal Sir John Dill, the British chief of staff. 'But in the case of investigation on the higher planes of secrecy [Enigma], we have discouraged as far as possible the duplication of our work in the USA or elsewhere.'

In late March, Travis told a meeting of the senior staff at Bletchley that the US Navy had agreed to supply some 'special analysing machinery', advanced bombes built by the US National Cash Register Company that were capable of producing much faster solutions to the four-wheel Shark Enigma used by the U-boats. Some of the equipment would have to be bought, some of it loaned. But while the exchange of naval material was presenting few problems, things were 'not going too smoothly' in the negotiations with the US Army over a similar deal for military and air intelligence, Travis said. 'A deadlock seems to have been reached. General Strong is still demanding the exploitation of E by Arlington with our assistance.'

A US mission, including Friedman, was sent to Britain in April

1943 and was involved in 'difficult and protacted negotiations' with Travis and Menzies. But in mid-May, the two sides signed a groundbreaking accord.

The BRUSA agreement set out a division of responsibilities between Bletchley Park and Arlington Hall. The British would control the interception and decryption of German radio messages while the Americans concentrated on Japanese. US liaison officers would be based at Bletchley Park where they would have access to 'all decoded material' and the right to pass those they selected back to Washington or on to US commanders in the field.

'The proposal is now that the Americans, though not exploiting E in the USA, should have a party in this country working either here at BP or elsewhere,' Travis told the BP management committee. 'Moreover some American officers would be attached to Hut 3 and would report to the USA from there. In this way General Strong would make certain he was not cheated of information.'

But with concerns over American security a predominant factor in the negotiations, it was agreed that all this material should be passed 'through existing British channels'. Information that was to be sent to field commanders would be passed via the British Special Liaison Units, the agreement said.

> Where an American officer is commander-in-chief, an American officer, properly trained and indoctrinated at Bletchley Park, will be attached to the unit to advise and act as liaison officer to overcome difficulties that may arise in regard to differences in language.
>
> The preservation of secrecy is a matter of great concern to both countries and, if the highest degree of security is to be maintained, it is essential that the same methods should be pursued by both countries at every level and in every area concerned, since a leakage at one point would jeopardise intelligence from these sources not in one area only but in all theatres of war and for all services.'

Friedman flew back to Washington, leaving Colonel Telford Taylor, a US Army Special Branch intelligence officer, in Britain to take charge of liaison between Bletchley Park and Arlington Hall. Taylor persuaded Travis to send someone from Hut 3 over to America to pick out US intelligence officers who would fit into the hut's somewhat rarified atmosphere. The man selected for this task was Jim Rose, who was to remain close friends with Taylor for the rest of the latter's life.

When Telford came over in 1943, he asked me to go out to Washington to interview candidates for Bletchley. Most of the officers who came to Bletchley I chose. There were some very bright people. One of them was Lewis Powell, who became a judge of the US Supreme Court. There was the man who became managing editor of the *Washington Post*, Alfred Friendly. There were quite a lot of lawyers and their reception in Hut 3 was extremely friendly and they all felt integrated.

While the Hut 3 reporters selected by Rose came, like Taylor, from the Special Branch, the US Army equivalent of the Intelligence Corps, the codebreakers came from the Signal Intelligence Service of the US Army Signal Corps and were under the command of Captain Bill Bundy, a law student from Harvard whose studies had been interrupted by the war. He recalled his first experiences at BP.

> I went to Arlington Hall in the spring of '43. And I remember vividly, a group of us, a very small group, were convened in a room there and told: 'What you're going to hear today is something you will not discuss.' They went on with the briefing about what was then in that circle called Yellow, which was the whole Enigma-breaking operation.
>
> After considerable sparring back and forth an agreement had been reached between the American and the British governments that the Americans would keep the major role on Japanese material and the British would maintain the major role on German but as a sort of codicil to that it was agreed that a small American contingent, thirty to fifty, should go to Bletchley Park to integrate right into the organisation there and I was picked to be the commanding officer of that outfit.

In great secrecy they were sent to England on the SS *Aquitania*, Bundy recalled. 'I think we were twenty in our advance contingent and on the way over we had to bunk with other services. Our cover story was that we were pigeon experts in the Signal Corps. I don't think we used it very often, Lord knows it would have broken down very quickly, you didn't really have to explain what you were doing on a troopship, but that was the cover story we used.'

Art Levenson, a young Jewish mathematician, was one of Bundy's advance party.

> We were a somewhat select group. But this was the first experiment in cooperating in the code-breaking business between any two countries in history. And I guess I don't know if you want to put your best foot forward, but you want to put one of your better feet. I don't think I'd ever met an Englishman in my life until that point.

We went to Lichfield, which was the repo-depot, the reporting depot where everybody who was coming to the UK or the European theatre went to. Then we were in London for a few days, and then we were sent up to Bletchley. We were introduced to Brigadier Tiltman and they treated us like visiting generals.

Despite those initial courtesies, the Americans were still regarded with suspicion by some of those not involved in the negotiations including Jean Howard who worked in Hut 3.

I remember with horror the American invasion when every section had an American. We believed they had no sense of security and were terrified that material they took out of the Hut would go astray. We felt strongly that they would never have come into the war but for Pearl Harbor.

They were different animals, and the English they spoke had different meanings. They were fat, we were emaciated. They were smart (eleven different sorts of uniform), we were almost in rags. They were rich, we were poor. They brought in alcohol: 'Have a rye, sister.' 'We don't drink here.' We were overworked and exhausted, and having to teach people who barely knew where Europe was, was the last straw.

The mutual mistrust came to a head on the Fourth of July, recalled Barbara Abernethy.

We were challenged by the Americans to a game of rounders. They nearly went home. Now in the United States, you don't need to get all the way home in one go to score. As long as you get all the way home eventually you score. Now our rules for rounders of course were very tough. You had to go all the way round in one go.

It was a lovely day, we all played well, and at the end of the game we all sort of clapped each other on the back and the Americans said: 'Well, we're sorry we beat you' and the British captain said: 'I'm sorry, but we beat you.' The Americans were a little touchy. They were convinced that they'd won and it took a bit of explanation on somebody's part to soothe ruffled feathers. It all ended with drinks all round, actually we agreed we'd won by our rules and they'd won by their rules. So that was all right. But they never asked us to play again.

While the row over the result of the rounders match was sorted out over a few drinks, the sparring continued over what access the US

Army should have to the German material. The British, led by
Menzies and de Grey, were reluctant to allow anything other than the
barest outlines of what Hut 3 was reporting to cross the Atlantic and
there were no arrangements in place capable of handling the amount
of material the Americans wished to see, Hilles recalled. 'There were
serious delays in transmittal and perceptible irritation on both sides.'

It was not until late August that anything was sent to Washington.
But within days, after being told that General Strong was flying to
Britain for talks aimed at sorting things out, the British stopped
Taylor from sending anything more until the talks had been held. At
a conference attended by Menzies, Travis, de Grey and Eric Jones on
the British side and Strong and Taylor for the Americans, it was
agreed that Taylor could select and transmit Ultra to Washington but
that his selection should be 'conservative'. Hilles said that the accord
was short-lived.

> Soon after the meeting General Strong reversed the previous decision
> and agreed with General Menzies that no Ultra should be sent from BP.
> There followed numerous consultations. While these were being held,
> General Strong returned to Washington, conferred with Colonel
> Clarke, decided that he had made a mistake and directed Colonel
> Taylor to try to reinstate the previous arrangements.

After several weeks of 'frequent parleys', it was eventually agreed
that Taylor should be responsible for the selection of what was
passed to Washington but must keep the War Office or the Air
Ministry informed of what items he was sending. On 27 September
1943, the service from Hut 3 to Arlington Hall was resumed.

The relationship with the US Navy was much better. Since early
1943, Op-20-G's codebreakers had been cooperating well, with Hut 8,
assisting them in decyphering 'Offizier', a double-encyphered
version of Enigma used for high-level communication by German
Navy officers. By September 1943, the new faster bombes produced
by the National Cash Register Company had come on line at Op-20-
G's headquarters in Nebraska Avenue, Washington.

But if the official negotiations with the US Army were concluded,
the atmosphere was still clouded by mutual suspicion, recalled
Valerie Travis.

> My father organised a dance to welcome the Americans to Bletchley
> Park. It was Trafalgar Day so we said it was a Trafalgar Day dance and
> one of the Americans was furious. He said: 'I don't believe it's Trafalgar

Day. When we came into port in Liverpool there were a lot of little boats running about and I said what on earth are all these little boats doing and somebody told me it was for Guy Fawkes Day.' He was furious. He was going around saying to everybody: 'What is today?' and when they said Trafalgar Day, he wouldn't believe them. That's the sort of silly thing that happened.

On the American side, there was a belief that the British were too 'stiff-upper lipped' to get on with, Bundy recalled.

We thought they'd be aloof, hard to reach, buttoned up, as we say. That it would be very hard to get to know them and that they'd probably be rather cold. Well that broke down, I should say, in the first forty-eight hours and certainly the first time that you had a mug of beer with a Britisher. If we're talking original stereotypes, they didn't last.

The Americans won even the most suspicious of British code-breakers over with their openness and enthusiasm. 'The infusion of US blood brought us Bill Bundy – everyone's ideal of the New England gentleman, tall, slim, handsome, fresh-faced, and courteous and others representing different traditions in American society, such as the exuberant Bill Bijur,' recalled Derek Taunt, a member of Hut 6. The occasion when he celebrated his promotion to first lieutenant by handing out cigars at midnight to all and sundry is a vivid memory, perhaps because it typified his generous, extrovert nature tinged with a touching naivety.'

Bundy fitted in well and was universally popular largely because he accepted the British concerns over American security.

One felt right away a concern on the British side whether Americans could keep their mouths shut. And they dealt with this, I thought, brilliantly, as they dealt with the whole security problem throughout. No stern lectures or anything of that sort, just quietly saying how important it was not to let a bit of this come out.

So very quickly and in a very low-key but totally persuasive way we were indoctrinated with the basic security principles that governed all the Enigma material and all the cypher and codebreaking materials at all grades, all levels throughout the war, it was just terribly well done.

I don't expect ever to work in a group of people that was more thoroughly dedicated and with a range of skills, insight and imagination that the Bletchley people had, the people in Hut 6 specifically. There were top mathematicians. There were these very competent people who ran the mechanics of the thing. It was an extraordinary group, and that was true right across the board in BP, whatever system of selection they used, and I've heard lots of narratives and lots of colourful stories about it, the result was an extraordinary group of people in an extraordinary organisation.

Their whole structure was one where you might readily find a major working under a lieutenant or under a civilian, somewhat younger. Whoever was in charge was the person who had been judged to be more effective at doing it. It was meritocracy in spades and without regard to where you came from or whether you were a man or a woman, although I think we had a very large majority of men in the senior positions. But we had absolutely superb women in a lot of key roles. It was very much integrated in that sense and every other, and it was the only way to do it really. The old remark attributed to Churchill, 'I told you to leave no stone unturned, but I didn't expect you to take me literally,' certainly did describe the varied and in some cases rather raffish British civilian contingent.

Gradually as the two sides got to know each other, a level of mutual respect replaced the suspicion and relationships between the two sides became very much closer, Bundy said.

We didn't have a separate American unit within the Enigma cypher-breaking structure. We were integrated on an individual basis in the various offices of Hut 6, or on the translation and exploitation side of Hut 3, and it was, from the standpoint of personal relations, a terribly good relationship, taking people as they came, as they were, laughing about the national differences and customs, a very relaxed, very giving and taking relationship.

Art Levenson recalled having a 'pretty heavy' social life at Bletchley Park.

We were a handful of Americans and we were, I guess, somewhat exotic. There were lots of Wrens around. They invited us to lots of parties and we had a great time. I made many friends that I still have. It was great fun, they were wonderful people, a great crowd. I had been full of stereotypes about the English. 'They're distant and have no sense of humour, they won't speak to you unless you're introduced' and all kinds of nonsense. But these were the most outgoing people, who invited us to their homes and fed us when it was quite a sacrifice, and with a delightful sense of humour. Maybe there were some English that fitted the stereotype but there were none at Bletchley, they were all a delight and just enough screwballs to be real fun.

Selmer Norland, a German teacher from Minnesota who was one of the first Americans to work in Hut 3, shared Levenson's happy memories of the reception they received from the British code-breakers.

I think that for most of them their only contact with Americans had probably been cowboy movies and they had preconceived notions of what Americans were like. And so we approached each other as sort of sensitive to differences and biases and so forth.

I was sort of in awe of many of them, they were Oxford and Cambridge dons and equivalent people from some of the other British universities and I just had a college minor in German. I had never lived in Germany, most of them had been able to spend summers in Germany or Austria, living and breathing the language. Fortunately we were dealing with military German. I couldn't discuss the finer points of Schiller and Goethe, but I did know military German. Still I thought they were terrific. I developed some very strong friendly relations with the people I worked with, they were great.

One of the most striking things about the Americans to the British, used to the weak wartime beer sold in the Bletchley Park beer hut or the local pubs, was their ability to drink spirits, and in particular whisky. 'It was astonishing,' said Christine Brooke-Rose, who was newly married to one of the other members of Hut 3.

I don't know if it was just the war or me being terribly innocent. I remember my husband and I being invited to dinner at the local hotel in Leighton Buzzard where all the Americans were billeted, and after dinner, all the Americans, each one would order another whisky and another Drambuie and another round.

It was absolutely amazing and we had to cycle back to the billet where we were living and I remember being really very zig-zaggy. It wasn't that they were alcoholics. It was just the war atmosphere. They did drink far more and very strong drinks. The British drank beer. There was a beer hut and people would have a beer before going on to the canteen for lunch but they wouldn't drink this strong stuff. That was part of the American culture.

The Americans also had their own rations and were happy to share them with the British, which certainly helped to ease any lingering mistrust and improve their popularity. Although there were relatively few US naval officers, they were officially designated as 'a detached unit' and entitled to their own supplies, Joe Eachus recalled.

> A detached unit covers a multitude of sins, from an individual to a ship. So when I went to London I got my supplies from the same place that ships did, sugar in one hundred pound bags and coffee in twenty-five pound cans. So my office was always very well supplied with sugar. Consequently when I would go to some other office to ask them to tell me about what they were doing, I would take a cup of sugar with me, which made me a good deal more welcome than I might otherwise have been.

The other thing the Americans brought with them was the Japanese game of Go, a replacement for chess. Turing had learnt the game at Princeton, though he was scarcely any better at it than at chess. But many of the British chess players quickly took to it, Eachus recalled.

> Go is a Japanese game which has a very very simple board. The pieces are like small marbles. You have marbles of one colour and your opponent has those of a different colour. If you can surround somebody you take all the pieces inside yours. That is the major principle in Go. So if you can get a thing the shape of a figure eight, then no one can take it. As soon as they fill one eye you take their piece. So the secondary objective as a defensive strategy is to get a figure eight.

As relationships became closer, there were inevitably romances between the Americans and some of the British women, a number of which would lead eventually to marriage. Telford Taylor, who was a married man, became involved in a torrid affair with the unhappily married Christine Brooke-Rose. 'It was just one of those things that happen,' she said.

> I was twenty-two and he was in his late thirties. He was very handsome, he looked like Gary Cooper, and he was a very interesting person. He was in charge of the American liaison section which was in one room just opposite where we were in Hut 3 so they would all come in for coffee and I knew them quite well.
>
> Telford had first arrived on his own and I was detailed to explain things to him. It was quite an odd experience because he was much too high up to be interested in this kind of routine work. I don't know how these things happened. He was a very serious person. He had quite a

good sense of humour. He was a nice man, a lawyer. He liked to tell me all about the American law system. But he was very musical.

After her husband was taken into hospital with pneumonia they began an affair, sharing trysts in London away from the gossip of Bletchley Park. When her husband was released from hospital, Brooke-Rose told him of the affair.

He was very, very British and he and Telford talked together. Telford was terribly amused afterwards because he thought my husband was so British, shaking hands and saying that everything was all right which of course it wasn't because our marriage broke up. It just made him laugh because Americans don't face things the way gentlemen used to. It was so British.

Despite the vastly different cultures and the early suspicions, the Americans settled in well and few of the codebreakers on either side have bad memories of the wartime alliance. Ralph Bennett conceded that some of the Americans had problems getting to grips with the workings of Bletchley Park.

But they were no worse off in that respect than we had been and the Americans, when they do things, they do them quickly and with great aplomb. They had no back-up, no training, but then nor did I when I went there. I'm still amazed at how quickly they did cotton on. They learned darn quick and were very good at it. No complaints about them at all.

Chapter 10

FISH AND COLOSSUS

One thing the British held back from the Americans for some time was the fact that they had gone on from breaking the Enigma cypher to cracking the even more complicated encyphered teleprinter transmissions used between Hitler and his generals. These messages, known at Bletchley by the overall codename 'Fish', were to become increasingly important as the Allied invasion of Europe approached.

The earliest indications that the Germans were using an encyphered teleprinter system came in the second half of 1940 when the Metropolitan Police unit at Denmark Hill under H. C. Kenworthy picked up unidentified German non-Morse signals. No effort was put into intercepting these transmissions until mid-1941 when an RAF station at Capel-le-Ferne, near Folkestone, picked up similar signals. 'The transmissions were erratic,' said Kenworthy. 'But on one occasion, a secret teleprinter message in clear was intercepted reporting the removal of a Flak battery to the Eastern Front.' Denmark Hill was asked to take a closer look at the teleprinter signals with the assistance of the GPO intercept station at St Albans.

The first regular transmissions intercepted by the British were on an experimental *Wehrmacht* link between Vienna and Athens which used the Lorenz SZ40 cypher machine. The codebreakers gave this traffic the codename Tunny. Another teleprinter encyphering system, the Siemens and Halske *Geheimschreiber*, was also detected in use by the Germans, mainly by the *Luftwaffe*, and was codenamed Sturgeon. But because of the lack of Army Enigma, the codebreakers decided to concentrate on the Tunny material produced by the Lorenz machine.

This worked on a system invented in America in 1918 by Gilbert Vernam. Teleprinter transmissions are based on the international Baudot system, a binary code in which each letter is made up of a series of five elements, or 'bits', each of which is either a 'mark' – the equivalent of the binary 1 and denoted by a cross – or a 'space' – the counterpart of the binary 0 and represented by a dot. Each element is transmitted as a separate negative or positive impulse.

'The letters were in the form of five elements, always preceeded by a start signal and always followed by a stop signal,' said Ken Halton, one of the GPO teleprinter engineers who worked at Bletchley. 'So they were basically seven units in length, the middle five being the active code elements. The start signal and the stop signal were there to start and stop the machine at the receiving end.'

The Baudot Code, as it is known, was not secret and remains in general use. But Vernam's cypher system combined the five elements for one letter with those of another letter 'randomly' selected by a cypher machine to produce a third encyphered letter. Each of the five elements that made up the letter under the Baudot code were added to each other on the basis that like and like, either two marks or two spaces, would produce a space, while like and unlike, i.e., a mark combined with a space, produced a mark. The new combination of marks and spaces constituted a third, encyphered letter. For example, if the letter A – which in the Baudot Code is represented by XX. . . – is added to B – which is X..XX – the result would be .X.XX or the letter G.

$$
\begin{array}{cc}
\text{x x . . .} & \text{A} \\
\underline{\text{x . . x x}} & \underline{\text{B}} \\
\text{. x . x x} & \text{G}
\end{array}
$$

The beauty of this system lay in the decyphering process. Because in binary maths addition is the same as subtraction, an identically set cypher machine at the receiving end had only to add the same pattern of 'random' letters to the encyphered letters, or effectively re-encypher the message on the same setting, to come up with the original clear text. The Lorenz SZ40 took Vernam's idea one stage further, adding not one but two separate 'random' letters to the original letter in an attempt to make it even more difficult to decypher.

The Lorenz machine had twelve wheels, ten to encypher the message, split into two separate rows of five, and two drive wheels. Each of the encyphering wheels had a number of sprung teeth equally spaced around its circumference which could be put into an active or inactive position to form either a mark or a space.

The five elements of the letter were passed through the first set of five wheels, each element through one wheel, and were either

modified or left unaltered depending on the addition principle
described above and whether or not the pin at that point was active
or inactive. They were then passed through the second set of wheels
where a similar process took place. But unlike the first set of wheels
which turned continuously, the second set turned intermittently,
stopping occasionally for a few turns.

The intercepted transmissions were converted into the
encyphered letters and sent to Bletchley Park where they were
examined by Tiltman. He quickly identified the messages as being
encyphered using the Vernam system and began to work on a
method of unravelling the messages by hand. Tiltman realised that,
because of the way that binary maths worked, if two messages were
sent using the same setting, and they could be lined up so that the
starting points matched, adding them together would eliminate the
'random' letters that the Lorenz machine had introduced. What
would be left was a combination of the letters in the two original
messages. Ken Halton described how the laziness of the operators
helped them to do this.

> Imagine that a message is sent using a machine that has been set up in
> a certain way and then another message has to be sent. The operator is
> lazy and simply resets his machine to the same position as before,
> which you can do with a simple operation, and puts the next message
> through so that it has exactly the same encoding pattern superimposed
> on it.
>
> If you can identify that, which you usually can because the operator
> has to tell his colleague what he's doing, and you then add those two
> messages together, one to the other, the two encoding patterns will
> cancel one another out and you are left with two clear texts added
> together. If you then carry out a statistical analysis of the distribution of
> letters in that combination of two clear texts, it will not be random. It
> will clearly have language characteristics. So you know that you have
> got two clear German texts added together and from that you should,
> with a lot of hard work, be able to go on to separate them out.

A number of messages sent on the same setting, or as the codebreakers described it, 'in depth', were recovered. But Tiltman was
having difficulty separating the clear texts out. Then a lazy German
operator came to his assistance. On 30 August 1941, the operator sent
a message 3976 characters long. When asked to repeat it, he sent it
again with exactly the same settings.

It should have produced exactly the same message, which would have been no help to Tiltman at all. But although the codebreakers knew from the operator chat that the two messages were the same and they certainly began identically, within a few letters they had become different. The vital clue that allowed Tiltman to work out what had happened was the fact that this message had fewer characters. The operator had left something out of the original message.

Anxious to cut down the length of time the job would take, he had abbreviated a number of parts of the message, beginning with its introduction. He had cut the word *Spruchnummer*, message number, using the German abbreviation for number to make it *Spruchnr*. Tiltman now knew that if he lined the subsequent apparently different parts of the two messages up and added them together, it would strip off the keys, leaving him with two identical clear texts added together.

Because each character of the combined text represented only one letter, albeit it added to itself, the stripped text would have similar characteristics to the German language and could be recovered relatively easily by exploiting basic cryptanalytical tools such as letter frequency.

Sadly, it was not quite as easy as that because the message had been abbreviated in a number of places. But Tiltman, who preferred to work alone, standing at a custom-built high desk, was a brilliant codebreaker. Gradually he worked his way through the message recovering the clear text up to the next abbreviation, working out what that was, realigning the two texts and reconstructing the next piece of plain language. Eventually, he managed to recover the complete text. This was in itself an amazing feat. But it was to be followed by one that was perhaps even more remarkable.

Once Tiltman had completely deciphered the message all he had to do was add the clear text to the encyphered version to find the elements that had been added by the Lorenz machine. He gave these to Bill Tutte, a young Cambridge chemistry graduate, who was working in the Bletchley Park research section, and asked him to devote all his energy to using them to try to find out how the Lorenz machine worked.

Tutte wrote out vast sequences of the individual 'bits' from the encyphering characters by hand, looking for some form of pattern. When he wrote the first elements in sequences of forty-one, he began to notice various patterns which were more than random and deduced correctly that the first wheel had forty-one teeth. Over the next two months, Tutte managed to work out its complete internal structure and how it operated right down to the intermittent movement of the second row of wheels.

Given that no one at Bletchley had any idea what a Lorenz machine looked like, Tutte had achieved a near miracle but he remained unassuming and modest about his feat, recalled Shaun Wylie, who later moved from Hut 8 to work on Tunny. 'You could get hardly anything out of him,' Wylie said. 'I once wanted to hear from him the saga about how he'd done this astonishing bit of work and I think we got interrupted after about half an hour but I really hadn't got much out of him.'

But the importance of the breakthrough was not lost on those in charge. 'That the Research Section was in fact able to achieve this feat within a matter of a few months was one of the outstanding successes of the war,' said Nigel de Grey. With Tiltman and Tutte having shown that it was possible to break the Tunny traffic, it was decided to set up a section to exploit it, de Grey added. 'The system was being fairly rapidly extended by the Germans over their high command networks and such messages as could be decyphered by "depth" reading left little doubt that their contents would have considerable intelligence value.'

The new section would become known as the 'Testery' after the man put in charge of it. Ralph Tester was a 39-year-old accountant who, having spent much of his working life in Germany, had an exceptionally deep knowledge of both the country itself and the language. He had been working with Tiltman on police cyphers having only recently arrived at Bletchley on a transfer from the BBC Monitoring Service at Caversham, near Reading, which intercepted German public radio broadcasts.

A farm on the North Downs at Knockholt, near Sevenoaks in Kent, was bought as an intercept site for the Tunny material and Frank Morrell of the GPO's Dollis Hill research station produced a machine which used standard post office relays and contact switches to simulate the actions of the first row of wheels.

The station, which was staffed mainly by ATS operators, came on line in mid-1942. The German transmissions were recorded on an undulator. 'That's a thing that draws a wriggly line on a piece of tape, a bit like the old-fashioned ticker tape,' Halton said.

> The girls at Knockholt were adept at reading these characters on the undulator tape and they used to type them up on a keyboard to produce a perforated teleprinter tape. A fair number of these perforated

tapes were brought to Bletchley Park by dispatch rider but a lot of them, particularly the ones they wanted there quickly, were sent over telegraph lines.

Everything was done twice to ensure there were no mistakes, Kenworthy recalled. 'An error in one character in several thousand was enough to cause trouble. A system was introduced to overcome this on the principle that two separate people would hardly be likely to make the same mistake. All tapes were therefore measured by two girls before being read up.'

There were six dedicated teleprinter lines between Knockholt and Bletchley, said Halton.

> They were used in pairs so that a message was sent by two separate lines and went on to two separate machines at Bletchley and so the message came out in step on both machines together. The Wrens used to take the tapes as they came out and put one on top of the other and look through them to make sure that the holes matched up. If they got more than six errors in a message they had to reject it and we had to start again, and probably check the line or the machines. So it was quite a task getting long messages into Bletchley with not more than six errors in them.

As the Germans increased the number of links and the amount of Tunny traffic grew, new outstations were opened at Forest Moor, near Harrogate; Wincombe, near Shaftsbury in Dorset; Kingask, near Cupar in Scotland; and Kedlestone Hall, near Derby.

The codebreakers recruited to work in the Testery included Roy Jenkins, who subsequently became Chancellor of the Exchequer and, as Lord Jenkins of Hillhead, Chancellor of Oxford University; Peter Benenson, the founder of Amnesty International; Donald Michie, a classics scholar from Balliol College, Oxford, whose wartime experience turned him into an expert on computers and led him to become professor of machine intelligence at Edinburgh University.

Peter Hilton, later a distinguished professor of mathematics at the State University of New York but brought into Bletchley Park as a twenty-one-year-old student, was one of those working in the Testery.

> I was recruited by a team looking for a mathematician with a knowledge of German. I wasn't a mathematician at the time. I was in my fourth year at Oxford. My knowledge of German was what I had taught myself in one year so I wasn't what they were looking for at all

really. But I was the only person who turned up at the interview and they jumped at me and said: 'Yes, you must come.' So I had no right really in a sense to have this job. But I loved it. There is this enormous excitement in codebreaking, that what appears to be utter gibberish really makes sense if only you have the key and I could do that sort of thing for thirty hours at a stretch and never feel tired.

Sometimes the German operator made the mistake of encyphering two successive messages using the same wheel setting. When he did this, we could combine the two encyphered texts and what we got was a combination of the two German messages. So you had one length of gibberish which was, in a certain sense, the sum of two pieces of German text. So you were tearing this thing apart to make the two pieces of text. And it's absolutely a marvellous process because you would guess some word, I remember once I guessed the word *Abwehr*. So that means you have a space and then *Abwehr*, eight symbols of one of the two messages.

By subtracting the Baudot elements for those letters from the characters in the combined text, Hilton would then be left with eight letters from the other message.

The eight letters of the other message would have a space in the middle followed by *Flug*. So then you would guess: 'Well that's going to be *Flugzeug* – aircraft. So you get *zeug* followed by a space and that gives you five more letters of the other message. So you keep extending and going backwards as well. You break in different places and try to join up but then you're not sure if top goes with top, or top goes with bottom.

Then of course when you've got two messages like that, as a codebreaker, you have to take the encyphered message and the original text and add them together to get the key and then you have the wheel patterns. But for me the real excitement was this business of getting these two texts out of one sequence of gibberish. It was marvellous. I never met anything that was quite as exciting, especially since you knew that these were vital messages.

One of the most common methods of getting into the Tunny transmissions by hand came when a message broke down mid-stream and the operators were forced to start again. This became known to the codebreakers as 'a go-back' and was the most common method of acquiring 'a depth', said Ken Halton.

Where it was likely to happen was if the message got halfway through and then went all awry. The Germans used to say: 'It's swallowed its teeth. Stop the message and start again.' Now what they were supposed to do was to agree on some starting position for all their twelve wheels on the machine. But very often they were lazy and they wouldn't bother to do that. They would say to one another: 'We'll just go back and reset.'

So they wouldn't start the message from the beginning but they would start the code wheels from the beginning so you would get the first half of the message with a certain key added and you would get the second half of the message with the same key added and if the intercept operators realised that was happening they would note this down and the codebreakers would add the bit after the interruption to the bit before it and see if it came out in depth, if it exhibited the language characteristics that showed it was two pieces of plain text added together.

Throughout 1942, the work on the Tunny material had to be done by hand and, although some useful material was gained on the German campaign against Russia and from the links between Italy and north Africa, many of the messages took several weeks to decypher.

Max Newman, one of the mathematicians working in the Testery, became convinced that, using the principles advocated by Turing in his pre-war treatise on a computing machine, it would be possible to build a machine that, once the patterns of the wheels had been worked out in the Testery, would find the settings of the first row of wheels, thereby making the codebreakers' task immeasurably easier.

Newman, an academic from Manchester University, took his ideas to Travis and received the necessary backing and promise of funding to set up his own section, which became known as the Newmanry. He then went to Wynn-Williams at the Telecommunications Research Establishment in Malvern and asked him to design the machine.

It was known as 'Robinson', after Heath Robinson, the cartoonist designer of fantastic machines, and the first version was delivered to Bletchley Park in May 1943. It worked on the principle that although the encyphering letters were supposed to be random, they were not. No machine can generate a truly random sequence of letters. Robinson compared a piece of teleprinter tape carrying the encyphered text with a piece of tape on which the wheel patterns had been punched to look for statistical evidence that would indicate what the wheel-settings were.

But while Robinson could clearly do its job, there were problems, Travis told the weekly meeting of senior staff. 'Although Mr Newman's new research machinery is still going through teething troubles, it is likely to prove better than anything they have yet produced in the USA. The only snag is that it needs a lot of personnel. It should be able to handle twenty-eight to thirty Tunny messages a day which would be invaluable.'

Robinson was designed to keep the two paper tapes in synchronisation at a thousand characters a second but at that speed the sprocket wheels kept ripping the tapes. Turing who, while working on the bombe, had been impressed by the abilities of a bright young telephone engineer at Dollis Hill called Tommy Flowers, suggested to Newman that he might be just the man to get Robinson to work.

'I came into the project when the Robinson machine didn't work properly, because it was made almost entirely of telephone parts, telephone switching parts, which was my area,' Flowers said. 'I was brought in to make it work, but I very soon came to the conclusion that it would never work. It was dependent on paper tape being driven at very high speed by means of spiked wheels and the paper wouldn't stand up to it.'

Tester recalled long conversations with Flowers, Turing, Tutte and Newman over what should be done. Flowers, who had been developing telephone exchanges containing valves instead of the old-fashioned relays used in Robinson, suggested that he could make an electronic machine built with valves that would do the same job much faster without the need for the synchronisation of the two tapes. The data on the wheel patterns would be generated electronically using ring circuits while the tape reading the cypher text would be read photo-electrically and could be run on smooth wheels rather than sprockets so it wouldn't rip.

Flowers said the codebreakers were highly sceptical of his suggestion.

They wouldn't believe it. They were quite convinced that valves were very unreliable. This was based on their experience of radio equipment which was carted around, dumped around, switched on and off, and generally mishandled. But I'd introduced valves into telephone equipment in large numbers before the war and I knew that if you never moved them and never switched them off they would go on forever.

They asked me how long it would take to produce the first machine. I said at least a year and they said that was terrible. They thought in a year the war could be over and Hitler could have won it so they didn't take up my idea. They decided they would proceed hopefully with the Robinson, which is what they did, and they left the question of whether the valve-based machine would be constructed or not to me.

I was so convinced that Robinson would never work that we developed the new machine on our own at Dollis Hill. We made the first prototype in ten months, working day and night, six-and-a-half days a week, twelve hours a day sometimes. We started with the design of what was to be called Colossus in February 1943 and we had the first prototype machine working at Bletchley Park on 8 December.

The purpose of the Colossus was to find out what the positions of the code wheels were at the beginning of the message and it did that by trying all the possible combinations and there were billions of them. It tried all the combinations, which processing at 5000 characters a second could be done in about half an hour. So then having found the starting positions of the cypher wheels you could decode the message.

When we'd made it for them and they saw it work, they were really astounded. It had about 1500 valves in it, which horrified Bletchley Park. But one of the disadvantages of Robinson was that it didn't always give you the right answer. The answer that they got from the machine was in numbers, a counter counted the number of times that certain letters appeared and the counter was a bit unreliable so they didn't always get the same count.

What they did with Colossus, the first day they got it, was to put a problem on it to which they knew the answer. It took about half an hour to do the run. They let it run for about four hours, repeating the processes every half hour, and to their amazement, it gave the same answer every time. They really were amazed. It was that reliable, extremely reliable.

Colossus was the first practical application of a large-scale program-controlled computer and as such the forerunner of the post-war digital computer. Although it had a specialised function, it showed that Turing's theory could be turned into practice. The sequence of operations was determined mainly by setting of external switches and plugboards, which were controlled by Wrens on the orders of the Newmanry codebreakers. Just like the Robinson, it was looking for sequences that were not random. 'The work on Tunny divided roughly between what you might call the machine work and the hand work,' Halton recalled. ' Machine work was of course putting messages on to Colossus which was a process whereby we would determine the starting positions of the first set of five wheels which were involved in making up the key. Then after that process had taken place, that is to say a process based on statistics, mathematics, the message shorn of part of its key would come to the codebreakers in the Testery who would then have the job of using their knowledge of expected pieces of text in order to set the remaining wheels.'

George Vergine was an American codebreaker posted into the Newmanry in December 1943, shortly after Colossus had been installed.

> When I arrived, the first Colossus was in a new area that they had acquired for expansion and I think two of the Robinsons, the previous diagnostic machines, were operating. There must have been probably fifteen mathematically minded analysts. There were probably ten Wrens on a shift, processing the tapes. There was a lot of background of mathematics and techniques to catch up on.
>
> Colossus was the epitome of an adult toy. For the mathematicians it was marvellous. It would tabulate five thousand frames of teleprinter tape a second so if you did a run for ten minutes you were probably getting close to three million tallies. It was fascinating really. You didn't see plain text, the Testery was the one that recovered the plain text. You were dealing entirely in a statistical world.
>
> You would toss out the random scores and look for anything that looked like it was causal. The operator had to make a decision when he got the final scores, on the spot. You made that decision right there, in your head, sitting on a stool in front of Colossus. You depended entirely on the probability of being right as far as the random scores were concerned. If you got a causal score you would try to confirm it one way or the other on some of the other wheels, or by another run.

Each codebreaker was assisted by two Wrens who set the machine up. Jean Thompson was just nineteen when she was posted to Bletchley in 1944 to work on Colossus.

> Most of the time I was doing wheel setting, getting the starting positions of the wheels. There would be two Wrens on the machine and a duty officer, one of the cryptanalysts – the brains people, and the message came in on a teleprinted tape.
>
> If the pattern of the wheels was already known you put that up at the back of the machine on a pinboard. The pins were bronze, brass or copper with two feet and there were double holes the whole way down the board for cross or dot impulses to put up the wheel pattern. Then you

put the tape on round the wheels with a join in it so it formed a complete circle. You put it behind the gate of the photo-electric cell which you shut on it and, according to the length of the tape, you used so many wheels and there was one moveable one so that could get it taut.

At the front there were switches and plugs. After you'd set the thing you could do a letter count with the switches. You would make the runs for the different wheels to get the scores out which would print out on the electromatic typewriter. We were looking for a score above the random and one that was sufficiently good, you'd hope was the correct setting. When it got tricky, the duty officer would suggest different runs to do.

Another of the Wrens working in the Newmanry was Odette Murray.

I was offered the chance of joining what was known as Pembroke V, not knowing what it was all about. A group of us turned up at Bletchley Park where we were taught to be touch typists, still not knowing what it was all about, and eventually I got into the Park itself in the Newmanry. I was head of a watch and I was given instructions by whoever was in charge at the time and, still not having the remotest idea what I was doing, I worked with a slide rule producing a lot of figures and gave the result to the next person who gave it to the next person and eventually it was run on a tape.

One of the duty officers was Shaun Wylie, who had been transferred over from Hut 8 shortly after Odette Murray arrived at Bletchley.

All the Wrens were swooning about Shaun Wylie. They thought he was absolutely wonderful: 'Oh, Mr Wylie this, oh Mr Wylie that.' I didn't think much of him. I couldn't see what they saw in him. However, he thought something of me.

He tried to explain to me exactly what my contribution had been in a successful thing. I just didn't understand. I'm not a mathematician, I'm not a linguist. I'm just somebody who's given instructions and does little funny calculations with a slide rule and bingo. A few days later a smiling Shaun comes in. I don't know what my contribution is but OK, it must be satisfactory.

She was billeted in Woburn Abbey and on their days off, Wylie would cycle over there to visit her.

Most of our courting was in Woburn Park. The Abbey is a huge imposing building and the central part has a large podium on top of it, very high up, and I used to go casual climbing, leaping across two-foot, three-foot chasms so that I could sit on the top of this to watch Shaun on his bicycle coming up the drive. No way would I go up there now.

Fortunately Wylie was a civilian so their decision to get married did not cause as many problems as it might have done. 'If he had been a naval officer we would have been separated at once,' Odette said. 'That would not have been allowed, but a civilian and a Wren, that was all right.' Nevertheless, the Wren administrative officers were unhappy and did try, albeit unsuccessfully, to separate them, Shaun Wylie recalled. 'They tried to get me turned out of the Newmanry because she was in there too but that didn't work so we just worked on different shifts, it was a bit awkward.'

Nevertheless the atmosphere in the Newmanry was very happy, largely because of Newman's influence, Vergine recalled.

Max Newman was a marvellous fellow I always sort of felt grateful to have known him really. We used to have tea parties. These were just discussions on problems or developments, techniques, to a great extent mathematical. We used to meet in the small conference room. Somebody would write a topic up on the blackboard and all of the analysts, including Newman, would come with their tea in hand and chew it around and see whether or not it would be useful as far as cracking more communications. They were very productive and after it was over somebody would summarise it in the research log.

Peter Hilton believed that Newman was the perfect example of a great facilitator.

He realised that he could get the best out of us by trusting to our own good intentions and our strong motivation and he made the thing always as informal as possible. For example, he gave us one week in four off. We would be just encouraged to do research on our cryptanalytical methods. Of course, the research work should always be related to the job and we always wrote down what we were thinking in a huge book so that it could be preserved and some of those ideas were adopted and became part of the procedure. So I think Newman was the model of an academic administrator.

Once the encyphered messages had been stripped of the effect of the first set of wheels, the part decyphered message was passed to the Testery where the cryptanalysts worked out the setting of the second row of wheels, said Ken Halton.

They worked this out by hand. All this depended on language characteristics and a very great deal of it depended on the fact that the second row of cypher wheels kept standing still. They weren't driven every step like the first row of wheels were. So there were times when the second row of wheels just stayed stationary for three, four or five characters and the codebreakers were adept at spotting these groups of characters.

The work in the Testery was much more like that in Huts 6 and 8 where the Enigma material was decyphered. The human brain had to take over from the machine. Roy Jenkins described the work:

We had to operate on a semi-intuitive basis and sometimes your intuition worked and sometimes it didn't. It was a curious life. It could be very wearing, particularly if it didn't succeed. You could spend nights in which you got nowhere at all. You didn't get a single break, you just tried, played around through this bleak long night with total frustration and your brain was literally raw. I remember one night when I made thirteen breaks. But there were an awful lot of nights when I was lucky if I made one. So it was exhausting.

The codebreakers looked for differences between the Baudot elements for regular sequences of letters which occur commonly in German, or characters that denoted a common sequence of teleprinter instructions. One of the Testery codebreakers was Alan Rodgers.

With most codebreaking, it is done on the frequency of the letters. But with Fish it is done on the differences between the letters that come up regularly together in German, like 'sch'. It was Ralph Tester who had the mammoth task of working out all those differences and how often they would come up. Some of the messages were thousands of letters long and you can build up a statistic over that length much easier than you can over a short message.

One of the methods used in the Testery to get into the Tunny transmissions originated from the tests conducted by the German operators before sending the message, Peter Hilton recalled.

We were fortunate that the Germans seemed to have been so convinced that we couldn't possibly be reading Tunny that they didn't take the precautions they should have done.

At the beginning of each message, the German operator would

transmit by hand some little piece of text of his own in order that the other operator would be able to report: 'I am receiving you clearly'. He could then switch over from hand transmission to automatic and put through the tape of the real message. Some of the German operators began to reveal their own personalities by referring to their own conditions and circumstances.

I remember one message which the operator began: '*Mörderische Hitze*' – murderous heat. Well once I'd broken the first few letters to guess he was talking about *mörderische* and it was quite likely, because that's a sort of natural expression of an ordinary German when something is terribly bad. What could be bad? He was writing from southern Italy, so it was very likely it would not be the food. It was probably the heat.

So you got to know people. There was another one I remember from outside Leningrad who said: '*Ich bin so einsam*' – I'm so lonely. The next day came a message that said: '*Hier ist so traurig*' – It's so sad here, and this fellow, I had the feeling that he didn't want to be there. He didn't want to be fighting the Russians. He didn't want to be besieging Leningrad, but he had to do it.

The officers drafting the messages made equally stupid mistakes, repeating predictable, and often completely useless, phrases, Hilton said.

I remember '*Nieder mit den Englander*', down with the English, as a phrase that certainly appeared very commonly in these messages and of course '*Heil Hitler*' was enormously valuable. You should never inculcate in your military the tendency to have exactly the same phrase opening every statement.

Once the settings of both rows of wheels had been worked out, the tape of the encyphered message was taken into the Tunny Room where there were a number of Tunny machines that had been built at Dollis Hill to replicate the action of the Lorenz cypher machine, said Ken Halton. 'They then ran it through a Tunny machine that was set up in exactly the same way as the German cypher machine was set up and the clear German tape came out.'

The Tunny machine was sometimes used in the codebreaking process as well, Halton recalled.

It was very versatile and you could set it so it only used one of the two rows of wheels. That meant that the codebreakers who were doing most of their work by hand used to often come into the Tunny Room and sit down at a Tunny machine and use it for typing in little bits of text that they had got with various wheel settings to try and get an edge to break into the message. So it was a very versatile machine that helped with codebreaking but was principally for doing the final decyphering.

Since they were Army messages, they were then passed to the Hut 3 intelligence reporters. The first really important reports to result from the decyphered Tunny messages covered the Eastern Front. They came between April and July 1943 when the complete German plans for the forthcoming Battle of Kursk were sent on the link between the headquarters of the German Army Group South and Berlin. A sanitised version, disguising the source, was passed to Moscow but this assistance was unnecessary. Stalin was already receiving full transcripts. For despite the strict security in force at Bletchley Park, a member of one of the watches in Hut 3 was a KGB spy.

John Cairncross, codenamed 'Liszt' by the Russians because of his love of music, had already given Moscow Centre details of Bletchley Park's network of intercept sites, while working in the section of the Treasury that dealt with the GPO in the months before the war. He had then become private secretary to Lord Hankey, minister without portfolio, and passed the Russians details of the Anglo-American atomic weapons project, providing them with the information that formed the basis for their own atomic weapons programme.

But at the beginning of 1942, Cairncross was called up and was instructed to try to get himself into Bletchley Park, which the KGB codenamed *Kurort*. Moscow Centre was aware from one of its other agents that Colonel F. W. Nicholls, the head of MI8, was looking for new codebreakers, and told Cairncross to seek him out. 'In the course of his professional duties, Liszt became acquainted with Nicholls and by rendering small services established friendly relations with him,' Cairncross's KGB handler told the Centre.

> During lunch at the Travellers Club, Liszt complained to Nicholls that he was about to be called up by the Army where he would be unable to use his knowledge of foreign languages. Nicholls started to persuade him to come to work in *Kurort*. After he received his call-up papers, Liszt told Nicholls about this, remained in his unit for one day and was then put at the disposal of the War Office which conditionally demobilised him and seconded him to *Kurort*.

Cairncross smuggled decrypts that were due to be destroyed out of Hut 3 in his trousers, transferring them to his bag at the railway station before going on to London to meet his KGB contact. The information that he handed the Russians is probably rightly credited with helping them to win the Battle of Kursk, the turning point on the Eastern Front. Despite the fact that a sanitised version of the Tunny messages was being passed to Moscow, Stalin was highly suspicious of any intelligence passed to him by the Allies, particularly if the source was unclear. But Cairncross was supplying the German language signals and it was coming via the KGB. 'The Russians were convinced,' Cairncross said, 'that in its German version the Ultra I supplied was genuine, giving the full details of German units and locations, thus enabling the Russians to pinpoint their targets and to take the enemy by surprise.'

Shortly after passing the Russians the information that helped them to win the Battle of Kursk, Cairncross was transferred to MI6 from where he continued to receive, and pass to the Russians, Bletchley Park decrypts in the form of the ISOS traffic that was being used for the Double Cross system. It is impossible to tell how vital his contribution to the Battle of Kursk was. But the Russians' codes were being decyphered by the Germans and their brief liaison with Hitler had left them riddled with Nazi agents. His breaching of the Ultra secret risked informing the Germans that their most secret cypher systems had been broken.

Chapter 11

THE INVASION OF EUROPE

The Germans had been concerned for some time that their cypher equipment might be broken. As early as April 1943, the German Army's cryptography bureau had warned: 'The enemy has excellent decoding personnel, and all auxiliary equipment. We know that messages have been decoded in two hours, so it is extremely difficult to create an encyphering procedure which is uncomplicated but safe.' Nevertheless, they believed that the addition of the plugboard to the Enigma machine had ensured that in practice it was secure. They also thought that the irregular movement of the second row of wheels on the Lorenz encyphered teleprinter machine had made it more safe rather than, as was in fact the case, easier to break.

Even so, in February 1944, the Lorenz machine was further modified in an attempt to prevent the British from decyphering it. With the invasion of Europe known to be imminent, it was a crucial period for the codebreakers but Colossus ensured that Bletchley Park was able to break the main link between Berlin and Field Marshal Gerd von Rundstedt, the Commander-in-Chief of German forces in the west.

The intelligence obtained from the traffic passing on this link, known as 'Jellyfish' to the codebreakers, was vital in the run-up to D-Day, keeping the Allies informed of German preparations to meet the coming invasion. It included the complete order of battle of the *Panzerarmee* drawn from the detailed itinerary of a tour of inspection by its commander, General Heinz Guderian.

It also updated the Allied assessment of the German military defences. This was already fairly good, based on traffic analysis, photo-reconnaissance and agent reports as well as a detailed description by General Hiroshi Oshima, the Japanese ambassador in Berlin, of a tour he made of the German defences in October 1943. The Magic decrypts emanating from the Japanese Embassy in Berlin were extremely important in keeping the Allies up to date on the German defensive preparations.

Among his many achievements, Tiltman had helped to crack the cypher used by the Japanese naval attaché in Berlin, assisted by the latter's tendency to begin each of his reports with the phrase: 'I have the honour to report to your excellency that . . .' In early May, the attaché reported back to Tokyo on a tour he had made of the German defences in northern France. Rommel, who had been appointed to lead the main force resisting an invasion, intended 'to destroy Allies near the coast, most of all on the beaches, without allowing penetration inland,' the attaché said. 'As defence against airborne operations he plans to cut communications between seaborne and airborne troops and to destroy them individually.'

The report gave detailed appraisals of the German dispositions and intentions and, worryingly for the Allies, said Normandy was regarded as a prime target for the Allies and was being reinforced. This trend was confirmed by a report from Oshima of a meeting with Hitler at which the Führer had told him that the British were expected to establish an initial bridgehead in Normandy before launching a second front against the Pas de Calais.

It was this information that enabled the British to use the Double Cross agents to refine 'Fortitude', the D-Day deception operation, to weaken the defences in Normandy by reinforcing Hitler's suspicions of a second front. The Double Cross agents built up the impression that the Normandy landings would be a feint. The real assault was to be mounted on the Pas de Calais by the First US Army Group, a completely fictitious organisation created with false reports from the double agents, dummy invasion craft planted in east coast ports and mobile wireless vehicles travelling around south-east England broadcasting messages from a number of different locations to fool the German radio interception units.

The number of staff at Bletchley Park had been dramatically increased in anticipation of the Allied invasion of Europe, reaching a total of seven thousand by June 1944, Bill Bundy recalled.

We were told the entire available output from the Scottish universities came to Bletchley Park. These were fine stalwart ladies for the most part, wearing tweeds and the flat shoes that we in Boston called butter-spreaders. They were vigorous and very, very good at their jobs. They also had a great sensitivity to temperature in the huts. This was not kept exactly torrid at any time. But when the Scottish ladies got there, if the temperature crawled above 60, you would hear this anguished cry: 'Stuffy in here,' and the windows would be flung open to let some fresh air in.

Morag Maclennan had by now been transferred out of the bombe section into Hut 4, the Naval Section, where in the run-up to D-Day, there was a minor security scare.

The girl who was most closely concerned with the Normandy beach landings went up to the Admiralty and was fully briefed. 'Bigoted' was the name for anybody who was let into the great secret in the weeks leading up to D-Day. She was bigoted and immensely pleased with herself. We had this enormous map all the way down one wall of the coast of Holland, right down to the south of France, and she carefully underlined the beaches that they were going to land on. We were horrified at this and went along underlining every beach we could see from Holland down to the south of France because the cleaners would come in and might notice.

Tommy Flowers and his team at Dollis Hill had meanwhile been working on a Mark II Colossus which had 2500 valves rather than the 1500 of the Mark I version and could process the tapes five times as fast. 'We were told if we couldn't make the machine work by June 1st it would be too late to be of use,' Flowers recalled. 'So we assumed that that was going to be D-Day, which was supposed to be a secret, so we worked to June 1st and we just made it.'

The decyphering girls in the Big Room of Hut 8 went on night shift just before midnight on 4 June 1944, unaware that the Allied invasion was about to be launched, said Pat Wright.

They told us that D-Day was today and they wanted every possible message decoded as fast as possible. But then it was postponed because the weather was so bad and that meant we girls knew it was going to take place, so we had to stay there until D-Day. We slept where we could and worked when we could and of course then they set off on June 6, and that was D-Day.

Although the heads of the main sections were all bigoted and most people at Bletchley Park knew that the invasion of Europe was imminent, even fairly senior staff were not told when it was to come. Bill Bundy was on the nightshift on June 5.

There was no point speculating when the balloon was going to go up.

So you didn't give day-to-day thought to it really and it just so happened that the evening of June 5, there was a long-scheduled party. I'm sure there was a moment's thought given on high as to whether this ought to be kept and the instantaneous decision was that to cancel it would be far too much of a signal. So it went ahead and I remember we had a very pleasant group and drank martinis in which the role of vermouth was played by sherry and one had a really very nice time.

Anyway, at midnight those of us who were on the night shift reported to our sections to work, and there waiting in the outer room just outside the watch was the head of Hut 6, Stuart Milner-Barry. He had been at the party and he was just sort of standing there on one leg watching the whole proceeding and one said: 'Why is Stuart doing this at this hour?' So we went to work and suddenly about 3 o'clock there was a real rustle in the room that got the traffic first and it was patent that something was happening on a big scale.

Very shortly the word spread that there had been German traffic in clear, saying that paratroopers were dropping all over the place and it happened to be nearer Calais than Normandy so I'm sure it was one of the deception operations. We later learned that they were not paratroopers, they were bunches of straw, something that would show up on the radar in the same way.

But the most important element of the Fortitude deception operation was that played by the Double Cross agents, and in particular Juan Pujol Garcia, codenamed 'Garbo', who ran a completely notional network of agents throughout Britain. He reported that the Allied forces were on their way before they hit the beaches but too late for the Germans to do anything about it. This helped to persuade them that his intelligence was accurate and paved the way for the next stage of the deception.

A few days later, as the Allied advance faltered and with the elite 1st SS *Panzerdivision* on its way, together with another armoured division, to reinforce the German defences in Normandy, Garbo reported troops massed across East Anglia and Kent as well as large numbers of troop and tank transporters waiting in the eastern English ports.

From the reports mentioned, it is perfectly clear that the present attack is a large-scale attack but diversionary in character to draw the maximum of our reserves so as to be able to strike a blow somewhere else with ensured success. The constant aerial bombardment which the area of the Pas de Calais has suffered and the strategic disposition of these forces give reason to suspect an attack in that region of France which at the same time offers the shortest route for the final objective of their illusions – Berlin.

Garbo's warning went straight to Hitler who ordered the two divisions back to the Pas de Calais to defend against what he expected to be the main invasion thrust. The Allied commanders were able to follow this order on the Fish and Enigma decrypts knowing that if the two divisions had continued to Normandy, the Allies might well have been repulsed.

Don Bussey was one of Telford Taylor's Special Branch intelligence officers.

Ultra made a tremendous contribution to the success of the deception planning for the Normandy landing because we were able to follow through Ultra not only what the German forces were doing but also that Fortitude was working so well. The Germans still believed well into July that Patton had an army in south-eastern England that was going to come across to Pas de Calais so they couldn't send reinforcements to Normandy. This is a very important aspect of how Ultra contributed to strategic consideration. That's big stuff and not to be minimised.

Amid concern at the damage the U-boats might inflict on the invasion forces, Frank Birch had arranged for a number of Royal Navy radio intercept positions to be set up in Bletchley Park. All signals indicating danger to the invasion force were dispatched from the Hut 4 Z Watch on what was known as a 'Rush' basis and the OIC was normally able to pass them on to the naval escorts within thirty minutes of the Germans sending them. Birch's initiative was the first and only time that any messages were actually intercepted at Bletchley Park, said Harry Hinsley.

This step was taken with some hesitation in view of the risk associated in having GC&CS associated with masts and aerials. But it was fully justified by the exceptional speed with which the naval Enigma was decrypted during the crucial days in which the assault forces were crossing the Channel and getting ashore. We were able to watch the expedition going across as well as getting the first German response. We quickly realised they weren't expecting an invasion and as soon as the assault waves were ashore we started reading all the emergency messages from the German Navy and sending them straight on to the invasion force leaders in their command ships off the beaches.

In Hut 3, Eric Jones told his staff that one signal alone had already allowed the Allied planners to move a dropping zone away from German troop concentrations, saving an airborne division of 15,000 men.

> At this moment, in far the biggest combined operation in history, the first of the airborne troops are down. Sailors and airmen are facing frightful dangers to transport the first ground troops across the Channel and protect them on their way; more sailors and airmen are daring everything to blast holes in the German defences; and the ground troops themselves, in their thousands, will soon be literally throwing away their lives in the main assault by deliberately drawing enemy fire so that others may gain a foothold; and we are in complete, or almost complete, safety; some of us are even enjoying something akin to peace-time comfort.
>
> It's a thought we cannot avoid and it's a thought that inevitably aggravates an ever-present urge to be doing something more active; to be nearer the battle, sharing at least some of its discomforts and dangers. Such feelings cannot be obliterated but they can be subjugated to a grim resolve to serve those men to the very utmost of our capacity. There is no back-stage organisation (and I think of Hut 3, Hut 6, Sixta and the Fish Party as an indissoluble whole) that has done more for past Allied operations and Allied plans for this assault; and none that can contribute more to the development of the invasion once the bloody battles for the beaches have been won.

Within forty-eight hours of the initial landings, the first of the twenty-eight British and American Special Liaison Units set up to pass the Ultra intelligence on to the Allied commanders were reporting that their positions were secure and they were on the air. Don Bussey was a member of one of the SLUs.

> Shortly after the Normandy landings, I was assigned to the European theatre to be one of the field representatives handling the Ultra information with the US military command, both Air Force and Army. All US commands had these Ultra representatives who would ensure the security of this information and that it was handled in the proper way. I had a special communications unit manned by British officers, both Army and RAF, that supported me, and they were the ones who would receive the messages over the air from Bletchley Park.
>
> It's very important to realise that day in, day out, the most important thing that Ultra had to tell us was the complete German order of battle.

We would know their divisions by number. We would know where they were. We would know their subordinations by corps and Army and by Army group. We'd know the boundaries between division and between other units, and all this gave us the kind of information which is absolutely indispensable. I would process all this information and pass it on to the people at headquarters who were authorised to receive it.

The mobile Y Service units were already producing large amounts of information about the German reaction. In conjunction with Bletchley Park, they produced the position of one of the most important German headquarters, allowing the British to mount a series of air strikes that put paid to a counterattack which would have driven a gap between the American and British armies, said Ralph Bennett, one of the Hut 3 intelligence reporters.

One of the very first things that was noticeable was that there was a radio station very busy indeed in Normandy, near the front. Now Y Service could locate this place exactly and could monitor the number of signals coming in and out, it was obviously a very important headquarters. But on 10 June, Enigma revealed that it was the headquarters of *Panzergruppe West*, the headquarters of all the tanks in the invasion area. Monty knocked it out for three weeks and lots of the senior staff officers were killed.

There were gaps in the information provided by Ultra. The codebreakers had been unable to provide a precise location for 32nd *Panzerdivision* which was defending the vital British objective of Caen and held up Montgomery's advance for more than a month. They had also missed the presence of a German infantry division defending Omaha Beach. But these were the only blank spaces in an otherwise complete and detailed picture of the German order of battle, said Bill Williams, Montgomery's intelligence officer.

Few armies ever went to battle better informed of their enemy. Ultra played a positive part in the formulation of the plan of invasion in that late reports of changed enemy dispositions in the Cotentin peninsula enabled us to re-allot the dropping zones of the American airborne troops: one of the most contributive elements in the overall scheme.

Intelligence officers at BP were briefed before D-Day and thereafter we made it our business in Normandy to send a daily Intelligence Summary from 21st Army Group saying what we thought was happening in front of us and in general attempting in a friendly and unofficial fashion to keep the Park aware of what we were trying to do.

The whole series of signals was conversational. One felt one was talking to friends and from that feeling of gratitude, which we hoped was reflected in the casually worded terms sent to the Park, emerged at least from the point of view of one consumer, a belief that because of them he was getting a better service. The people at the other end knew what he wanted and there seemed to be no hesitation in the answer.

Although the *Luftwaffe* Enigma remained a constant source of intelligence, there was still very little Army Enigma and von Rundstedt's Fish link to Berlin had become temporarily unreadable, said Art Levenson.

Until D-Day, they changed the wheel patterns once a month. So once you had them recovered, you were in. But after we invaded, they changed the patterns every day, so the job became much more difficult. We went to the boss Edward Travis and said: 'We need four more Colossi because they're changing the patterns too often.' He went to Churchill who said: 'Anything they want.' So we got the four new Colossi and they were absolutely necessary. We used them to recover the links, which we never would have done without them.

On 20 July, a group of senior German Army officers, among them Colonel Claus von Stauffenberg, attempted to assassinate Hitler. Von Stauffenberg took a bomb, hidden in a briefcase, to a staff conference at the Rastenberg Führer HQ and placed it under the conference table. As soon as he heard the explosion, and unaware that Hitler had escaped serious injury, he left for Berlin to tell the generals planning the military takeover that the Führer was dead.

Alec Dakin was on duty in the Hut 4 Z Watch when the premature message announcing the military takeover came through.

I looked at this tray and it didn't seem to have anything in it and when I looked closely there was this message, one of the most exciting messages ever. It said: 'Naval Headquarters to all. Operation Valkyrie. Officer only. Setting D. The Führer Adolf Hitler is dead. The new Führer is Field Marshal von Witzleben.' That was the day of the July Plot and von Stauffenberg was quite sure he was killed so he sent this signal.

By 11 o'clock that night, the attempted military coup was over and von Stauffenberg and a number of other senior officers were already dead.

As the Allied forces poured into Normandy, they had been held back by heavy German resistance, orchestrated by Field Marshal Günther von Kluge. But at the beginning of August, the American

12th Army Group under General Omar Bradley swept south through Avranches, turning west into Brittany and eastwards behind the German tanks.

'I remember after the invasion there was a long period of time when Montgomery's forces and the US forces under General Bradley were being built up,' said Selmer Norland, one of the Americans working in Hut 3.

> Units were being ferried across the Channel and, after they captured the initial bridgeheads, they were sort of pinned down for quite a long period of time while this build-up was taking place. And I remember a particular night when I was working on a message and some German unit reported that the American tank spearheads were in the outskirts of Rennes. I told the Army adviser who was on duty at the time and we dashed for a map to find out where Rennes was. We were astonished to find that it was almost all the way across the Brittany peninsula.

Convinced of his own infallibility as a military strategist, Hitler now decided that von Kluge should force his way through to the western Normandy coast at Avranches, cutting the American thrust in half.

> We must strike like lightning. When we reach the sea the American spearheads will be cut off. We might even be able to cut off their entire beachhead. We must not get bogged down in cutting off the Americans who have broken through. Their turn will come later. We must wheel north like lightning and turn the entire enemy front from the rear.

There was a certain element of reason in the idea but with more than a million Allied troops now firmly established in Normandy, von Kluge had little hope of carrying it out and, far worse, with Montgomery's 21st Army Group pressing down on him from the north and the Americans sweeping westwards along his southern flank, he risked becoming trapped in an Allied pincer movement.

The Allies, fully informed by Bletchley Park of the German plans, ensured that the initiative failed. As von Kluge's counter-attack faltered with its only route of retreat through a small gap south of the town of Falaise, Hitler insisted that it should be carried through to the bitter end. 'On its success depends the fate of the Battle of France,' the Führer said in a message sent in the early hours of 10 August and decyphered in Hut 6 almost immediately. 'Objective of the attack, the sea at Avranches, to which a bold and unhesitating thrust through is to be made.'

John Prestwich was on duty in Hut 3 when Hitler's orders came through the hatch from Hut 6.

> I remember it. My goodness I remember it. I remember we queried it at the time. We said: 'It cannot be true.' It seemed to us inconceivable. But what made sense was that the Americans had broken out of their base in the Cotentin peninsula and the Germans had made what was a perfectly sensible limited spoiling attack on the American lines of communication. Then there came through this detailed order that four or five German armoured divisions were to go hell for leather for Avranches and this opened up the whole possibility of wiping out the cream of the German armed forces. All you had to do was to close the Falaise Gap and there was this great pocket. But it was an order from Hitler. The German generals might have thought it was lunatic, and Rommel clearly did on at least one occasion, but they obeyed on the spot because they were under oath.

Within a few days, it was clear that von Kluge had no hope of carrying out Hitler's orders and, fearing that at any moment the Allies would surround his forces, he ordered the withdrawal. Susan Wenham was one of the codebreakers on duty in Hut 6 on 16 August when von Kluge's orders came through.

> It was the most exciting night I had. The Germans were making plans to make their last terrific push to try to get out of the pincer they were in. I was on the night shift and the day shift had had an enormous message. They came in sections, they weren't allowed to do them more than a certain length. It was a ten-part message and only six of the parts of the message, the *Teile*, came through. They had managed to break those during the day and the message was to say how the Germans were planning to get out of this impasse. Then during the night, a very obvious re-encodement of this came in, all ten of the parts, and we could see by looking at it that it was a word-for-word re-encodement, which was absolutely not allowed. So we let Hut 3 know and we got all the bombes cleared. We worked like mad on this thing during the night and by morning it was all put through and finished. So that was a very exciting night.

Allied timidity allowed 300,000 German soldiers to escape from the Falaise Pocket, but a further 250,000 were either killed or captured. With the Germans now in full retreat, the Allies poured out of Normandy towards the the Belgian and German borders. Paris was liberated on 25 August as Montgomery's 21st Army Group raced towards Belgium, heading for the Ruhr and, with the newspaper headlines trumpeting 'Berlin by Christmas', an unwarranted level of confidence set in.

The intelligence supplied by Bletchley Park had proved invaluable to the Allied generals, giving them a comprehensive picture of their opponents' positions and plans. But now the picture coming out of Hut 3 seemed to contradict that generated by the speed of the breakout from Normandy and the race across northern France.

Montgomery, whose reputation had been built on the back of the codebreakers' advance knowledge of Rommel's plans in North Africa, foolishly ignored their reports that Hitler had ordered his troops to maintain control of the Scheldt estuary in Holland. This prevented the Allies from building up their supplies through Antwerp and caused Montgomery's own troops immense logistical problems.

His arrogant decision to disregard yet more Ultra information was to lead to a major defeat for the British on the banks of the Rhine. Anxious to beat the Americans to Berlin, Montgomery pushed on into Holland to mount Operation Market Garden, a three-stage airborne offensive with landings at Eindhoven, Nijmegen and Arnhem – the infamous 'bridge too far'. Elements retreating from the pocket in August and September filled the air with reports of their movements and stength,' said Ralph Bennett.

> Among much else these showed that II SS *Panzerkorps* was to refit in the general area of Arnhem where Montgomery was planning to make a bridgehead across the lower Rhine. So firmly entrenched however was the conviction that German resistance was nearing its end that this knowledge was not enough to cast doubt on the wisdom of launching Operation Market Garden.

Although the American airborne troops dropped on to Eindhoven and Nijmegen secured their positions and managed to link up with the main advance, the British 1st Airborne Division which was to seize a bridgehead across the Rhine at Arnhem was not so fortunate. It succeeded in capturing the only surviving bridge across the Rhine and held it for several days, expecting reinforcements to arrive at any minute. But surrounded by vastly superior forces, the British paratroopers were eventually forced to withdraw. Only 2200 of the 10,000-strong division managed to get out.

Yet even the mistakes of Antwerp and Arnhem failed to dissuade the Allied generals from their over-optimistic belief that the

Germans were finished and that there was little they could do to slow the advance on Berlin. They continued to ignore the evidence of the Ultra decrypts which now pointed to a major counter-attack being prepared in the Ardennes.

Jim Rose, one of the Hut 3 air advisers, and Alan Pryce-Jones, one of the military advisers, flew to SHAEF headquarters in Paris in November. They briefed General Kenneth Strong, Eisenhower's intelligence officer, on the Ultra decrypts, Rose recalled.

> Strong had a very weak chin. He said: 'This is the way we read it. Right across the front from the North Sea really to Switzerland the Germans are losing a division a day and this can't be maintained. They're bound to crack.' Alan Pryce-Jones was just a major. He had his own form of battledress, he wore suede shoes. He just sort of sat on the corner of the desk and he said to Strong: 'My dear sir, if you believe that you'll believe anything.' Three weeks later was the Ardennes offensive.

The warning signs that the Germans were planning a major counter-attack were not as obvious from Ultra as they had been at other times during the war. Nevertheless, there was no failure of intelligence collection, simply a lack of long-term analysis of German intentions borne out of the belief that the war was virtually over, said Ralph Bennett.

> The high-ups on our side became convinced that the Germans were weakened by their failures and they couldn't do any more. By that time we'd got too damn cocky. I still don't understand and I don't think I shall understand, how it was that sign after sign that they were planning something was ignored. Who knows what it was, we never did know until it happened. They never told us. They were getting very security conscious by then. Time after time, we simply neglected to add two and two together and say well it might make a total of four rather than seventeen and a quarter.

The clearest evidence from the codebreakers came in the Magic decrypts from the Japanese diplomatic representatives in Berlin speaking of 'the coming offensive'. But there was plenty more beside, said Bennett.

> The evidence about what turned out to be the Battle of the Bulge began in September 1944 and went on until 16 December when the attack happened. If anybody had ever thought of putting all the bits of

information together they would surely have come to the conclusion that there was going to be an attack.

We had continual signals recording that the rest of the Panzer divisions were moving across from the Rhineland into Belgium and no one was saying: 'Why are they doing all this? That's very funny it happens to be just the area where Ike and Bradley have put our defences at their thinnest.' Because the Ardennes is very difficult countryside, Bradley had weakened that front, put the least-trained divisions there because it was most unlikely they'd be involved in urgent operations. Damn it, Rommel and 7th Panzer had gone through there in 1940.

Easily the most striking evidence was that the Germans had just brought in the ME262s, the first jet aircraft, and these ME262s, the latest, fastest kind of aircraft were making almost daily aerial reconnaissance of the same area, the area in front of the Ardennes, over and over again every day. No one seems to have thought: 'This is rather a rum thing.' So consequently we were deceived into thinking there was nothing going to happen, and when I say we, I don't mean Hut 3, I mean the British. It never occurred to us to think that something might happen down there.

Hitler intended a massive armoured attack to rip through the Allied forces, splitting them in two before recapturing Antwerp and cutting off their lines of supply. It was a massive gamble. Hitler's attempted reprise of his earlier blitzkriegs was checked by the Americans, first at St Vith, and then, fatally for the Germans, by the US 101st Airborne Division at the Battle of Bastogne. His refusal to shift the weight of the attack to that part of 'the Bulge' in the German lines that was making most forward progress prevented his tanks from overrunning the Allied fuel depots to replenish their supplies and within four weeks the counter-attack had run out of steam.

The Battle of the Bulge was a massive defeat for the Germans, who lost 120,000 men killed, wounded or captured, compared to a little over half that figure for the Americans. But it had held up the Allied advance by around six weeks. 'Hut 3 was asked to do a post-mortem,' said Jim Rose. 'It was done by Peter Calvocoressi and F. L. Lucas. It was an extremely good report and showed the failure of intelligence at SHAEF and at the Air Ministry.'

The Germans had dropped the complications to the Lorenz machine by October 1944, easing the problems faced in the Newmanry and Testery, and in January 1945, as the Allies advanced towards the Rhine, a new intercept station for Fish was set up at Genval, near Brussels. 'This was the only station connected with Knockholt which received any damage from enemy action,' Kenworthy recalled. 'A V1 dropped very close to the building rendering it unserviceable. Very little damage was done to the gear and it was then installed in the wireless transmitter vans. The Brussels station moved up later in the year with the 21st Army Group advance.'

Colossus was constantly updated as new variants were introduced, allowing an early form of computer programming. By the end of the war, there were around ten Colossi actually operational, said Donald Michie, another member of the Newmanry.

> Each one was like a very big wardrobe in size and the place looked almost like an aircraft hangar. At the end it was looking like a scene that you didn't see again until about 1960 with huge mainframes all over the place, the whole thing going flat out around the clock, 24 hours a day, 365 days round the year. A total staff of 300 Wrens, maybe 50 on duty on any particular shift, and a duty officer taking decisions.
>
> Very often when things got really hot in the sense of being on to something which had been resisting, you would work on. So that there would be people who were officially on shift and people who weren't but just couldn't tear themselves away and would catch another transport out of the place and flop in their digs for a few hours and then come back again. It was a very exciting time.

Another machine, the 'Dragon', was built to search for common sequences of characters in order to help the Testery codebreakers to break the second set of wheels, Ken Halton said.

> The job of the Dragon was to pull a dragword along a tape to see if it showed signs of fitting in any particular place on the tape. There were certain characteristics that they could look for which would appear together. So you set up a dragword which was not necessarily a word at all. It might be something like figure shift; figure shift; full stop; space; space; letter shift; letter shift, which was a sequence that you got regularly at the end of a sentence, or a very common sequence of letters or something that was likely to appear in this message. You set up this dragword and compared it position by position all the way along the tape until you got an indication that it was likely to appear at that point in the tape.

The first people to produce a Dragon were the Americans and they sent it across with this American technical sergeant and we installed it and I don't know that we ever got it going properly. It made a lot of noise but it never did very much and while we were still struggling with that they made one at Dollis Hill. We were much more familiar with that because it used British equipment, British relays which we were able to adjust properly. The American version was called Dragon One and the one made at Dollis Hill was called Dragon Two and that worked very well and I can remember the intelligence corps code-breakers coming in to sit at that and look for things and going away with smiles on their faces when they had found what they wanted.

At the end of the war, Dragon Three came in and that had valves in it which speeded up some of the processes. It helped to find the starting positions of the wheel. If you could find where a word fitted in, you could run the Dragon backwards, which was something you couldn't do on a Tunny, back to the beginning of the message and just read off the starting positions of the wheels and that saved us a lot of time. Otherwise you would have to do it by hand.

By now Bletchley Park had little effect on the Allied advance across Germany although its intelligence on the V-bomb launch sites at Peenemünde and the ISOS traffic carrying the reports of the Double Cross agents was invaluable in Operation Crossbow, the effort to counter the last-ditch German bombardment of London.

The double agents were repeatedly being asked for information on where the missiles were falling. The mean point of impact of the V-bombs was in south-east London, four miles short of their target. But by carefully manipulating the times and locations of the blasts reported back by the double agents in conjunction with the times of the launches reported by an RAF Y station sent to the Continent to monitor them, the Double Cross Committee persuaded the Germans that they were overshooting and the range of the V-bombs was short-ened, moving the danger still further out of London.

As the threat from the Germans receded, increasing numbers of people were moved on to Japanese codes and cyphers. They were taught Japanese in an off-shoot of the Inter-Service Special Intelligence School, a detached house in De Parys Avenue, Bedford, before being shipped out, either to the Far East Combined Bureau, which had moved to Colombo following the fall of Singapore and where most of the British work on Japanese cyphers had taken place, or to the Wireless Experimental Centre just outside Delhi in what had been a part of the city's university campus, from where they monitored the Japanese retreat from Burma.

In early 1945, some of the sections within Bletchley Park that had previously concerned themselves primarily with German codes and cyphers had to start dealing with Japanese material. They were not always happy to take on this new role, recalled Phoebe Senyard, head of the the Hut 4 registry.

> The dreaded day came when we had to take over the sorting and distribution of the Japanese raw material. I must say that it was the part I disliked the most. At first I was too busy to tackle the Japanese traffic, owing to the vast amount of German signals which were pouring in, but I was gradually able to cope with it.
>
> At last the day arrived for which we had all worked so long and so patiently, VE Day, 8 May 1945. Strange to say, we took it very quietly and gravely but with a sense of relief. German plain language began to pour in as anticipated and was rushed to the Z Watch. Changes began to take place all round.

Travis issued a Special Order to all the staff at Bletchley Park to mark VE Day.

> On this historic occasion I want to express my personal thanks to all of you for your loyal cooperation in our common effort to defeat the enemy. The general standards of keenness, discipline, personal behaviour and security have been admirable and have combined to produce a direct and substantial contribution towards winning the war. But our work is by no means ended yet. Three main problems face us now: to finish off the Japanese war; to ease the transition from war to peace conditions as much as possible for everyone; to ensure that nothing we do now shall hinder the efforts of our successors.
>
> I cannot stress too strongly the necessity for the maintenance of security. While we were fighting Germany it was vital that the enemy should never know of our activities here. We and our American Allies are still at war with Japan, and we are faced with great responsibilities arising out of the preliminaries to peace in Europe. At some future time we may be called upon again to use the same methods. It is therefore as vital as ever not to relax from the high standard of security that we have hitherto maintained. The temptation now to 'own up' to our friends and families as to what our work has been is a very real and natural one. It must be resisted absolutely.

Chapter 12

The End of Station X

The need to look ahead to 'the next war' with the Soviet Union dominated the Allies' post-war planning. Codebreaking had proved itself during the war and was expected to have just as important a role in peacetime. 'The opportunity for the practice of signal intelligence does exist in peacetime if the means exist to seize it,' wrote one codebreaker. 'In the brave new world, we have got to be prepared to follow trouble around the globe – vultures ready to take wing at the merest indication of corpses.'

As early as September 1944, Menzies had set up a committee 'to study and set out a plan for the post-war organisation of GC&CS'. Travis, Hinsley, Tiltman and Welchman were all heavily involved in the discussions. Their conclusion that the codebreakers needed to be 'closely fused with SIS under the director-general [Menzies] as the one and only intelligence-producing service' flies in the face of suggestions that they resented the fact that the head of MI6 was in overall control of their work.

Welchman identified a need to coordinate the work of GC&CS with the services and the certainty that machine cyphers would become more difficult to break, adding: 'Developments of the last year have convinced me that as yet we are only scratching at this problem.'

In an attempt to find out as much as possible about the German systems, and to prevent them getting into the hands of the Russians, a top secret Anglo-American mission known as TICOM, the Technical Intelligence Committee, was sent into Germany to seek out the latest communications technology. Originally it was to be dropped by parachute into Berlin with the US 101st Airborne Division for protection. But wiser counsels eventually prevailed and a TICOM team, including Ralph Tester, Selmer Norland, Art Levenson, and Major Edward Rushworth, one of the senior officers in the Hut 3 Fusion Room, was sent to the border between Bavaria and Austria, where the Nazis were expected to make their final stand in the Alpine National Redoubt.

Tester went south to the Austrian town of Pfunds, close to the Swiss and Italian borders, where he found a number of Enigma machines and a Lorenz machine that had been used on the teleprinter link between Field Marshal Albrecht Kesselring, the German commander in Italy, and Berlin. It was in perfect working order. A few days later, the team travelled to Hitler's Alpine retreat at Berchtesgaden where more communications equipment was discovered. Tester and Levenson drove it back to England in a convoy of German signals trucks.

The TICOM team had achieved its objective but it was about to receive an unexpected bonus. Rushworth, Norland and the rest of the party drove to the headquarters of a German signals intelligence unit at Rosenheim, thirty miles south-east of Munich, where the captured German codebreakers gave them some startling news. They had hidden a mass of cryptographic machinery which they believed the British and American officers might be interested in, the equipment they had used to decypher some of the Red Army's most secret radio communications.

Soviet technicians had devised a system of encrypting teleprinter communications which split each message into nine different elements, each of which was sent on a separate radio channel. The message was then reassembled by the receiving station. The German codebreakers had developed a technique to intercept and decypher these transmissions and were hoping that the Allies might allow them to remain free to set up their equipment to continue monitoring the Russians on their behalf.

Rushworth and Norland were ordered to take the equipment and its operators back to England, as Norland recalled.

I'll never forget leaving Rosenheim fairly early one morning. Major Rushworth was riding up in the front of the convoy of five lorries and I had the dubious honour of riding in the fifth lorry. That turned out to be slower than all the others. So with a very sinking feeling, I saw the other four lorries disappear out of sight. I felt very much alone because the four ahead had all of the equipment and all of the German personnel were riding in my lorry. I was surrounded. I had a German driver and assistant driver in the cab with me and all of the other German personnel, I don't remember how many, fifteen or twenty, in the back of the lorry.

I didn't realise then, I only discovered later, that neither hell nor high water would have kept them from following their equipment, they were so devoted to it. But I did have some very uneasy moments. Most of the overpasses on the autobahn had been blown up. So there was a detour every time you came to an intersection and that would run down through German villages and as soon as the population, mostly women of course, saw there were German prisoners on the back of this truck, they came rushing out with food and coffee and things of that sort. So I felt very much alone and very insecure I can tell you.

The top secret equipment was taken, together with its operators, to a country house near Bletchley where it was set up and tested against real Soviet transmissions. Large numbers of the codebreakers were already being trained in Russian. 'At the end of the war, you were given a choice,' said Jean Faraday Davies, one of the Fusion Room analysts. 'You could go and work on Russian intercepts, which most of us didn't want to do, or you could leave.'

Apart from the encyphered teleprinter communications the Germans had been monitoring, the Russians also began using captured Enigma machines. But having been told of Bletchley Park's success by John Cairncross and Kim Philby, they modified them to make the cyphers more difficult to break, said Roy Jenkins.

> The Russians knew pretty well what we were doing at Bletchley. When they came into Berlin at the end of the war, they took over the German machines and used them for communication within their new empire, to Belgrade and other places. But when we tried to break the Russian cyphers, they had made the settings more complicated which suggests they knew how much we had been doing.

The Soviet Union was not the only new target the codebreakers were asked to look at, recalled Jimmy Thirsk, a log-reader in Sixta.

> I remember there being almost a mutiny at the end of the war with Germany because we started working on French intercepts. Quite a lot of us objected to this and a delegation of fifteen or twenty of us went to one of the officers in charge and made our complaint and said we didn't want to do it. Someone else was called in and we were given a lecture and told: 'Well, if you don't want to do it, you're redundant.' But there was a definite revulsion against spying on our former Allies.

Thirsk and his friends were not the only ones made redundant. The number of people at Bletchley Park had reached a wartime peak of

8995 in January 1945. But after the atomic bombs on Hiroshima and Nagasaki led to the end of the war with Japan, the numbers of codebreakers dropped rapidly.

The proposals of Tiltman, Hinsley and Welchman for a single foreign intelligence service had been ignored. In June 1946, GC&CS adopted its wartime covername Government Communications Headquarters as its new title and, completely independent of MI6, moved from Bletchley Park to Eastcote, near Pinner in Middlesex.

Two of the Colossus computers and fifty bombes were taken to Eastcote but the rest were destroyed as was all hint that the world's first programmable electronic computer had ever existed.

'I was given instructions to destroy all the evidence we had of Colossus, for some reason which I didn't understand and which I couldn't challenge,' said Tommy Flowers. 'So I took all the information on paper, all the drawings and the records of what we'd done down to the boiler room and put them in the boiler fire and that was that.'

That decision almost robbed Colossus of its place in history as the world's first programmable electronic computer. Even now there are those who seek to play down its significance. But Donald Michie is in no doubt. 'It was not a universal computer, the universal machine having been spec-ed out in mathematical terms by Turing in 1956,' he said. 'But it was semi-programmable, it had some of the properties of a universal computer and it was a first in terms of high-speed electronics by a very wide margin.'

The Colossus computers were taken to Cheltenham when GCHQ moved there in 1952 and at least one was still working into the early 1960s. The bombes were put to work almost immediately at Eastcote, presumably on eastern bloc cyphers. The Poles, without whose brilliance the British codebreakers would have struggled to get started, were now one of the enemies. But such was the power of the bombes that the modifications made by the Soviet technicians apparently had little effect.

'Some of these machines were to be stored away but others were required to run new jobs and sixteen machines were kept comparatively busy on menus,' the official history of the bombe sections recorded. 'It is interesting to note that most of the jobs came up and the operating, checking and other times maintained were faster than the best times during the war periods.'

Barbara Abernethy was left to close down Station X.

People were being declared redundant which meant they got one week's pay and off they went. I was established, as they called it, so it didn't affect me. But I saw my friends going, that was sad. Rumour had it that the GPO was going to take the place over. So we just left everything as it was. I and a guy called Colonel Wallace closed up the place. We just closed down the huts, put all the files away and sent them down to Eastcote. I was the last person left at Bletchley Park. I locked the gates and then took the key down to Eastcote. That was it. The dons happily went back to Cambridge. The permanent military, like Brigadier Tiltman as he then was, went to Eastcote, and the organisation went back to London three times the size it was before the war.

Not only was the new GCHQ much larger than the small group that had arrived at Bletchley Park in Captain Ridley's shooting party, the relaxed air of the country house weekend had gone forever, to be replaced by a highly mechanised organisation that was to play a key role in the Cold War.

That it was able to do this was largely a result of the alliance forged with the Americans at Bletchley Park. A few weeks after VJ Day, President Truman authorised a continuation of the Signals Intelligence cooperation into peacetime and in March 1946 a conference in London attended by Harry Hinsley laid down the basis of what was to become the UKUSA Accord, tying Britain, America, Canada, Australia and New Zealand together in a unique cooperation arrangement, splitting up coverage of the world between them to maximise their intelligence effort.

'The British and the Americans wrote down rules for exchanging material,' said Art Levenson, who worked for the National Security Agency, the US equivalent of GCHQ. 'It got very thick indeed. We became very, very chummy with our British opposite numbers.' That close relationship owed a lot to the close friendships built up between the two sides at Bletchley Park.

Bill Bundy continued to work for the American intelligence services after the war and would eventually became Assistant Secretary of State. But nothing he ever did was as enjoyable as his time at Bletchley Park.

It was a terrific human experience and I've never matched it since. I think virtually every American who was involved at any level felt roughly that way. I had other jobs with superb people, important and worthwhile pursuits but certainly for me personally this was the high point. Nothing gave the total personal satisfaction that Hut 6 did. Because this was a totally dedicated group working together in absolutely remarkable teamwork.

Those feelings were shared at every level, from the leading codebreakers to the junior servicemen and women. 'It was just a marvellous place to be,' said Ann Cunningham, who as Ann Lavell was PA to Josh Cooper.

> I'm terribly grateful to have been there for the five years I had there. It was something quite out of this world. I met people I wouldn't have otherwise met. Josh Cooper said a stint at Bletchley Park should count as a university degree. I think he had got something there. It was a very broadening experience, because of all those extraordinary people gathered together, and so many of them were extraordinary.

Gwen Watkins, who as Gwen Davies, had worked on low-level *Luftwaffe* codes and cyphers, said that for a lot of the young people who came to Bletchley it was quite literally the time of their lives.

> Many of us who had come straight from school were lifted up immediately into an atmosphere that perhaps we would never have met or that would only have come to us very, very slowly in our different lives. To be with people for whom books, music, art, history, everything like that, was a daily part of their lives, it was an absolute blossoming for me and I have to say that, though I've had many wonderful friends since, I've never again experienced that atmosphere of happiness, of enjoyment of culture, of enjoyment of everything that meant life to me.

The story of Station X was not a good one for all its participants. Alistair Denniston, who retired at the end of the war, was never given the credit he deserved. Certainly, he was neither the tub-thumper that GC&CS needed in the early days of the war, nor the skilled political operator required to manage the much larger organisation it became.

Yet it was Denniston who created the relaxed atmosphere between the wars in which brilliant codebreakers like Knox, Tiltman and Strachey could develop their skills. During one minor dispute with the senior cryptanalysts at Bletchley Park, he uncharacteristically put the more belligerent Commander 'Jumbo' Travis firmly in his place.

> After twenty years' experience in GC&CS, I think I may say to you that

one does not expect to find the rigid discipline of a battleship among the collection of somewhat unusual civilians who form GC&CS. To endeavour to impose it would be a mistake and would not assist our war effort.

More importantly, Denniston was the man who decided, before the Second World War had even begun, that codebreaking was moving into the machine age and called in large numbers of young mathematicians like Turing and Welchman, the two men whose early contributions were crucial in breaking Enigma and reorganising GC&CS into a highly efficient intelligence organisation. As Josh Cooper said, his critics 'did not realise that Denniston, for all his diminutive stature, was a bigger man than they.'

Sadly, although Turing and Welchman's contributions have now been well-recognised, both were poorly treated after leaving Bletchley Park. Turing left to continue his pioneering work on computers, first at the National Physical Laboratory and then at Manchester University. He was awarded an OBE for his war work but in 1952 was arrested and put on trial for homosexuality. As a result, his security clearance was taken away. Two years later, he killed himself by taking cyanide. But according to Donald Michie his legacy lives on all around us.

Alan Turing is one of the figures of the century. His consequences are everywhere and nobody knows now where it's going to take us. The world of computing and now the world of the Internet stems from Alan Turing's fundamental ideas. There were other great men in Bletchley Park, but in the long long wall of history I think Turing's name will probably be the number one in terms of consequences for mankind.

Like Turing, Gordon Welchman was also awarded an OBE for his wartime work. He left to become director of research at John Lewis Partnership before emigrating to America where he helped to develop computer systems for the US forces. Although his publication in 1982 of *The Hut Six Story* followed the announcement by the British Government that restrictions on former codebreakers discussing the work done on Enigma had been relaxed, he too lost his security clearance and, only months before his death in 1985, was accused by GCHQ of 'direct damage to security' and threatened with prosecution and imprisonment.

Edward Travis remained as director of GCHQ, assisted by Nigel de Grey, the man who broke the Zimmerman Telegram during the

First World War continuing as deputy director for the first five years of the Cold War. Eric Jones, the head of Hut 3, went on to become director of GCHQ as did Leonard 'Joe' Hooper, the young man found by Josh Cooper reading an Italian dictionary on that first chaotic day at Bletchley Park. Having joined when the cryptanalyst's only tools were a pencil and a piece of paper, Hooper was the man who took GCHQ into the satellite age.

Stuart Milner-Barry switched to the Treasury, becoming an assistant secretary within two years, Ralph Tester went back into business with Unilever, while Max Newman and Harry Hinsley returned to academia. Josh Cooper, Frank Birch, Hugh Alexander and John Tiltman all continued with GCHQ after the war. Tiltman retired from the Army to take charge of the cryptanalysis division. He continued to work at Cheltenham until his seventieth birthday in 1968, evidence enough of how highly valued he was. But even then he did not stop codebreaking, moving to America to work for the NSA for a number of years.

These men and around 10,000 other people, the vast majority of them women, who worked at Bletchley Park did not win the war, but they certainly shortened it, saving countless lives on both sides of the conflict, said Ralph Bennett.

> Its impact was very great indeed, no question. Whatever theatre you look at you'll find the impact is very great indeed. I don't want to say more than that because it becomes speculative, but it undoubtedly must have shortened the war. How much I don't know, others have been prepared to guess, I'm not.

One of those who was prepared to attempt to put a length of time on the effect Bletchley Park had on the war was Harry Hinsley, whose authorship of the official history of British Intelligence in the Second World War put him in a unique position to judge. 'The U-boats would not have done us in, but they would have got us into serious shortages and put another year on the war,' he said. 'Operation Overlord would certainly not have been launched in June 1944 without Ultra. Or at least, if it had been launched, it would probably not have been successful.'

It was still possible that the Russians might have gone on to capture Berlin in 1945 or that Britain might have been so badly hit by Hitler's V-bombs that the Allies might have responded by using the atomic bomb, he said. 'But my own belief is that the war, instead of finishing in 1945, would have ended in 1948 had GC&CS not been able to read the Enigma cyphers and produce the Ultra intelligence.'

Arguably, however, the transatlantic alliance forged at Bletchley Park was just as important as the codebreakers' effect on the war. It is no coincidence that large parts of the Station X story were only declassified once the Cold War came to an end. Not only were some of the methods employed at Bletchley Park still in common use against the Warsaw Pact countries but they gave the British and Americans a vital advantage as the Iron Curtain came down across Europe and the Soviet threat grew.

One leaked GCHQ memo showed that British codebreaking techniques were still making a major contribution to transatlantic cooperation in the early 1980s. US officials frequently based their foreign policy decisions on reports derived from intercepted messages decyphered by the British. That superior codebreaking ability had its roots in the advances in cryptanalysis made at Bletchley Park. The extent of the British codebreakers' wartime capabilities was so fantastic, that although the Germans were warned by their own experts that it was possible, they refused to believed it.

After the war, Alan Turing and Tommy Flowers travelled to Germany to find out if there was anything that the victorious Allies could learn from the Nazi technological research programmes. When one of the Germans they met showed them a Lorenz cypher machine, they had to pretend they did not know what it was, Flowers recalled.

'This chap then explained how it worked and said didn't we think it was a marvellous machine and we all said yes. "But nevertheless," he told us in an incredulous voice, "Our codes people said the enemy could break these messages in two years." I asked him if he had changed the machine after two years. "Oh no," he said. "Our factories were so disorganised by the bombing that we weren't able to make another machine. But it was safe, absolutely safe." That was quite a moment,' Flowers said. 'It was a great temptation to turn to Turing and wink.'

Sources

Andrew, Christopher, *Secret Service: The Making of the British Intelligence Community* (William Heinemann, London, 1985)

Baring, Sarah, and others, *Hut 4 Naval Section: Bletchley Park 1941–1945: Wartime Drawings and Poems, and Recollections after 50 Years*, Unpublished, Dated 1995

Beesley, Patrick, *Very Special Intelligence* (Hamish Hamilton, London, 1977)

Bennett, Ralph, *Ultra in the West: The Normandy Campaign of 1944–45* (Hutchinson, London, 1979)

Bennett, Ralph, *Ultra and Mediterranean Strategy 1941–45* (Hamish Hamilton, London, 1989)

Bennett, Ralph, *Behind the Battle: Intelligence in the War with Germany, 1939–45* (Sinclair-Stevenson, London, 1994)

Cairncross, John, *The Enigma Spy* (Century, London, 1997)

Calvorcoressi, Peter, *Top Secret Ultra* (Cassell, London, 1980)

Currier, Prescott, *NSA Oral History OH-38-80* (November 1980)

Denniston, A. G., 'The Government Code and Cypher School Between the Wars', *Intelligence and National Security*, Vol. 1, No. 1 (1986)

Denniston, Robin, 'The Professional Career of A. G. Denniston', in Kenneth Robertson (ed.), *British and American Approaches to Intelligence* (Macmillan, London, 1987)

Denniston, Robin, 'Diplomatic Eavesdropping, 1922–1944: A New Source Discovered', *Intelligence and National Security*, Vol. 10, No. 3 (1995)

Denniston, Robin, *Churchill's Secret War* (Sutton Publishing, Stroud, 1997)

Erskine, Ralph, and Weierud, Frode, 'Naval Enigma: M4 and its Rotors', *Cryptologia* Vol. 11 (1987)

Erskine, Ralph, 'Naval Enigma: The Breaking of Heimisch and Triton', *Intelligence and National Security*, Vol. 3, No. 1 (1988)

Erskine, Ralph, 'Naval Enigma: An Astonishing Blunder', *Intelligence and National Security*, Vol. 3, No. 1 (1988)

Erskine, Ralph, 'From the Archives: Tunny Decrypts', *Cryptologia*, Vol. 12 (1988)

Erskine, Ralph (ed.), 'From the Archives: U-Boat HF WT Signalling', *Cryptologia* Vol. 12 (1988)

Erskine, Ralph, 'Kriegsmarine Short Signal Systems – and How Bletchley Park Exploited Them', *Cryptologia*, Vol. 12 (1998)

Erskine, Ralph, 'The First Naval Enigma Decrypts of World War II', *Cryptologia*, Vol. 11 (1997)

Erskine, Ralph, 'When a Purple Machine Went Missing: How Japan Nearly Discovered America's Greatest Secret', *Intelligence and National Security*, Vol. 12, No. 3 (1997)

Erksine, Ralph, 'Churchill and the Start of the Ultra-Magic Deals', *International Journal of Intelligence and CounterIntelligence*, Vol. 10 (1997)

Filby, P. W., 'Floradora and a Unique Break into One-Time Pad Ciphers', *Intelligence and National Security*, Vol. 10, No. 3 (1995)

Harris, Robert, *Enigma* (Arrow, London, 1995)

Hinsley, F. H., Thomas, E. E., Ransom, C. F. G. and Knight, R. C., *British Intelligence in the Second World War*, Vols I–III (HMSO, London, 1979–1984)

Hinsley, F. H., and Simkin, C. A. G., *British Intelligence in the Second World War*, Vol. IV (HMSO, London, 1990)

Hinsley, F. H., *British Intelligence in the Second World War* (Revised Abridged Edition), (HMSO, London, 1994)

Hinsley, F. H. and Stripp, Alan (eds), *Codebreakers: The Inside Story of Bletchley Park* (OUP, Oxford, 1993)

Howard, Michael, *British Intelligence in the Second World War*, Vol. V (HMSO, London, 1990)

Jones, R. V., *Most Secret War* (Hamish Hamilton, London, 1978)

Jones, R. V., *Reflections on Intelligence* (Mandarin, London, 1990)

Jones, R. V., 'A Sidelight on Bletchley', *Intelligence and National Security*, Vol. 9, No. 1 (1994)

Kahn, David, *Seizing the Enigma* (Souvenir, London, 1991)

Keegan, John, *The Second World War* (Viking, New York, 1990)

Keegan, John (ed.), *Who's Who in World War II* (Routledge, London, 1995)

McKee, Alexander, *El Alamein: Ultra and the Three Battles* (Souvenir, London, 1991)

Masterman, J. C., *The Double-Cross System* (Pimlico, London, 1995)

Richelson, Jeffrey T., *A Century of Spies* (OUP, Oxford, 1995)

Richelson, Jeffrey T., and Ball, Desmond, *The Ties That Bind* (Unwin Hyman, Boston, 1990)

Sale, Tony, *Origins of Colossus* (Bletchley Park Trust, Bletchley, 1998)

Smith, Bradley, *The Ultra-Magic Deals: and the Most Secret Relationship 1940–1946* (Presidio Press, Novato, California, 1993)

Smith, Michael, *New Cloak, Old Dagger* (Victor Gollancz, London, 1996)

Stripp, Alan, *Codebreaker in the Far East* (Frank Cass, London, 1989)

US Naval Cryptologic Veterans Association (Turner Publishing, Paducah, KY, 1997)

Wallwork, Jean F. (Ed.), *Bletchley Park: The Fusion Room 1942–45* (Unpublished recollections of Jean F. Wallwork; James Thirsk; Joan Thirsk; and Joyce Rushworth)

Welchman, Gordon, *The Hut Six Story* (Baldwin, Cleobury Mortimer, 1997)

West, Nigel, *GCHQ: The Secret Wireless War 1900–86* (Weidenfeld and Nicolson, London, 1986)

Winton, John, *Ultra at Sea* (Leo Cooper, London, 1988)

Public Record Office, Kew, London: HW1 series: GC&CS Churchill Files; HW3 series: GC&CS Official Histories and Personal Memoirs; HW14 series: GC&CS Correspondence Files; AIR20 series: Air Intelligence Files; WO208 series: War Office Intelligence Files; ADM223 series: Naval Intelligence Files

KGB, Moscow: File No. 83896 (Liszt), Vols I and III

INDEX